THEORETICAL and PRACTICAL TREATISE ON DANCING

by

GENNARO MAGRI
Naples, 1779

Translated by
Mary Skeaping

with
Anna Ivanova and Irmgard E. Berry

Edited by
Irmgard E. Berry and Annalisa Fox

DANCE BOOKS
Cecil Court   London

First published in 1988 by Dance Books Ltd, 9 Cecil Court, London WC2N 4EZ.

ISBN 0 903102 99 4

Distributed in the USA by Princeton Book Co., P.O. Box 109, Princeton, N.J. 08540.

Design and production in association
with Book Production Consultants, Cambridge.

Typeset by Alacrity Phototypesetters, Banwell Castle, Weston–super–Mare
Printed and bound in Great Britain by
Biddles Ltd, Guildford and King's Lynn

British Library Cataloguing in Publication Data

Magri, Gennaro
    Theoretical and practical treatise on
    dancing.
    1. Ballet, Techniques
    I. Title   II. Berry, Irmgard E.
    III. Fox, Annalisa
    792.8'2

    ISBN 0-903102-99-4

Contents

Acknowledgements

M any people have played a part in bringing this translation into being. Sadly, Mary Skeaping died before she could express her gratitude in writing and therefore I apologise to anyone who may be inadvertently omitted from the following.

Most grateful thanks to the Calouste Gulbenkian Foundation, UK branch, for continued sponsorship of this project, to the Radcliffe Trust (Secretary, Ivor Guest) for providing additional funds to complete the editing, and to the Friends of the Drottningholm Court Theatre for funding the photography of the notation plates in Part II and the staff of the Drottningholm Theatre Museum for overseeing this.

Deepest thanks to Anna Ivanova, who spent the best part of four years working on this project, to Annalisa Fox for her invaluable contribution in checking and helping to edit the final translation, to Sarah Bertaglia and Gillian Cornish for their invaluable help during the proofreading process, and to Peter Brinson for his constant support and encouragement, without which the work would not have been accomplished.

Thanks are also due to:

the late Professor Agne Beijer for introducing Magri's work to Mary Skeaping;
the late Melusine Wood and Jane Carroll for providing preliminary translations;
the late Professor Friderica Derra de Moroda OBE and the late Marian Hannah Winter for ferreting out information in Europe on Gennaro Magri, other dancers and dances mentioned in the text;
Professor Pierluigi Petrobelli, Professor Reinhard Strohm and Iris dell'Acqua for advice on the translation of the sections of music;

John and Deborah Chapman, who worked on the book with Mary Skeaping during 1978;

the dancers of the Royal Swedish Ballet, who acted as 'guinea pigs' in the reconstruction of many of the steps;

all the people who offered possible translations for various Neapolitan expressions;

and last but not least, Michael Fox, who sustained us with delicious teas throughout the editing process.

Irmgard E. Berry
London, September 1987

Introduction

by Mary Skeaping

For those interested in dance history there is a wide choice of fields for specialised study. The line chosen may depend upon many factors. My interest began in rather a casual way in the 1930s, when a producer attached to a repertory theatre asked me if I would arrange an Italian renaissance dance for a Shakespeare play. I was interested in the idea, but with a little thought I realised that in spite of having devoted years to training in classical ballet I had no material at my disposal which would warrant my taking on this task. Since I had a strong desire to be able to do this, I turned to Melusine Wood, of whom I had heard, and hereby began a long and very fruitful relationship of pupil and teacher, and later of co-worker, which only ended with her death in 1971. I cannot be grateful enough to this remarkable lady who devoted so much of her life to original research on European dance, making the subject come to life by relating the dance to its historic 'milieu', to country, costume and manners. Her lessons were no 'talking shop': one had to work very hard under the eagle eye of this teacher who brooked no nonsense. She could get very testy if she suspected that one were not serious. However, if one were, there was no trouble too great for her to take: an irreplaceable teacher and friend.

The first time I actually handled an original copy of Magri's *Trattato teorico-prattico di ballo* was at the Drottningholm Theatre Library in Stockholm in the early 1950s. The theatre historian Professor Agne Beijer showed it to me saying, 'I think this is something for you'. I thought so too, but at that moment I could not give any attention to it, as I was embarking on the interesting but very exacting task of attempting to rescue the Swedish Opera Ballet (as the Royal Swedish Ballet was then called) from the doldrums. Magri had to wait. However, he was rarely far from my thoughts. At last the time came when I could study this treatise. On enquiring, I found that it had disappeared from the Drottningholm Library, but I am glad to say that much later it turned up again, having apparently been 'lost' in the library itself. In the meantime, I had obtained a microfilm copy from the Paris Opera Library. Armed with xerox copies from this microfilm, I began to study the steps with Melusine Wood, who was keen to add to her material of the late 18th century, though this treatise, as she said, was somewhat off her beaten track with the names and range of the steps and their execution being nearer to 'modern ballet' than the ballroom.

When I returned to Stockholm after the summer break of 1960, I began to experiment with my Swedish dancers, putting some of the steps described by Magri and the ideas I had gained from them into the work I was doing at the Drottningholm Court Theatre. This gave me great pleasure. Magri was a dancer after my own heart, or better said, he was a dancer. Every facet of the work I have done in research on theatrical dance techniques has really been from the standpoint of a performer with choreographic interests, so practical application of whatever I was studying was always my aim.

Since Magri in the first part of his book was not describing dances but simple and compound steps, there is always an area of freedom in making the required linkage between steps, and how one does this will depend on the quality and knowledge of the performer. I did not know that I would ever find the conditions in which this interest and way of working could find its most satisfying expression, yet that is just what happened when I had the very good fortune to come across the Drottningholm Court Theatre in Sweden, although, on looking back, it seems that I had been working towards this end over a long period of time, collecting material with special emphasis on the second half of the 17th and through the 18th centuries.

When one comes to work in an 18th-century theatre such as that at Drottningholm, one is made very aware of the marvellous support the perspective stage gives to the three categories of dancer so clearly alluded to by Magri, i.e. the *serio*, the *mezzo carattere* and the *grotesco*. The very shape and arrangement of the traps make it possible to bring on a variety of evil spirits, furies, winds of which Magri speaks to convincingly, and here they can, on occasion, usurp the heavenly regions, which are rightly the province of the good spirits, angels, gods and goddesses. But no unwanted fury can usurp for long the crowning glory of the *Big Char*,[1] with its beautiful cloud decoration, where Parnassus reigns supreme.

Two of the most valuable books for re-creating theatrical dances of the 18th century are Lambranzi's *New and Curious School of Theatrical Dancing* (1716) and Magri's *Trattato teorico-prattico di ballo* (1779). In the former, the character of the dances is shown by means of illustrations and accompanying airs, the types of steps to be used indicated by name but with no description given. In the latter there are no illustrations but there is a full description of all the steps mentioned. Although there is a gap of over sixty years between these two books, they complement each other splendidly.

Although Magri's treatise is not presented in a scholarly manner, it nevertheless contains much valuable and interesting material, coming, as it does, at the beginning of a new period of development. It is an excellent guide to approaching the pre-Romantic Ballet: how to widen the scope, how to broaden the field to the further development of the earlier steps. One finds oneself with a greater sense of freedom. In considering the fundamental steps, Magri's thoughts were never far from their application to theatrical conditions. This is not surprising since he was a dancer, and when he is writing from the point of view of a dancer he is writing at his best, particularly where the special steps of the *grotesco* are concerned. He gives very good advice on how to avoid the pitfalls and how to get the maximum effect from one's labours. He insists on the importance to a dancer of perfect stance and footwork for a successful outcome, and his careful explanation of the *ports de bras* (Part I, Ch. 59), with the placing of the body in this, and in the *attitudes* he describes, lead us forward to the pre-Romantics.

My chief interest in making a translation of this book was, originally, for the practical use of the steps, and thus to add to my vocabulary for choreographic purposes, an interest which I hope can be shared with others who will receive equal pleasure and reward from their use. For those specially interested in research, there are several points of historic interest which could be followed up. For example, the events connected with the festivities given by Ferdinando IV, King of the Two Sicilies, when Magri was engaged to compose the *Contredances*. It is interesting to note here that it was the success of these dances which prompted Magri to publish the fine collection of *Contredances* which occupy so much of Part II of this treatise.

Much has been written about the *serio* dancers. One can look up records and obtain the dates of their birth, death and details of their careers. There were contemporary accounts and anecdotes, letters and theatre records, and biographical information about the most outstanding interpreters of this genre. In contrast to this, accounts concerning the *groteschi* are much harder to come by. Gennaro Magri belonged to this latter class of theatrical performer. His career is difficult to trace because his birth and death do not appear to have been recorded.

However, one can obtain a glimpse of Gennaro Magri's performing career, thanks to some biographical details collected by the late Marian

Hannah Winter which record his theatrical engagements between the years 1755 and 1764:

1755-6	Teatro San Carlo, Naples. 'Magri our Napolitano, known as Gennariello, for his grace in dancing and strength and agility in jumping, prerogatives of which he has shown clear signs from the very first time he appeared at the Royal Theatre' (Croce, 1891).
1759	Burgtheater, Vienna. Engaged by the ballet master Hilverding (from the manuscript daybook prepared by the assistant ballet master Philip Gumnhuber, now in the Harvard Theatre Collection).
1760	Teatro San Angelo, Venice. Engaged as choreographer and *primo ballerino*.
1760-1	Still in Venice. The programme specified that Gennaro Magri was appearing along with the French *grotesco* Pierre Bernard Michel.
1762-3	Still in Venice, but with his old associate Giuseppe Salomoni and two couples of *primi ballerini*. Magri was the *primo grotesco* with this group.
1763-4	Returned to Vienna as dancer. Paid the unusually high salary of 2062 Fl. (from the yearbook of the Burgtheater in Vienna 1754-64 by Fr. Radamovsky, p. 126).

Magri later returned to Venice to dance at the Teatro San Crisostonio in Gaetano Cesari's company as *primo ballerino grotesco* before returning to Naples.

To sum up, this brief account connecting Magri with the important centres of Vienna and Venice is enough to place his position as a dancer during a period rich in reassessment, innovation and invention. One which witnessed the work of Franz Hilverding, Angiolini, Onorato Viganò, Lepicq and Noverre, to mention a few. In this treatise the specialities of several dancers are recorded, some of whom are familiar to us, others not. For example, he mentions Cesarini when describing the *salto tondo* (a form of *tour en l'air*): 'only Cesarini has ever done all three turns easily and perfectly and this was the *capriole* reserved for him' (p. 161), and again when describing the *salto morto*, a step requiring a fine controlled jump: 'This step was a specialty of Sig. Cesarini, who remained suspended in the air longer than anyone else' (p. 166).

Magri's remarks, concerning a fellow *grotesco*, show an awareness of the importance of very high technical achievement 'where only the best is good enough', so to speak, a note which runs throughout this work.

One of the many values of this treatise is the wide range of material dealt with. A very careful study of this will be of real educative value to teachers and students alike.

London 1983

Commentary

M ary Skeaping had intended to write an account of how this translation was accomplished but as her account had unfortunately not been written by the time of her death, I will attempt to chronicle the translation process on her behalf.

Mary had been familiar with Magri's treatise for over fifteen years when, in 1978, she was finally able to devote most of her time to translating it. Mary felt that the translation from Italian to English would only be acceptable if all the steps could be reconstructed from the English description. She was then seventy-six years old and unable to work out the steps physically herself. She needed another pair of legs. That was where I came in. I had just finished my dance notation training at the Benesh Institute of Choreology and was studying dance history with John Chapman. He and his wife Deborah had done some work with Mary on the book but other commitments intervened. John suggested me to Mary as a possible assistant and in November 1978 I began working with her. Mary also invited her lifelong friend Anna Ivanova to join us. Mme Ivanova gave us the benefit of her formidable knowledge of Spanish and Portuguese dance history, as well as her experience of working with Melusine Wood.

My first task was to see what I could make of the steps from the preliminary translation which had been made by a non-dancer. There were chunks of descriptions left in Italian because to a non-dancer they were ambiguous or there were several possible translations. I decided it was quicker to work out the steps from the original Italian and this I did through Benesh Movement Notation. By notating every movement given for every step, I was then able to dance the steps from my notation. When the three of us came to work together, our method was for Anna to read the English translation, while I demonstrated the steps from my notation with Mary watching to check that the practical demonstration corresponded to the written word. When there was a discrepancy between my demonstration and the English text, we would go back to the original Italian and much discussion would ensue. I can say, happily, that it was usually the English translation that was at fault and we were able to amend it. As with all written descriptions of dance steps, there is the problem of describing actions happening simultaneously. In notation the problem is obviated by having a complete picture of each step. This proved invaluable in my demonstrations. I usually had to perform each step at least three times, the first two times being in slow motion to correspond to the detailed description of the action. The first time Mary would watch my right leg as its actions were described and the second time she would watch the left leg. Then I would perform it once more without the text being read so that she could have a picture of the whole step performed at a danceable speed because, once the mechanics have been worked out, the step must be made to dance. The process was slow and painstaking, not to mention occasionally painful as I balanced on one leg for what seemed an eternity, but through this practical demonstration any ambiguities or discrepancies in the translation were obviated. Phrases and terms which to a non-dancer could have several translations usually had only one in practical dance terms.

Using my notation of the steps, we were able to reconstruct the *Minuet* and the *Amabile*, two dances described in Part II. The *Amabile* works beautifully but the description of the *Minuet* runs into problems with the giving of left, right, then both hands. Magri does not seem to have given enough sets of the *minuet step* for the circling figures.

This translation process took over four years as we checked and rechecked the work. Mary's almost annual trips to Sweden during this period afforded an opportunity to try out our reconstructions on the dancers of the Royal Swedish Ballet. This was most useful in the case of the *caprioles*, which I had only been able to mark. These can be seen in her last choreography for the Drottningholm Court Theatre, six dances for *Arlequin's Death*, created in 1981 and based entirely on the results of our work.

In 1983 I accompanied Mary to Drottningholm for a festival in which all her ballets and collaborations with Ivo Cramér were presented. It was fascinating for me to see how almost twenty years of working with the Magri material had altered Mary's conception of the technique. In *The Return of Springtime* (1965), for all its charm, there is a certain stiffness to the steps. In *Arlequin's Death*, created sixteen years later, the steps flow into each other and therefore give a more dance-like quality.

During the course of our work together, Mary was often ill and in great pain but she soldiered on, the thought of completing the project being uppermost in her mind, even during her last days. She died on 9 February 1984, having entrusted to me the completion and editing of the translation. I spent the year following her death checking the translation once more, in consultation with Annalisa Fox, an Italian expert and early-dance enthusiast. Her knowledge of dance was very important because this is a book written by a dancer for dancers. Just as Magri himself explains steps in a way that is only fully comprehensible to other dancers, so in the translation we have made no concession to readers who do not have a basic physical understanding of the art of dancing. Had Mary lived a few more years, she may have made detailed annotations but she did not.

In 1985, as I finished checking the translation, I sent it to Regina Beck-Friis, Mary's former rehearsal assistant for the Drottningholm repertoire, so that she could use the material in her choreography of *Don Juan*, being created for the Drottningholm Court Theatre. I was able to attend the première and I was anxious to see if the translation had been clear enough for her to re-create the steps as I knew them. I immediately recognised the *grotesco* jumps (*caprioles*) but it took me longer to recognise the other steps, which underlines my belief that Magri's clearest explanations are for the *grotesco*.

Regina Beck-Friis was fulfilling Mary's fervent desire in making the translation, and that was that the material be used for performance. I hope that other choreographers will find the same delight in the book and, like Mary and Regina, be inspired to use the technique on stage.

I will be forever grateful for the opportunity of working with Mary Skeaping and Anna Ivanova and for the firm friendships which ensued. With a lifetime's professional dance experience behind them, they welcomed me, a relative 'novice', as an equal, always ready to listen to and consider my opinions. Through the generosity with which they shared their wealth of knowledge of dance and the theatre, they have both played an enormous role in cultivating my appreciation of dance. I consider it a privilege and an honour to be counted among the friends of these true Ladies of the Dance.

Irmgard E. Berry
London, September 1986

Mary Skeaping's Work and Influence
An Introduction

by Peter Brinson
Head, Postgraduate Studies, Laban Centre for Movement & Dance

This introduction attempts a context for Mary Skeaping's translation of Gennaro Magri's *Trattato teorico-prattico di ballo*, published in Naples in 1779. Magri's work is one of the most important of all dance technique books because it links the style and technique of Noverre, in the latter half of the 18th century, with early-19th-century technique, from which developed the technique of dancers of the Romantic Ballet later in the century. Magri's pages, notes Marian Hannah Winter in her *The Pre-Romantic Ballet* (1974), manifest his knowledge and his eagerness to show future dancers how to accomplish the wealth of steps he recorded for their benefit. It is 'the most important body of general technical information at that date ... the most complete source of information on the *grotteschi*, including 12 pages on the steps and the dance style of the Commedia dell'Arte characters ... [It] is the most invaluable 18th century treatise on ballet technique'.

Such was the work which Mary Skeaping undertook to offer English readers and to which she brought all her enormous scholarship and practical theatre experience. For this reason it seems to me important to set down the nature of the knowledge which informs her translation. I have done so in the ways suggested by her career: her background, early influences and training; her development into choreographer and producer of international stature after leaving the Sadler's Wells Ballet in 1951; her appointment to the Royal Swedish Ballet and her historical productions and choreography for Drottningholm from 1956; her dialogue with the 18th century. Later I try to indicate her legacy and assess the two sides of her contribution to dance knowledge, historical and philosophical. Finally comes Magri.

This, though, would be to present the career, the scholar and the choreographer but to forget the person. That person I knew well in her flat in Paddington, West London, an enormous quantity of music, books and papers spread across her grand piano and piled on little tables. She was seen best, however, in a rehearsal studio. Here her profound mastery of her profession, her conviction and expertise carried the day in every situation, no matter what the odds. Young dancers in most places were inclined to smile when first they met her – an oldish lady with thick glasses, an out-of-date hair-style, wearing a brown, tweedy skirt (rumoured to have come from several bales bought cheap at a sale of damaged cloth after an air-raid during the war – she was nothing if not economical) and wearing for demonstration what *looked* like carpet slippers. The smiles disappeared when they experienced her discipline, realised her knowledge and noted her respect for them as dancers. She never ceased to remember that whatever she created would have to be communicated to an audience by the dancers she was rehearsing. Her ultimate task was to move audiences. In this she seemed touched by the spiritual nature of dance, its capacity for magic.

Such is the translator of Magri.

Mary Skeaping was born at Woodford, England, on 15 December 1902. She died in London on 9 February 1984, an internationally respected choreographer, dance producer and teacher. In particular she changed the image and status of classical ballet in Sweden through her training of the Royal Swedish Ballet and her choreography in 18th-century styles and techniques of original ballets and opera-ballets produced for the Gustavian Court Theatre at Drottningholm near Stockholm. For these productions and others in Britain she carried out extensive researches which added substantially to international knowledge of dance techniques and dance production in styles from the Renaissance to the late 19th century.

Her mother was a pianist; her father a portrait painter; her brother John became one of the most respected English painters of his generation; her four nephews, of whom she was very fond, became significant musicians. She herself turned to dancing, influenced by a sister who took dance lessons. Dancing became her contribution to the remarkable Skeaping talents, but the influence of the broad artistic education received from her family background shaped all her creative vision.

The second significant influence upon her life's work was a professional training from some of the best classical ballet teachers of the day. These included Novikov, Trefilova and Egorova among the Russians, and the great English teacher Margaret Craske. Through Craske she acquired a lifetime's devotion to the principles and methods of Enrico Cecchetti, one of the most influential teachers of classical ballet in the 20th century. As a result she became a leading member of the Cecchetti Society, formed to codify and develop the master's teaching. Equipped with such a training she moved almost naturally into the Pavlova Company. This third formative experience ended with the dispersal of the company after Pavlova's death in 1931. Thereafter Skeaping, the dancer, began to acquire the wide range of theatrical experience which was the fourth major element in her artistic development.

She belonged to a dancer's generation for whom a career exclusively in classical ballet was, to say the least, problematic. Ninette de Valois, Frederick Ashton, Marie Rambert, Peggy van Praagh, among others, belonged to the same, or a slightly younger, generation. All, without exception, mingled early experience in classical ballet (Skeaping danced with the Nemchinova-Dolin Ballet and other companies) with experience in operas, musicals and a range of different forms of dance theatre. In every case these experiences were important. Skeaping also drew all she could from the increasing number of dance visitors to be seen in London during the 1930s, showing the inquisitive mind which is the mark alike of an artist and of a creative research worker. Apart from the Ballets Russes of Colonel de Basil and appearances of the Pavlova Company at the Royal Opera House, Covent Garden, the Skeaping papers today include from this early period programmes from visits to the American Southern Syncopated Orchestra Singers in 1919; a European folkdance festival in 1935; an appearance by Uday Shankar at the Savoy Theatre in 1937; performances by Basque dancers in 1938 with comments and reactions noted on the programme in her own hand; and a first visit by Indonesian dancers to the UK in February 1939. She was eclectic, curious – and never threw anything away. Thus one can trace the development of some of her choreography and many of her ideas through dozens of postcards, mostly of historical scenes; catalogues from museums and galleries; and large quantities of music from many periods.

All these background influences and personal explorations began to come together in her work as a teacher and choreographer/producer. She was part of the great experience in popularising ballet throughout Britain during the war years fostered by the Government and the armed forces entertainment organisations. Three years after the war, in 1948, she became ballet mistress of the Sadler's Wells Ballet at Covent Garden. Throughout this period she developed her own ideas and personal inquiries into the great classical legacy, into teaching methods and into the history of her art. Perhaps it was this independence of mind, perhaps it was the natural end to a particular experience, which caused her to leave Covent Garden in 1951 and move into the international field. She became guest producer of various productions of ballet classics between 1952 and 1954 in Cuba, Canada and especially Sweden, where her production of *Swan Lake* in 1952 led to an invitation to direct the Royal Swedish Ballet from 1953 onwards. Her appointment lasted nine years during which she reshaped the company. She not only produced the standard 19th-century repertory of classical ballets, and brought in choreographers of international stature like Antony Tudor, but also created a repertory of original choreography of her own, appropriate to the 18th-century Drottningholm Court Theatre. The two developments went in necessary parallel. She could not have created her historical productions without the good dancers she trained. Their dancing in the great classics and the modern repertory, and their careers as professional dancers, were enriched by the Drottningholm experience. Thereby the international status of the Royal Swedish Ballet was enhanced immeasurably.

It was during the early years of her work in Sweden that I met Mary Skeaping for the first time. An historian of dance and teacher of dance history myself, I earned also part of my living writing about dance for *The Times, The Sunday Times, Observer* and some foreign journals including the *Herald Tribune* and *Svenska Dagbladet* in Stockholm. Accordingly, I was asked to cover festivals in various parts of Europe, including Stockholm. Thus I met the director of the Royal Swedish Ballet and came to observe the extraordinary results of a coincidence which brought a choreographer in 18th-century dance styles to the one theatre in the world which could stage her work authentically and could be stimulated boundlessly itself by her creative spirit.

The Drottningholm Court Theatre stands by the Royal Summer Palace of Drottningholm overlooking Lake Mälar, only five miles from Stockholm. It is the second theatre constructed on this site and dates from 1766. Like its predecessor it was erected under the inspiration of Lovisa Ulrika, Queen of Sweden and sister to Frederick the Great of Prussia. A typical product of 18th-century enlightenment, she developed greatly the cultural life of the Swedish Court but always in the French manner and French language. Her son, Gustav III, who succeeded in 1771, inherited to a high degree his mother's love of fine arts, literature, music and theatre, but with an ambition to make the general cultural life of Sweden Swedish rather than French based. The theatre received his particular attention so that he is the founder of the Royal Swedish Opera and the Royal Dramatic Theatre. From 1777 onwards Drottningholm became the centre of court life during the Swedish summer. Towards the end of the 1780s an average of four different theatrical entertainments took place there every week, with all the necessary scenic and musical support. This activity ended when Gustav III was assassinated at a masked ball in 1792. The theatre fell into disuse and the stage at Drottningholm, with all its scenery, equipment and costumes, remained inert throughout the whole of the 19th century.

It was rediscovered in 1921 by Agne Beijer, an official of the Royal

18

Library in Stockholm, who recognised some superb 18th-century scenic sets standing still intact on the old stage. Still intact, too, and in working order was the stage machinery. The theatre itself was, in general, untouched. Nothing was missing, except artists and audience and the ropes which animated the machinery. A year later, on 19 August 1922 – 150 years to the day after Gustav III's revolution – the theatre re-awoke from its long sleep with the public performance of an 18th-century divertissement by members of the Royal Swedish Opera. Since then, particularly in summer, the theatre has been alive, as theatres should be, with rehearsals, performances and the applause of audiences. Performances were shared between drama, opera and dance, but on 14 June 1956 an event occurred which gave dance a special place in what can be called today the Drottningholm repertory. The curtain rose on the first performance of *Cupid out of his Humour*, a baroque ballet to music by Purcell created by Mary Skeaping to celebrate the first official visit to Sweden of Queen Elizabeth II of England. The ballet was inspired by a ballet of the same title presented at the court of Queen Christina on 1 November 1649 to a libretto by the Swedish poet Georg Stiernhielm.

This Skeaping production has achieved a significance for Swedish dance today, and for wider historical dance studies, much greater than its transitory political significance in 1956. It demonstrated that the ancient court theatre, the only theatre of its kind in the world in full working order, had acquired a choreographer able to exploit and explore all its possibilities.

Through original works in choreographic styles of the theatre's own period, Mary Skeaping brought to life on stage the most formative period of Swedish theatrical history. Thus she illuminated choreography, dance history and theatrical life in the 18th century. The many ballets which followed in the thirty years to Mary Skeaping's death helped to create collaborators who carry forward now this unique work, and dancers whose training today encompasses historical styles far outside the experience of classical dancers in other countries. Moreover, unlike the productions which followed the re-opening of Drottningholm in 1922, these productions since 1956 have been recorded on film and video. The result justifies visibly the claim to have created a coherent Drottningholm dance repertory appropriate to an 18th-century theatre which possessed still its 18th-century stage designs and scenic effects. Skeaping's good fortune was that Beijer discovered in 1921 not only a working theatre but many 18th-century costumes, and more than thirty complete 18th-century stage sets, painted, dated and often signed by distinguished European artists of the time. Extraordinary as this great discovery was, no less remarkable was the chance conjunction of theatre, settings and choreographer able to inspire each other to vivid life. Hence Skeaping's historical work lives in Sweden whereas all but her *Giselle* has been lost in England.

Artistic judgements of her productions and choreography can be read in critical assessments of the time. What needs to be added here is the context in which her work took place, including her translation of Magri. If, in a literary sense, the translation of *Trattato teorico-prattico di ballo* lacks the written notes which Mary Skeaping planned to add, these 'notes' in fact exist. They can be seen at Drottningholm whenever *The Fishermen, The Return of Springtime* and other, later Skeaping ballets are danced. She drew on Magri over many years, both for particular steps and as an example of a certain kind of dance style at the end of the 18th century.

In the same way Skeaping's *written* contribution to the study of dance history is comparatively small whereas her *danced* contribution is very great. She was the rare historian who made dance studios her laboratory as well as her place of creation. The written contribution, therefore, can be listed quickly. Besides this translation of Magri (by far her most important literary commitment), she is the author of the monograph *Ballet under the Three Crowns*, published by Dance Perspectives, New York, in April 1967. Later this was enlarged in Swedish to become *Den Svenska Hovbaletten* (1983). In 1979 she was the co-author with Anna Greta Ståhle of *Balett på Stockholmsoperan*. Throughout her life she wrote also a number of articles for dance journals.

The Skeaping legacy, therefore, lies mostly in the practice of dance and in historical knowledge communicated through dance. The range of her work thus becomes important because it informs the nature of the dance knowledge she communicated on stage out of her researches. The researches, for example, brought intimate understanding of styles, both in the creation of individual dances and in comprehensive choreography for an entire ballet. Today, she used to point out, we underestimate so much the importance of the mimetic element of dance. This element cannot be divested from dance because dance is presented always by a live human body. Thus the element of mime, of bodily conversation, is present even in the most modern of modern dances. It changes, of course, with each period and does not have to take the form of arm or hand gestures. A noble dance of the 18th century required that a dancer's gestures should embrace the whole body and should be able to express the full range of human passions. For this purpose the theatrical codes of the 17th and 18th centuries offered a rich resource of gestures and stylised movement. There were signs which communicated by imitating and stylising character, feelings and emotions, and there were signs which animated action. These resources were translated onto the Drottningholm stage according to the period of the ballet Mary Skeaping created. Towards the end of the 18th century, for example, it became customary to group ballets under headings which indicated their chief characteristic, such as Ballet-Dramatique, Ballet-

Héroique, Ballet-Pantomime, Ballet-Comique, Ballet-Historique and Ballet-Anacreontique. *The Return of Springtime* is an example of the last type, as Mary Skeaping explained in an introductory programme note, but she was remarkable for being able to work in the styles of many periods. *Cupid out of his Humour* draws on the early-17th-century technique of de Lauze; *Il Pastor Fido* presents the noble style of the early 18th century; and comedy dances in Ivo Cramér's *The Death of Harlequin* draws on Magri in a style of the 1770s.

The other part of the range of her historical work is what she created in Britain. This is much wider than is generally supposed. It includes a continuing series of Handel productions for the Handel Society, usually at Sadler's Wells Theatre, with Charles Farncombe conducting; a number of period films for which she did the choreography; her work for the Royal Ballet's Ballet for All group, distinguished particularly by representatives of the fourth *Entrée* of the *Ballet Royal de la Nuit* (1653), John Weaver's *The Loves of Mars and Venus* (1717) and *The Return of Springtime* (1818); and, of course, her *Giselle* created in 1971 for London Festival Ballet. She never received in Britain from critics or from television the kind of attention her work received in Sweden. Consequently, only her *Giselle* can be seen today on a British stage. On film there is a long sequence of Tudor Court dances in *Anne of the Thousand Days* with Richard Burton; some inadequately presented extracts of her work for Ballet for All made by Thames Television in 1970; and a sequence of dances in Margot Fonteyn's television series, *The Magic of Dance*, mutilated by insensitive cutting and declared unacceptable by Mary Skeaping. There were also in this series a number of uncredited examples of her work.

Such records, therefore, are poor supplements to the Swedish record of her contribution to dance knowledge. This contribution was of two kinds, historical and philosophical. The one underlies the other. Part of her contribution to the study of dance history, for example, was to show that movement can be a source of historical knowledge and can communicate that aspect of history which cannot be described in words. Movement thus provides historical evidence. There are important aspects of the absolutism of Louis XIV and the role of the French court in the late 17th century which can be understood best through a study of *ballet de cour* and, if possible, a staging of its work. Similarly, it is difficult to comprehend fully the philosophy and aesthetics of 18th-century European society without reference to its manifestation in the lyric theatre descended from *ballet de cour*. Skeaping demonstrated this aspect of dance history especially through her work at Drottningholm. In so doing she extended our understanding of the significance of the non-verbal elements of human history and of ways in which such elements might be studied.

How did she do it? Over nearly thirty years I was privileged often to work with her and to be her discussant. She familiarised herself with all the written dance records of the period she was studying and with all the dance notations, mostly Feuillet, on which she could lay her hands. Thereby she seemed to enter into personal discourse with the dancing masters of the 17th and 18th centuries, and with the societies in which they lived. She spoke of them as friends, still alive, so that one of the joys of working with her in the late 1960s to create her representation of part of the fourth *Entrée* of the *Ballet Royal de la Nuit* was to hear her speak of ways in which the young Lully tactfully prompted the young Louis XIV, aged fifteen, dancing for the first time the role of the rising sun.

More important, she seemed to comprehend and adopt ways of thought of the dancing masters with whom she was in discourse. Among these ways of thought was a misty understanding, today clarified and debated in educated circles, that there are various kinds of thinking and various kinds of human intelligence. Part of the uniqueness of this intelligence lies in the way we appraise and communicate with each other. We do this through many different modes of understanding and communication, not only in words. We communicate, for example, through languages of numeracy, morals and religion; of gesture, posture and visual expression; and of aesthetic awareness expressing ideas and judgements of beauty, grace, harmony, ugliness and so on.

Not to enter into any of these communities of discourse is to that extent to be uneducated, to be, in 18th-century terms, uncivilised. This was the understanding and starting point of the dancing masters who sought to argue their case to the polite societies around them through books, which Skeaping studied. Beauchamps, Feuillet, Weaver, Pierre Rameau, Tomlinson and later Noverre, Angiolini, Magri and Blasis into the 19th century, all sought to place dance, in Kellom Tomlinson's words, among 'the other Arts and Sciences'. The dancing master who expressed this most clearly was John Weaver. He argued in his *Anatomical and Mechanical Lectures* of 1723 that 'the Rules and Institutions of our Profession are built upon the Fundamentals of *Anatomy*; Agreeable to the Laws of *Mechanism*; consonant to the Rules of harmonical Proportion and adorned with the Beauty of a natural and cultivated *Gracefulness*'. In this claim Weaver was applying to dancing the latest scientific knowledge of the day discussed in London intellectual circles, especially advances in anatomy and mechanics.

Mary Skeaping's research, which helped her to acquire this inside view of 17th- and 18th-century society – especially the 18th century – is one of the fundamental reasons, I believe, for the success of her historical productions. Her opera-ballets for the Drottningholm Court Theatre seem to me to bring to life not only the works of lyric theatre which belong there, but also much of the ethos and cultural values of Gustavian society from which they sprang.

It was the same with her work in the more restricted circumstances of Ballet for All in England. Here she concentrated more on the 16th, 17th and early 18th centuries because of interest in the Tudor period and the needs of the historical work of Ballet for All. Ballet for All was a small section of the Royal Ballet, founded in 1964, with the aim of taking classical ballet, performed by professional dancers from the Royal Ballet, to remote stages and places where ballet normally would not be seen. It comprised six dancers in rotation from the Royal Ballet, two actors and two pianists with a small support staff at the Royal Opera House.

The method of presentation mingled information with entertainment because the role of the group was to talk about, explain and introduce the story of classical ballet. For this a new *genre* was devised and called the ballet-play, mingling explanation with the dancing. The flexibility of this *genre* allowed presentations covering the history of ballet from the late 16th century onwards. About a dozen such ballet-plays were created, the earliest of them totally dependent on the historical work of Mary Skeaping. It was, in fact, characteristic of her approach that the small size of the group did not deter her from giving it all the knowledge and time its needs required. Supporting her the group had the work of designers like David Walker and of the wardrobe of the Royal Opera House to the extent that when the company closed in 1979, many of its historical costumes were passed to the new British Theatre Museum as examples of their kind.

Ballet for All was lucky that someone who drew together so many strands of contemporary ballet history – Cecchetti, Pavlova, the Sadler's Wells Ballet and many experiences overseas – should have been willing to combine all this to help a small educational group. Like Pavlova, Mary Skeaping was a missionary as much in her own special contribution to choreography as in every other way, as much in Britain as in Sweden, though she received much less acknowledgement in her own country. Working together – I as writer/producer, she as choreographer – I soon learned her persistence and ability in the detective work of historical research upon which her choreography rested. She often used Ballet for All to test ideas thrown up by this research, explorations for later, larger productions. She tried out notions, for example, which appeared years later in her full productions of *Giselle*, especially the 1971 version for Festival Ballet in London. Thus we became a willing laboratory of historical research. She created for Ballet for All the first version of *The Return of Springtime*, based on a libretto by Filippo Taglioni for a special occasion at the Spanish Embassy, Stockholm, in 1818. Taglioni used only three characters – Flora, Zephyr and Cupid – so the work was suited admirably to Ballet for All's restricted resources, being used in extract only to illustrate dance technique and styles immediately preceding the use of Romantic Ballet. Later, the full version was produced at Drottningholm where it remains in the repertory with great success.

Two creations, however, were exclusive to Ballet for All in England – her sequence from the fourth *Entrée* of the *Ballet Royal de la Nuit* and her condensed version of John Weaver's *The Loves of Mars and Venus*. We used these, of course, to illustrate key moments in our account of the history of ballet – the use of *ballet de cour* for political purposes by Mazarin, driving home the defeat of the Fronde in February 1653, and the creation by Weaver of the first *ballet d'action*, the first ballet without words, in London in 1717. For *The Loves of Mars and Venus* she could draw on Weaver's written description of the action of mimetic gesture to represent emotions – Neglect, Contempt, Detestation, Admiration, Upbraiding, Threats, Indignation, Anger, Coquetry and more. But nowhere, as we searched the sources, could we find the music Weaver used. In other writings he mentions collaboration with a composer Henry Symonds. After searches in the British Museum we found music by this composer, so were able to use music at least approved by Weaver. The incident illustrates Skeaping's integrity as a practising dance historian, refusing to use music on a purely speculative or convenient basis.

In the Louis XIV extract we have an example of her persistence in historical research. She recalled seeing in the Bibliothèque Nationale in Paris a libretto and music of the Ballet Royal. Once we had decided to attempt to restage this it took us several months to persuade the Bibliothèque the work was there as well as to release it. In the end we sent someone to photograph what we needed. This meant we were able to adapt the actual music of Camberfort and translate the actual poetry of Benserade to present on stage not only the central character of Louis XIV, aged fifteen, as the Sun, but Sleep and Silence (actors), who introduced the *Entrée*, and two of the many noblemen who supported the King's dancing – by exemplifying his virtues – the Duke of York as Victory, and the Duc de Joyeuse as Valour. The Royal Opera House wardrobe went to enormous trouble to match, as far as possible, the weight and actual material of the original costumes redesigned by David Walker. My main regret, therefore, was not to be able to reproduce for all this the elaborate stage machinery and effects of Giacomo Torelli, which were so important a part of the conception of many *ballets de cour* of the period. Nevertheless we could and did reproduce Benserade's words, which expressed so clearly, in Fergus Early's translation, Mazarin's political purpose in staging the work. Thus we could explain to our audiences the political connections of much *ballet de cour*. Standing before a large silver drop curtain representing moonlight, Sleep and Silence introduced the rising Sun –

On mountain tops glowing with my first fire

Already I shine for the world to admire.
On my vast course have I far to run
But already to all things I have begun
To give form and colour. And who does not meet
My light with homage, shall feel its heat.

The curtains parted, transforming the stage into gold with the light of the Sun. The young King, seated on his throne, rose and danced.

The task of staging an historical event, illuminated by historical choreography of this kind, often became a learning process on all sides. It could not be otherwise as Mary Skeaping explored the application of 17th- and 18th-century techniques on classically trained dancers of the 20th century. During long rehearsals, the young Royal Ballet dancer Sven Bradshaw could not capture the special placement of the body suggested by the famous illustration of Louis as Apollo in the Bibliothèque Nationale. When, however, the dancer assumed the costume with its head-dress, the weight of materials and the high heels researched by the wardrobe of the Royal Opera House, he *had* to stand the way Louis is shown. It was the only way to balance and move. The problem was solved.

In this sort of way, developing her knowledge through practical application on stage, the Skeaping researches and productions brought to life for many of us in England more than three centuries of theatre – from her long and brilliant sequence of 16th-century Tudor court dances for the film *Anne of the Thousand Days*, to the *Basse Dance, Tordion* and *Galliards* later in the century produced for Ballet for All (with an *Allegrezza d'Amore* thrown in from Italy in 1600), to the *Courantes* and *Contredances* of early-17th-century France, and then her ingenious, necessarily limited, production of a sequence from the *Ballet Royal*. This and her later work in England overlapped, of course, with her much greater work in Sweden on which her reputation is based. Her work in England complements this reputation, particularly through the sequence from the *Ballet Royal*, her production of the condensed version of John Weaver's *The Loves of Mars and Venus* and, much later, her great production of *Giselle* for London Festival Ballet.

The second part of Mary Skeaping's contribution to dance knowledge is consequential on her extension of the study of dance history to include not only its practical staging but also those elements of history which cannot be expressed in words. If dance and movement can provide historical evidence of areas of social development which cannot be expressed in words, it follows that this notion of knowledge raises issues about the nature of knowledge itself. For many centuries academic circles have sustained the fiction that only knowledge acquired and transmitted through the written word is knowledge worth having. That which is not acquired thus, like the results of scientific experiment or mathematical speculation, remains experimental or speculative until presented in words. Our European university systems are based on this premise. Only within our own century has it come gradually to be recognised that there are wide areas of knowledge which not only cannot be transmitted in words, but for whose acquisition words are unnecessary. Such is dance.

The nature of dance knowledge, as all dancers appreciate, is non-verbal. It is to do with gesture, motion and the movements of the body in response to stimuli within or outside the body, or to express feelings, qualities and knowledge which cannot be expressed in words. All dance is of this nature, East and West, North and South, because dance is part of the history of human movement, part of the history of human culture and part of the history of human communication. Without human movement there is no society, no economic production, no re-production, no relation to the environment, no communication with the unknown, no communication between human beings. Early on it was the special function of dance to explore the unknown, impersonate it and perform the magic task of communication with Powers who shaped human destiny. Universities have been slow to recognise that movement is a source of knowledge, a communicator of knowledge and, above all, a fundamental element in European society's concept of the arts. In dance, for example, lies a significant contrast between the Gustavian manifestation of cultured society, at least for the group around the Swedish court, and English society of the same period. By the late 18th century English society had long since abandoned the notion that a great part of the glory, even the wealth, of a society and its State should *necessarily* be reflected in State patronage of the arts. In this attitude England was isolated not only from the rest of Europe but from most of the rest of the world. The societies of Africa, India and China at that time all honoured and supported the arts, including dance, as embellishments of the social order.

This world attitude to the arts arose, I suggest, not only to enhance the person of the ruler under the political philosophy of the time, nor only as a means of social control. Each particular art made its contribution according to the temperament and traditions of its society. The dance element was linked, implicitly or explicitly, with an understanding of the significance of body language to that society or period. Such a notion of body language was well argued by Dr Kurt Johannesson in a paper on *Eloquentia Corporis* at an international symposium on 'Opera and Dance in the Gustavian Era, 1771-1809', convened in Stockholm, June 1986. Having regard to the subject of the symposium, Dr Johannesson drew attention to the special importance of body language in the 18th century, and the role of dancing masters like Magri in educating the bodies and minds of young pupils to communicate correctly the body language of the day. At no time was this verbal but a communication 'from the heart speaking only to the heart'. All Mary Skeaping's work in Sweden and Britain emphasises the accuracy of this view. The problem is that recognition of the importance of dance education and body language in the 18th century was lost in the 19th century. Today, therefore, in spite of the increased importance of body language in our multiracial society, we have to persuade much of the British education system that knowledge can be transmitted and acquired not only in words but also non-verbally, and not only knowledge of today but also historical knowledge.

Skeaping's work makes an important contribution to this conception. Yet she was no specialist in these matters. She was clear in the significance of her work for the study of dance history, less clear on the wider implications. Nor was she, as far as I know, religious, but she puzzled for a meaning in life and searched through authors, including classical authors such as Plotinus. For some time she was interested in Buddhism and sketched in her own hand in 1982 some influences of its teaching, which she supplemented with typed descriptions. Her search, as I recall, was a search for knowledge on two levels – of the senses, and beyond the senses. She argued that we need to see the world as process not structure, a conclusion born of contact with reality. Dance is contact with reality in its most direct form – contact with earth, space, the body and all the senses. It is also in some measure unpredictable because it links material reality with emotions and explores reality outside the Cartesian/Newtonian world view of a universe operating on predictable cause and effect like a clock. Thus the material world is not as predictable as was thought, and the magic of dance can be seen to be a view of man related to his universe in ways which go beyond the traditionally rational and explicable. Dance achieves this relationship by linking the emotional and material worlds.

This understanding and personal philosophy seemed to underlie her reverence for the styles of the 17th, 18th and 19th centuries. Consequently, few choreographers have been able to illuminate so clearly our comprehension of the manners and values of societies now gone for ever. All this was based on a careful study of sources and of the societies within whose context the dances took place. She insisted always that her work was original choreography. 'How could I', she used to say to me, 'pretend to be my predecessors, or know precisely how they worked?' She must be acknowledged, therefore, as a unique choreographer in her own right. This insistence illustrates also her modesty among other personal traits which made her a colleague always stimulating, if sometimes demanding and difficult. As a creator she was immensely ingenious. As a scholar wonderfully enthusiastic and generous with her knowledge. As an artist intensely professional so that to have worked with her creates a memory

27

which can never fade. As a human being she was dominated by a sense of time and its shortage. Right at the end, when she had tidied her flat and papers as if in preparation, she said in that energetic way of hers 'There is still *so much* to do.'

This was the woman whom I knew well by 1972 and who asked me that spring to come to her flat in Paddington to discuss a project. I had just become director of the UK branch of the Calouste Gulbenkian Foundation. So I guessed the problem was money. The project was a translation of Magri; the inspiration was the man himself. Having been familiar for so long with the dance technique and body language set down in his *Trattato*, she perceived him still only dimly. A small grant, she argued, would achieve two objectives. She would understand the man in his time more fully. From this she could achieve better the first English translation of a work which would fill a gap in our knowledge of the development of classical dance technique. How did the 18th-century classical dance technique she used so fruitfully at Drottningholm become the technique from which Vestris, Blasis and others developed methods to train the dancers who launched Romantic Ballet in the 1830s?

On the face of it Mary Skeaping was the ideal person for such a project. Knowing, as she did, the long history which formed the dance technique Magri inherited, and having translated already on stage elements of Magri's development of technique, the funding of a translation, as we saw it, would be a meeting of minds, hers and Magri's. She argued, moreover, for a very small grant, too small as it turned out. Since her Italian was not sufficient always to decipher Magri's very personal use of the language it was characteristic she wanted the grant not for herself, but to pay a specialist to help her. Apart from all this we knew as well as she did that her work would provide the English-speaking dance world of the five continents with one of its most invaluable treatises on ballet technique. It was not difficult, therefore, to persuade my trustees to provide a grant for such an enterprise by such a person, even though it lay outside the Foundation's priorities of the moment.

Mary Skeaping estimated the translation would take about two-and-a-half years. The grant of less than £3,000 was for translation help and for illustrations. She refused any fee for herself, a practice with which I was familiar from Ballet for All days. Generous to a fault with her time and knowledge, we used to have to insist on some financial recognition of her essential contribution to theatrical work which was entirely her creation. In the case of Magri she argued that the achievement of translation would be recompense enough. So it might have been except that twelve years later, after two more small grants, the work was still unfinished when she died. The translation, however, was virtually done. It needed some further small bits of translation, completion and editing by Irmgard Berry, her collaborator of the last four years. This translation is her final gift to the profession and art by which she lived.

Paradoxically, it was her international reputation as a producer of the classics and as an outstanding dance scholar which was the cause of the slow progress of her work on Magri. 'I live to work', she told Gerd Andersson and producers of a film of that title about her work in Sweden in 1984. Consequently, she found it difficult to reject the invitations which came to her from America and Britain as well as Sweden. It was equally difficult for us to argue she should stop making the often significant additions to dance knowledge her productions represented to concentrate only on Magri. I recall one period when she commuted across the Atlantic between two concurrent productions, the 18th century at Drottningholm and the 19th century of Petipa's *The Sleeping Beauty* in the United States. She was then in her late seventies.

Indeed, she only really started to work seriously on the guts of translation in 1978 when Irmgard Berry joined her and she was pressured by Gulbenkian. Until then she had worked mostly on the words. From 1978 she worked on the steps through long hours with Irmgard interpreting Magri in practice on the floor of her flat. Such practical work crucially validates the translation even though the translation itself is the fruit of moments between incessant theatrical activity. One of the outstanding characteristics of this activity, as I have pointed out, was ability to master historical sources and to enter the societies around the dancing masters on whose work she drew. In the same way she seemed to enter Magri's life.

Her productions and studies began usually, in my experience, with a book of the period, or, of course, a score or libretto. From this frequently a microfiche was made. Thus her association with Magri began through an introduction by Dr Agne Beijer some years before she undertook the translation or began to use his steps in her choreography. All or most dance scholars, I suppose, proceed somewhat in this fashion, especially when research involves practical reconstruction. At the same time each research becomes personal, adapted to the individual and subject. So it turned out with Magri.

The *Trattato* is written by a dancer for dancers. Before long, therefore, Mary came to feel she was working with a friend and colleague. Magri, however, was somewhat special among her other colleagues of the 18th century. He was a *grotesco*, a dancer we call today a character dancer, one of the three recognised physical types into which nature divides classical dancers. There are the noble dancers, the princes, tall and elegant; demi-character dancers, usually shorter in build, who dance many athletic, acrobatic roles while still having also much physical elegance; and character dancers, whose physique allows them to do much brilliant dancing but deprives them of a final elegance. Magri is especially interesting because he was a *grotesco* who wrote down his convictions and methods. Thus he has created a rarity of a book which carries us into a part of the 18th-century dance world hardly ever entered. Grotesque dancing was undertaken only by professionals whereas noble dancing through much of the 18th century could be undertaken by gifted amateurs. Clearly Magri was not only a professional who knew his stuff but one with a reputation which took him as a choreographer to many parts of Europe, although little is known of his life, birth or death. At the time of the *Trattato*, with its Neapolitan terms and usages which created particular difficulties for Mary Skeaping, he was ballet master at Naples, where the *Trattato* was published in 1779. He needs to be seen, therefore, very much in an Italian context and in the context also of his profession. Thus he deals in Part II of the *Trattato* with the social graces and manners of the day. Teaching these to the children of the nobility and gentry provided the bread and butter of most dancing masters in Europe. It was part of the non-verbal fabric of society to which dance provides an introduction. Part I is the real treasure house of the book because here Magri provides his detail of the dance profession of the time and fulfils his aim to show future dancers how to accomplish the wealth of steps he performed and set down for their benefit.

Such an aim also was Mary Skeaping's, except that she could offer her knowledge in partnership with Magri to a world of dance many times larger than Magri knew, and to scholars and critics whose professions hardly were thought of in his day. It was for all of these, and the students she never forgot, that Mary Skeaping undertook her work.

REFERENCES

Chesterfield, Lord (1774): *Letter to his Son*, London.

Gulbenkian Foundation (1980): *Dance Education and Training in Britain*, London.

Gulbenkian Foundation (1982): *The Arts in Schools*, London.

Lorraine, Philip L. (1956): *Drottningholm Court Theatre*, Stockholm.

Noverre, J.-G. (1760): *Letters on Dancing and Ballets*, Stuttgart; trans. Beaumont, London.

Read, H. (1943): *Education through Art*, London.

Skeaping, Mary (1967): *Ballet under the Three Crowns*, Dance Perspectives, New York.

Skeaping, Mary (1983): *Den Svenska Hovbaletten*, Stockholm; trans. Cramér.

Skeaping, Mary & Ståhle, Anna Greta (1979): *Balett pa Stockholmsoperan*, Stockholm.

Tomlinson, K. (1735/1720): *The Art of Dancing and Six Dances*, London.

Weaver, John (1723): *Anatomical and Mechanical Lectures*, London.
Winter, Marian Hannah (1974): *The Pre-Romantic Ballet*, London.
Andersson, G. & Aberle, V. (1984): *I Live to Work*. Documentary film on the work of Mary Skeaping in Sweden, Stockholm.

NB: Extracts from this introduction were presented at The Stockholm Symposium on Opera and Ballet in the Gustavian Era 1771–1809. June 9–14, 1986.

Notes on the Translation

by Irmgard E. Berry

1.   In coming to this treatise, it is essential to realise that it was written by a dancer for dancers and it is assumed that the present reader has a basic knowledge of theatrical dance technique. Therefore, bracketed additions are given only where a dancer would need further clarification. Specific notes are used to describe a term perhaps unfamiliar to today's readers, to offer an English equivalent of a step name or to point out discrepancies and possible misprints in the text.

2.   The biggest hurdle to overcome in the translation was the ungrammatical writing and idiosyncratic punctuation of the original Italian. Grammar has been corrected as far as possible without destroying the verbal style of Magri's writing. Punctuation has been amended accordingly, mainly by the use of semi-colons to break up his lengthy and complicated sentences. Only in extreme cases has one sentence been separated into two. Magri's erratic use of capitalisation and italicisation has been followed except for step names and non-English words, all of which have been italicised for easier reading.

3.   Following the example of English treatises of the period, step names have been given in French where possible, according to Magri's own example, but directions such as forwards and backwards have been given in English. The only direction in French is *sur place*, *sotto al corpo* in Italian, for a purely aesthetic preference to *on the spot*. Magri's faulty and archaic French spelling has been corrected so that *fuetè* becomes *fouetté*, *jettè jeté* and so forth. Italian corruptions of French terms such as *ambuettè* for *embôîté* have been kept, with a note giving the correct French term.

4. The term *cou-de-pied, collo del piede* in Italian, gives great problems in translation. Today this term can refer to any point between the instep and the part of the leg just above the anklebone, depending on which dance technique is being followed. The precise Italian meaning of 'instep' has been chosen as the most appropriate translation. However, in a number of steps, especially the beaten steps, the translation 'anklebone' is not an impossibility.

5. Generally the Italian term *fatto* ('done') corresponds to *en dehors* ('outward') and *disfatto* or *disfare* ('undone' or 'to undo') to *en dedans* ('inward'), but as there are a few exceptions to this, the terms have been left in Italian.

6. Magri uses the terms *avanti* ('in front') and *sopra* ('over') and *in dietro* ('behind') and *sotto* ('under') interchangeably throughout the text when indicating the action of closing one foot to the other. 'In front' and 'behind' have been chosen as the clearest translations except when describing some *pas de bourrée* and *glissades* in which 'over' and 'under' are accepted directions in today's dance terminology.

7. For the jumps described in the last chapter of Part I, the English translation *capriole* for the Italian *capriola* has been used in preference to the French *cabriole*. The term covers all big jumps (i.e. needing elevation) and is not restricted to one type of beaten jump as is the French term *cabriole*. Magri distinguishes between 'little jumps' (*salticelli*), which he includes amongst steps and which correspond to *terre à terre* style, and jumps which need greater elevation and are therefore termed *caprioles*.

8. In Part II, Magri uses the Italian word *figura* to mean several different things. The English translation 'figure' is given when Magri is referring to the pattern of set steps which mark out set patterns on the floor. When it refers to a couple or an individual dancer, these translations are used. The verb *figurare* is translated by the English verb 'to figure', meaning to perform the figuration. *Figurazione* ('figuration') is used interchangeably with *figura* ('figure') in reference to the floor pattern or sequence of steps.

EXPLANATION OF THE THREE CATEGORIES
OF THEATRICAL DANCERS:
SERIO, MEZZO-CARATTERE AND GROTESCO

Serio (Serious)

Tho' there are but few good Performers in the Sort of *Dancing*, yet is it of all other the easiest attain'd; and there goes but little towards the Qualification of the Master or Performer of it; but yet this Difficulty attends it, that a Man must excel in it to be able to please. There are two Movements in this Kind of *Dancing*; The *Brisk*, and the *Grave*; the *Brisk* requires *Vigour, Lightness, Agility, Quicksprings*, with a *Steadiness*, and *Command* of the *Body*; the *Grave*, (which is the most difficult) *Softness, easie Bendings and Risings*, and *Address*; and both must have *Air* and *Firmness*, with a *graceful* and *regulated Motion* of all *Parts*: But the *Artful* Qualification is a *nice Address* in the Management of those *Motions*, that none of the *Gestures* and *Dispositions* of the Body may be disagreeable to the Spectators. This *Address* seems difficult to be obtain'd and in effect is so; and it is this *Address*, that ought to take up the Thoughts of the Performer; and in which he must shew his Skill; nor will it perhaps be so easie a Matter, as some may think, to attain a Perfection in it!

(Weaver, 1721, p. 163–4)

Mezzo-Carattere (Demi-Caractere)

The demi-caractere dancer should be of medium height and a slim elegant build. A figure such as Mercury or the Hebe of Canova would be suitable for demi-caractere or mixed roles, and those with the good fortune to possess these physical assets will shine in this delightful style.

The demi-caractere is a blend of different styles in dancing and students who embrace it may make use of all the movements and steps that the art offers. Nonetheless, their manner should always be noble and elegant and their temps d'abandon accompanied by restraint and a pleasing dignity. They should avoid the grand temps of the serious style, as for them unqualified success resides only in steps appropriate to Mercury, Paris, Zephyrus, etc., and in the dances and graceful ways of an elegant troubadour.

(Blasis, 1820, p. 57)

Grotesco (Grotesque)

Grotesque *Dancing* is wholly calculated for the Stage, and takes in the greatest Part of *Opera-Dancing*, and is much more difficult than the Serious, requiring the utmost Skill of the Performer. Yet this sort of *Dancing* seems at first View not to be so difficult; by reason there are so many Pretenders to it, who palm themselves upon the Town for Masters: But Men of

Judgement will easily perceive the Difference between a just and skilful Performance, and the ridiculous Buffoonry of these artless Ignorants. A Master or Performer in *Grotesque Dancing* ought to be a Person bred up to the Profession, and throughly [sic] skill'd in his Business ... As a *Performer*, his Perfection is to become what he performs; to be capable of representing all manner of *Passions*, which *Passions* have all their peculiar *Gestures*; and that those *Gestures* be just, distinguishing and agreeable in all Parts, Body, Head, Arms and Legs; in a Word, to be (if I may so say) all of a Piece.

(Weaver, 1721, pp. 165, 166)

Notes

DISTINCTION BETWEEN THE TERMS BALLERINO, BALLANTE AND DANZATORE
by Anna Ivanova

Naples was occupied by the Spaniards in Magri's day; indeed he was employed by the Spanish court there as dancing master. In his Treatise he records that Italian dance technique was enriched by the Spanish dance influences he found there. He even took the trouble to describe the five Spanish positions (Part 1, Chapter 5, section 5). It would therefore seem probable that in Italy at this period, as in Spain, a clear line of demarcation was drawn between the diverse types of dance executants which Magri constantly refers to.

A Ballerino heads the list, for this was a title bestowed upon the dance artiste who had an acquired knowledge of the Art, and it was usually associated with the professional theatrical dancer at the peak of his profession.

A Ballante was a term applied generally to dancers of any rank. Magri refers to a *ballante grotesco* suggesting that likewise the ballante belonged to the theatrical hierarchy. However, a ballante might also be one who danced instinctively, without any academic training, as for example folk dancers, many of whom were brilliant executants.

A Danzatore was, as the name implies, that dancer excelling in the performance of danzas. Skill was required to do them well, since they called for refined deportment using the head, arms and shoulders. Magri warns his 'courteous reader': 'One who only knows how to move his legs will never make a good danzatore'. Obviously to acquire this skill required the services of a dancing master. The 18th Century masters had transformed these danzas into a highly developed dance form which they used profusely in their theatrical productions. They also became extremely fashionable in the aristocratic ballrooms. It was considered a mark of social distinction to be able to dance them well.

Bibliography of Works Referred to during the Process of Translation

Blasis, Carlo. *An Elementary Treatise upon the Theory and Practice of The Art of Dancing*, translated by Mary Stewart Evans. Dover Publications Inc., New York 1968.

Compan, Charles. *Dictionnaire de danse*. Paris 1787.

Croce, Benedetto. *I Teatri di Napoli secolo XV–XVIII*. Naples 1891.

Donnington, Robert. *A Performer's Guide to Baroque Music*. Faber and Faber, London 1973.

Duchartre, Pierre Louis. *The Italian Comedy*, translated by Randolph T. Weaver. George G. Harrap and Co. Ltd, London 1929.

Dufort, Giambattista. *Trattato del ballo nobile*. Naples 1728.

Enciclopedia dello spettacolo. Sansoni, Italy 1961.

Greenish, Arthur J. *The Student's Dictionary of Musical Terms*. Stainer and Bell Ltd, London 1953.

Lambranzi, Gregorio. *New and Curious School of Theatrical Dancing*, translated by Friderica Derra de Moroda. C. W. Beaumont for the ISTD, London 1928.

The New Groves Dictionary of Music and Musicians, ed. Stanley Sadie. Macmillan Publishers Ltd, London 1980.

Nivelon, F. *The Rudiments of Genteel Behaviour*. London 1737.

Rameau, Pierre. *The Dancing Master*, translated by C. W. Beaumont. C. W. Beaumont, London 1931.

Smith, William C. *The Italian Opera and Contemporary Ballet in London 1789–1820*. The Society for Theatre Research, London 1955.

Tomlinson, Kellom. *The Art of Dancing Explained by Reading and Figures*. London 1735.

Veilhan, Jean-Claude. *The Rules of Musical Interpretation in the Baroque Era.* Alphonse Leduc, Paris 1977.
Weaver, John. *An Essay towards an History of Dancing.* London 1712.
Anatomical and Mechanical Lectures upon Dancing. London 1721.
Winter, Marian Hannah. *The Pre-Romantic Ballet.* Sir Isaac Pitman and Sons Ltd, London 1974.

THEORETICAL AND PRACTICAL TREATISE ON DANCING

BY
GENNARO MAGRI
NEAPOLITAN

DANCING MASTER OF THE ROYAL ENTERTAINMENTS OF HIS SICILIAN MAJESTY, OF THE ROYAL MILITARY ACADEMY

AND

MASTER OF THE NOBLE ACADEMY OF MUSIC AND DANCE OF THE SIGNORI CAVALLIERI, TO WHOM THIS WORK IS DEDICATED

NAPLES 1779

PRINTED BY VINCENZO ORSINO
BY ROYAL LICENCE

Most Illustrious and Most Noble Gentlemen of the Academy

Having wished to introduce an Academy into this Metropolis, wherein it is desired to practise the fine arts of Dance and Music, as well as virtuous pleasures, is so commendable that it earns you universal applause, in showing that you wish to spend the hours remaining to you from your daily domestic duties in Chivalrous exercises, detaching yourselves from the company of idlers.

Now recognising in you these laudable principles of noble pastime, and seeing that you have chosen me as Dancing Master for such eminent Company from among so many other excellent Masters, I therefore esteem it my duty to show my gratitude for the honour bestowed upon me.

Nowhere is a confession of obligation made more public than in a Dedication. I have chosen to publish my appreciation of you, most worthy Gentlemen of the Academy, in this way. To you I offer and consecrate my work which, if having no other merit, cannot be denied that of new invention, especially regarding the second part, which brings to light new and original material. All the signs which appear therein are of my conception and, without vanity and presumption, I can aspire to the honour of being the first Inventor.

It is risky to set foot along an untrodden path, and it is easy to stumble, as could very well have happened to me in this new venture, in which undoubtedly the insolent Satirists, full of evil talent for insulting the labours of others, will find material to lacerate my name with all that malice and envy might suggest to them, without good reason, without pity, without understanding the difficulty of being the first to handle the enterprise. But they will not dare to attack it, seeing on the frontispiece

the name of not one, but so many illustrious Patrons, whom I devotedly salute and, with all glory, I boast of being your
Most Humble, Devoted and Grateful Servant,

Gennaro Magri.
Naples   15 August 1778

Preface

The birth of the Dance is concealed in the shadows of such remote antiquity, that it has never been possible to come to any definite conclusions about its origin, nor to obtain from the most renowned Authors any definite conclusions as to which era it belongs. The only thing that can be ascertained is that its invention was very long ago.

With the Greeks, it was much used in celebrating Sacrifices to their Deities and specifically in the Bacchanalian festivals. After having swallowed liberal quantities of alcohol, in a state of merriment, the whole bodily mechanism was put into motion and excitement. In that state of ecstasy, unable to remain still, each one felt a secret impulse to hurl himself, stretch himself, move himself and thus impatiently abandoning themselves, they improvised dances without artifice but as nature impelled the brilliant machine[1] enlivened by sweet goblets: whence it is usually argued it had its crude and simple origin.

However, I do not want obstinately to adhere to this; I would rather say that it was born of some spirited Group which happily enjoyed itself. In fact it can be observed even today that the Dance needs drive and to be enlivened by some external cause; and usually this is the Music which so awakens the aesthetic that often it moves one from melancholy to happiness, and impels the limbs to extend and to move according to its beat.

Among the many examples, one sees the sway that Music holds over the human mind in the healing of the *Tarantolati*[2] so that, at one sound of the music called *Tarantella*, in the highest state of their agony, the bodies begin to move automatically so that, shaken from that mortal lethargy, they set about jumping with extraordinary movement, causing the pores of the skin to open, expelling all the poison dissolved in sweat.

But let us leave this digression aside, and return to our subject. The most learned Signor Ludovico Antoni Muratori, in the *Antichità d'Italia*, relates that an Anonymous Author of a handwritten Chronicle of Milan, an Author of great Antiquity, describing the ancient Milanese Theatre writes that, as soon as the singing ended, the Dance began. *Finito cantu Busoni, & Mimi in citharis pulsabant, & decenti motu corporis fe circumvolvebant.*

Among the games called by the Romans *Ludi scenici*, there were also the Dances, especially those called *Mimes*. This sort of spectacle was performed by one Actor only, called *Pantomimus*, who, singing and dancing, comically portrayed all men's actions, imitating them in a thousand ways, putting himself in a thousand ridiculous postures to make the spectators laugh. His name is still maintained in the theatrical presentation called *Pantomimo ballato*.[3]

This festive custom was still used by the *Sannili* and *Tarentini*, who drew the ancient origin from the Spartans. These celebrated the Saturnalia, placing the God of Happiness on an ostentatiously decorated machine, weaving around it in varied and lively dances, which were then abolished by Pyrrhus, King of Epirus, in order to train the youths well for war and not divert them from military discipline when they defended themselves against the power of the Romans, who wanted to subjugate them.

Although all these people danced and jumped governed by musical harmony, they did not however perform dances with prescribed steps: wherefore without doubt it is required that the honour and glory of being the first to give rules to the Dance must go to our Italy, having formed its precepts and given it documentation.

As far as we know, the first to write about Dances was Maestro Rinaldo Rigoni, whose work bears the title *Il Ballerino perfetto*, printed in Milan in the year 1468. After this, Signor Fabrizio Caroso da Sermonetta wrote a *Raccolta di vari balli*, printed in Rome in 1630. In our century the *Trattato di ballo nobile* by Giambattista Dufort appeared, which went to press in Naples in the year 1728.

After the Italians, the Spaniards were to learn the Dance in the Italian manner, adding to it some *caprioles* and the sound of *nacchare*.[4]

Although the Italians can boast of being the first to invent rules for the Dance, nevertheless they did not bring it to perfection and, although they danced in cadence with the Music, the steps were so forced and affected that if their characters were put on the stage, it would be the most jocular and grotesque Pantomime, as was ingeniously executed by Monsieur *Filibois*, Dancing Master at the Imperial Court. We are obliged to the French for the precision which dancing shows today. They have refined it on the lathe of good taste. With this amazing and delightful spectacle they have added lustre to the Theatres. They have ennobled the ballrooms with this majestic and brilliant entertainment which takes place not only at noble and civil assemblies, but is also the greatest and principal festivity of the Sovereign Courts: where, seeing the pre-eminence of this diversion, I have applied myself to giving the truly strict rules both in Theatrical and Ballroom Dance according to modern taste, embracing that which is customary in our time and rejecting everything used by the ancients. I have endeavoured to explain with the utmost clarity possible in order to be intelligible to beginners, minutely describing all the steps, their diversity and the movements.

I have divided this Treatise of mine into two parts. In the first I shall speak of all the steps, of the material pertaining to them and of the *caprioles*; in the second I shall deal with Ballroom Dancing.

I ask nothing more from this my labour, other than it be of pleasure and benefit to others, entirely free of vainglory and the desire to immortalise my name in print. Having won general approval, I have accomplished my aims and, with this flattery, I find the reward for my toil. If any defect should appear within, it should be blamed upon my limited knowledge but it should not detract from the merit of the noble art of the Dance.

Warning
to the Courteous Reader[5]

As soon as I thought of publishing the present treatise, I immediately formed the grave suspicion that I should be subjected to the lashes of criticism employed by my rivals to discredit me. In fact the printing was not yet completed, when they brought onto the scene the miserable and obscure *Francesco Sgai* and, having dressed him up as a thinker, put his name to a most defamatory libel against me. On reading those fatuous thoughts, I realised that they did not have the strength to bring even the slightest discredit to my treatise, and I did not shrink from proceeding with the printing. Therefore I present this my work just as it was composed before the reflections, and I deem it necessary only to precede it with a few words on their nature, and condition.

Firstly, the frontispiece of my treatise is attacked, for having added *Theoretical-practical* to it as if to suggest that the term *theoretical* is unsuitable, that it is not within my understanding to deal with the art of theories. This is a temerity that can only be born from the depth of ignorance. In all arts, practice is necessarily the daughter of theory, and if the latter is ignored, the former cannot be exercised. Some may be good theorists but bad practitioners; however, it is impossible for one to be a good practitioner if one is not a perfect theorist. To my expertise in dancing, the public is witness, to whose impartial judgement I willingly submit without heeding the malicious voice of the thinker. Therefore it cannot be any wonder that I have set about expounding those ideas which I have obtained from experience and from reading the best works on this subject. Whether I have happily succeeded should be decided by the wisest professors after the publication of my treatise, and the thinker could not have anticipated their decision without the stamp of disgraceful effrontery.

Then the titles attributed to me on the same frontispiece are attacked and, with a ridiculous paraphrase, I am accused of presumptuously appropriating the offices of others. I venerate the professors who actually hold them. These titles are held by worthy people but they did not suffer when they were held by me. At the time my treatise was printed I was in fact exercising those duties and rightly attributed the titles to myself, which the thinker could well gather from my dedication to the Gentlemen Academicians, to whom it would have been dangerous to assume the title of the Director of their dances if I had not been so, since they could have made me appear disgracefully contradicted.

He then goes on to censure my preface, and leads one to suppose that somebody else had written it in my name. However, he does not provide any generic or specific proof of this plagiarism but is diverted by slander and ludicrous expressions.

Putting on airs of an antiquarian, he points out the first origins of the dance, which I judiciously left to the research of the learned. I did not enter into examining whether or not he was able to draw the truth from the mists of time, but I would only say that such scrutinies demonstrate the thinker's torpid indolence, bringing nothing useful to those who cultivate the dance, and they are quite improper in a booklet of ill intentioned censure. I have never claimed to emulate the glory of the most learned investigators of Greek and Roman antiquity. I limited my talents to improve my own profession, and I flatter myself to have given no mediocre profit. That the dance might be invented by the *Corybantes* in Phrygia, or by the oldest Ruler of Egypt is as indifferent to me as it will be to all the dancers in the world. My only concern was to indicate the origins of some dances, so that their practice could be illustrated in a better manner. I marvel however that the presumptuous thinker, assuming the task of showing the first origins, should then have terminated his very inept research by confessing what I had already confessed, that the origins of the dance are entirely unknown.

In a treatise of dancing he would have desired the purity and clarity of the Tuscan language. This means that he does not know the rules of criticism, and in fact the thinker shamefully ignored them: where instead of writing a criticism which by its nature should have been gentle, benign and urbane, he wrote a malicious, impudent and rude satire. The true critic would have sought in my treatise facts and not words. *Stultum ac supinum* said old Scaligero, *rebus relictis consenescere in verbis*. In indicating the rules of dancing, I did not place before me the vocabulary of the Crusca[6] but the proportion, the decency, the intricacy, the beauty, and the means for the necessary agility. It is upon these that he should have made his expertise and ingenuity shine, and not waste paper and time going about dissecting Tuscan words and phrases.

In whatever manner I have expressed myself, it is sufficient that I have been understood, regardless of whether *vengasi* is written *venghisi* or *atteggio* instead of *atteggiamento*. For the rest the Critic should not lack knowledge of the subject he criticises. I am sure that nobody will pay heed to these most absurd reflections, but if someone should be drawn by curiosity, they will be disgusted by so many barbarisms, solecisms, idiocies and abuses of words, which are seen at first hand to be scattered by the supposed Florentine in those few papers with which he defiled the honour of the printed matter; I should have been glad if the rules of the art which I expounded had been amended, corrected or explained in a better form by him. But he did not take the trouble, perhaps because, indeed *undoubtedly* because, he did not have the help of expertise. He goes on to note some small things, which it suits me to review here in order to see how tediously he fulfilled the duties of a critic.

He censures me for having prescribed a too affected stance for the beginner, and wants it understood that in this matter the natural posture should not be violated. Whoever has the slightest common sense can understand how harmful this indulgence is to the spirit of the art, which absolutely requires of a dancer an unaffected decency, which is exactly what I sought. Leave the body in its defective condition, and there will be no regularity in the steps, no beauty of movements, and the spectators will be disgusted.

He is displeased that I want the musical instrument to serve the beginner, opining that, in this matter, he will never become used to dancing in time. But this is a sign of the scant knowledge that the thinker has of man. He who begins to apply himself to an art wishes to be as if led by the hand, and to be accustomed little by little. The rigorous, and uninterrupted playing of the music will render the dance impracticable rather than facilitate the measure of the beginner's steps, who, having first to learn the steps, cannot be forced to learn at the same time the rule of the cadence and of the speed. When order and system in teaching are not employed, much confusion and little profit ensues.

He derides the requisites that I describe as necessary for the *ballerino*. He is horrified by the arts and sciences which I require, and shows loathing for bodily gifts. Every art presupposes its own particular understanding. One will never become a professor while these are ignored. Those indicated by myself are so necessary to a *ballerino* that not having them he cannot be so called. As poetry is a speaking picture, so the dance is moving poetry. Can one be a good poet who only knows how to write verses? But no. Similarly one who only knows how to move his legs will never be a good *danzatore*. Whoever moves them with order, with symmetry, with judgement, with proportion and adapting his movements to the truth, to the probable, to the occasion, whoever invents new, surprising and pleasing things, will make an excellent *ballerino*. All this cannot be done if there is not a tincture of poetry, geometry, music, history, philosophy, geography and mythology; and those are the faculties that are requested.

Examining the rest of my principles, concerning the nature of steps and movements, he had nothing else to say, except that the formation of some of these is arbitrary, according to the modern school. The arbitrary has no school, and whoever admits the school of necessity submits the arbitrator to the laws of the selfsame school. Whoever seeks a Master to execute the art according to the really arbitrary? Therefore the thinker should have shown that the regulated manner of movement and of gesture prescribed by myself resulted in indecency, and corrected it by indicating another. Criticism should be fruitful. Discovering an error should propose the correction, it being the work of a fool to say *this is no good* without indicating how it could be better.

Finally he scorns me for having followed in the footsteps of certain able professors of dancing and transcribed their sentiments. The art of dancing did not originate from my hands. Others had already dealt with it, and many will after me. It was necessary that I made use of the thoughts of others, having found them judicious and correct, and on such occasions I have openly confessed from whom I have taken them. A learned Latin Writer said: *ingenui pudoris est fateri per quos didiceris.* I have not troubled however to mix up so many broken fragments of ancient Authors, as did the thinker in order to give conviction to his wide and varied reading. The public does not want to be so outlandishly wearied. And *Plautus, Terence, Phaedrus, Cicero* and *Martial* have about as much to do with dancing as crabs have with the moon. Moreover it is shameful pedantry to mingle Latin banter with Italian speech.

It was my intention to give a complete treatise for the dilettanti. If I was betrayed by the outcome, it was not through lack of will. Human understanding has its limits. However, I have forced myself not to introduce into the dance that charm which is directed to it. That this does not please the thinker does not bother me much, in fact not at all because he is not a competent Judge of such contests. When my work reaches the hands of good and dispassionate judges, I shall receive their modest corrections with goodwill. In social life first place must be given to *Maestro Galateo.*[7] However, whether or not any such corrections are undertaken, my courteous reader will be forewarned that, as ideas on dancing are enclosed within the human mind, while they may be well conceived, they may be badly represented, or badly understood by he who begins to read, stirred and agitated by the tyrannical passion of the faction. *Vivi felice.*

FIRST PART

1

Of the Utility of the Dance

The object of this pleasing faculty is not only to delight, as others believe, but the benefit that you obtain from it is more than grace; a hallmark, I would dare to say, of importance and necessity to a Gentleman. The manner of introducing oneself at a *Conversazione*, of receiving people with courtesy at home, the way to behave at a gathering and to distinguish persons with bows and salutations are all things learned from the Dance. Not only that, it also gives to the limbs a fine disposition which adds an air as well as a beautiful carriage to our body. I do not pretend to say that this disposition which the Dance gives to our body will give it a new symmetry but will only render it more prepared and better placed than that with which nature endowed the human body. We see men ordinarily holding their limbs in such a negligent posture, that in them one is unable to observe and distinguish all those fine dispositions and proportions to our mechanism which are distributed by nature. He who has learned the Dance however, does not neglect the symmetry of his body but he places each limb in the right position and shows the just proportion and order of the whole machine. As Signor Cavalier *Planelli*[8] sagely advised on this. Indeed in most cases a good artful disposition can hide certain little defects which are ascribed to certain bodies, either innately or by faults contracted through bad habits, as will be better seen by observing them.

2

How to Learn to Dance Perfectly

Those things in the world which are only practised, and denuded of theory, are only half learned. He who wishes to delve immediately into the heart of a subject, without first having applied himself to the rudiments, learns little or nothing and that little imperfectly. To learn the general rules, and to be instructed in their particular exceptions, is the only method by which man may reach perfection in whatever he wishes to learn. To some, it seems that Practice is master of everything. I say that the Practice is an edifice which needs a foundation to support it, and this foundation is the Theory. Some wish to reach the peak of perfection through experience alone. Experience convinces, but does not persuade; it demonstrates, but does not conclude; it is an art, and not reason. Some people will wish to show that the air is heavy by hanging on scales an hermetically sealed glass jar, balanced with a weight on the other side; then with a Boiliana machine, or a Pneumatic machine, extracting the air from the glass jar, so that they will see that the heavier side tips the balance. Will this demonstrate how the rule of gravity works, how with the Pneuma machine the air is extracted, and other intrinisic causes, without explaining the whole system? Not at all. In the same way they will be as ignorant as they were before watching the experiment. But let us convey a more easily understood example better suited to our purpose. Anyone who has a good ear, a sonorous voice, and who learns easily is capable of being able to sing any little tune which takes his fancy, after hearing it two or three times. But this man will never know Music, and what he hums approaching the melody will never be perfectly sung, in spite of attention given and outstanding natural ability. And then he can sing nothing else than those things which have been committed to memory through sheer practice; and they are sung with so many faults that not he, but those listening, who know something about the art, recognise the discords. Those however who have studied the principles of Music, and by these means have arrived step by step at singing a tune to perfection, similarly will be capable of intoning as many of them as ever have been created and as many as ever could be.

Now let us speak about the Dance. Those who have the will to learn it perfectly, if they do not diligently apply themselves to study thoroughly the principles, the rules, the precepts of our fine Art, will never know anything about the Dance but it is only through these that they will be able to dance all the possible dances existing in the world, and those that might exist; but those who, without knowing the principles, suddenly want to learn through practice this or that Dance to show that in a short space of time, thanks to their ability, they have been taught a great number of dances, these will not have learned anything and will not know how to form a step or a dance as it should be; and thus they are miserably deceived, and all that time has been wasted that they believed to have been doubly gained. Therefore there is no other means of succeeding in dancing than a long patient study of the first rudiments and then, little by little, bringing them together, adjusting them with precise symmetry and, in order to make great headway, taking them slowly. Therefore the foolish idea must be banished that one is going to be able to teach oneself a miscellany of Dances, of *caprioles*, of sequences of steps, as soon as the positions are barely known; from this it follows that, having only a light smattering of something, they suddenly wish to begin something else. Whoever wishes to learn to read, first has to know the letters, then how to form the syllables and thus gradually will achieve perfect reading: dancing is no more and no less; and whoever derides these my warnings, and executes the contrary, will find himself unhappily derided and deceived. I do not pretend other than to set forth the truth and to manifest not only what I think myself, because it is my understanding, but because through long experience, and in training the dilettante, I have found similar talents necessary.

53

3

The Qualities of the *Ballerino*

A *rs longa, vita brevis etc.*, says Hippocrates in one of his Aphorisms, speaking about Medicine. I say the same about the Dance; neither is it enough, as others think when speaking of the Theatre, for he who wants to be a *Ballerino* to learn only dancing. Many are the requisites sought in him. It goes without saying that firstly he must know how to read well, and to write better – most essential things – but it is also required that he should know something about the various sciences, not only because it is my firm opinion, but that of the celebrated Monsieur *Noverre*. Cavalier *Planelli*, worthy critic of Musical Works, gave enough proof that, although not a *Danzatore*, nevertheless he thinks so clearly about it that, it being lawful, I am pleased to quote him. *The Ballerino must endeavour not only to become agile and light in order to render the hands and the body eloquent (as Demetrius the philosopher said of a Danzatore in Nero's time), he needs to be initiated in many disciplines.* Lucien in his Dialogue on the Dance wishes that a *Ballerino* had understanding of Poetry, Geometry, Music, Philosophy. *Il faut que le Danseur Pantomime connoisse la Poésie, la Géomêtrie, la Musique, la Philosophie, l'Histoire et la fable, qu'il sache exprimer les passions et les mouvements de l'âme, qu'il emprunte de la Peinture, et de la Sculpture, les differentes postures, et contenances, en sorte qu'il ne le céni à Philias, ni à Apelles pour ce regard. Ce Danseur doit savoir aussi particulièrement expliquer les conceptions de l'âme, et Découvrir les sentiments par les gestes, et les mouvements du Corps: enfin il doit avoir le secret de voir partout ce qui convient (qu'on appelle le Décorum) et avec cela être subtil, inventif, judicieux, et avoir l'oreille très délicate.* Lucien on Dance. On such requirements I thus reason. Of Poetry, for the invention and formation of the dances, to compose them with lifelike characters, with interpolated ornaments, natural in the action, to observe rigorously the four *Unities* of the *Stage*, that is of *place*, of *action*, of *characters* and of *time*; nothing less than these, as the true and illustrious Poets of Tragedies, Musical Dramas, and Comedies observe and as Signor Salomoni states in one of his manuscripts *Dissertazione su la Tragedia*. Of Geometry, for the just proportion and the measure of the figures. Of Music, to adapt the time well, and the steps to the beats, so that the representation might be expressed by alternating the pathetic with the joyous, according to the passions of the action. Of fables and history, to weave the arguments with the qualities taught by Poetry. Of Painting and of Sculpture for the diverse gestures, to link the groups, to form the pictures, called in terms of the art *Tableaux*. In truth we see the Statues and Pictures thus speaking, expressed so vividly, that their passion shows in the eyes, in the posture by which emotion dominates them, whether anger, hate, love, sadness, happiness and such like. Thus the *Danzatore* must be impressed by these gestures to be able to execute them when he has to express this or that emotion, and he must have the secret of gratifying our senses and moving our emotions; the latter is the *Pathetic*, the former is the *Aesthetic*, which is the nature of the Fine Arts, without which the name of this Faculty would be improperly applied. To some it will seem to be claiming too much. It seems to me too much presumption for a *Ballerino*, in order to exercise his profession well, to begin to appear in the Theatre without knowledge of this necessary learning.

Beyond this understanding, Noverre in his Fifth Letter, already referred to, mentions that the *Ballerino* should study Anatomy in order to depict the skeletons.[9] He does not draw Michelangelo's foreshortened figures, but he places the *figurantes* disproportionately in their groups. These studies are absolutely necessary in order to render man in his just proportions, to portray him in his movement and in his attitudes; and with Anatomy, mechanics and drawings are desirable.

I would add to these Geography in order to know the rites, climates, places, customs, abuses, Islands, seas, Cities of different Nations, especially those of the African, Asiatic, and American ones, not known to us, so as to stage properly and express the character in a natural way, if wishing to put one of these Nation's dances into a spectacle. These are all necessary things, without which one cannot succeed as a first rate *ballerino*. And yet this is little. These are things which a man with a good intellect, and who has the possibility of cultivating himself in these studies, will be able to acquire. It is necessary that Nature has formed him well in limb and, according to *Polycletus*, the stature of the *Ballerino* should not be too tall or too short, neither fat, nor thin but of just proportions, attractive, and well formed, that he be strong in each of his limbs, and nimble.

4

Of the Equilibrium of the Body

L et us establish the whole basis of the steps before entering into their practice. The Equilibrium is one of the fundamental principles of the Dance. It keeps the body straight and upright. What matters most in equilibrium is that the line, which divides each body into two equal parts from top to bottom, falls in the centre of the base. This equilibrium has so much strength that the whole Terrestrial Globe or, rather than use hyperbole, the whole world might be sustained on the point of a sewing needle, if it were possible. By force of equilibrium, those tall machines are supported, vast on top but standing on a slender base, to the wonder of spectators; and if the fine art of Architecture were joined to the most perfect equilibrium, and the earth were stable, never would such machines and buildings be liable to ruin. But let us leave these digressions and return to that which concerns us about the fundamental basis of our art, the equilibrium of our body. We say that the equilibrium of the body holds the waist upright and well placed in the dance, preventing it from inclining to one side or the other, and a *Ballerino* taking a pose in the correct equilibrium could remain in it for days, unless lassitude should weaken his spirits and the agitation cause him to lose it.

There are six different ways of balancing the body in the dance. I. Naturally supporting the body on both feet with the torso very straight so that if a plumb line were hung from the *Sternum* or intercostal bone, called by Anatomists the *Pugio*, that is, the bone of the thorax to which the ribs are attached, the line would fall plumb in the centre of that space between the feet. II. The body is balanced on the balls of both feet with the same symmetry. III. On the sole of one foot, lightly touching the ground with only the tip of the other and then it is necessary to slightly incline[10] the body to the side of the foot which is flat on the ground, because otherwise it would be impossible to achieve just equilibrium, since the two feet do not form an equal base as before. IV. With one foot in the air, and the whole body supported on the sole of the other. V. On the ball of one foot, holding the other in the air. VI. Sustaining the body over both heels, without the rest of the foot touching the ground, and here the body will be perpendicular as in the first equilibrium.

I do not admit other kinds of equilibrium that others admit, which Sig. Dufort puts in fourth place, and that is balancing the body on the ball of one foot and the ball of the other hardly touching the ground. My feeling is that the foot is held entirely raised from the ground when the whole body is supported on the ball of the other, as is practised by the true *ballerini virtuosi*, and not by those who are not in this class.

Lack of equilibrium produces ill effects. In the *Ballerino serio* who is not able to achieve aplomb, the attitudes are feeble and fall flat; in the case of the *Grotesco*, when he lands from the *caprioles* he staggers and sometimes falls; in the *mezzo carattere* he does not do the set sequences of steps: all these defects coming from the body not being in perfect equilibrium.

5

Of the Movements of the Body

The Movements of the body are also an essential part of the Dance. They are nothing more than moving the body from one place to another, or turning it on the same place where one is standing; and there is no step that is not composed of one or more movements.

The movements may be either simple or compound. The simple ones are those done by themselves, without being linked to other kinds of movements. Compound movements on the contrary are an aggregate of many kinds of simple movements. For example, the *plié* is a simple movement; also simple are the rise, the walk, the turn. The *plié* movement is done by bending the knees; the rise by stretching the same knees or rising on the balls of the feet; the walk is done moving forwards, backwards or to the side; the turn is moving the body around without moving off the spot. The compound ones that, as was said, consist of several simple movements, are, for example, the *plié* taking one step, which is one movement only made up of the *plié* and the walk and must not be considered as two; the *plié* turning, the walk turning and such like are all composed of two simple movements. The *plié* walking with a turn is composed of three simple movements: of the *plié*, the walk and circling. And so every movement employed in conjunction with more than one is called a compound movement. The *plié* and the rise are two simple movements which nobody can really count as one compound. In jumps only two movements are counted; the first is the bending of the knees and the second is the stretching of the knees which thrusts the body into the air, which may also be called a rising movement, without which one cannot extend the knees or press into the ground to take the jump. The landing is not counted as a separate movement because it is a necessary motion produced by nature herself, since every weight demands the centre, and cannot remain in the air. This is what occurs to me when thinking about movements. Let us pass to the cadence, also an essential thing in this our Treatise.

6

Of the Cadence[11]

All the steps of the Dance will never be made attractive if they are not regulated by the harmony. A *Ballerino* may have all the grace, form the steps to perfection with all possible agility, but if he does not know how to adapt them to the musical metre he will never be numbered among the *ballerini*; if he goes out of cadence, everything else is rendered useless, and for this it is necessary for whoever wishes to know the Dance to also know Music. I do not say that this obliges him to know Music thoroughly, as he must who applies himself to this alone, but it is necessary that he distinguish perfectly the two metres: the *binary* and the *ternary*, for all the other diverse measures in Music can be reduced to these two alone in dancing. Indeed, strictly speaking, in Music there is no measure which is not *ternary* or *binary*; and just as all numbers have to be even, or uneven, so musical measures must by rights be *duple*, or *triple*. The Music Masters may divide and subdivide as much as they wish; they cannot avoid making it duple, or triple.

The *binary* time, which is a more lively time than the other, is used in those Dances that are done more quickly, as, for example, the *Gigue*, the *Gavotte*, the *Allemande*, and so forth. The *ternary* time, which is more stately, is used in Dances that are done with composure, like the *Chaconne*, the *Follia*, the *Amabile*, and the like. The *three-four*, in spite of being ternary time, can also be played very quickly and the furies[12] and others dance to it. There are other times which seem to be slower, and composed in ternary, called *twelve-eight*, to which are danced the *Entrata grave*,[13] and the airs which the French call *Loure* and the *Passacaglie*, nevertheless these times may be reduced to the binary whilst still preserving their gravity.

The *Major Triple* time or *three-one* needs three *Semibreves* to fill one bar;

three-eight, likewise ternary time, requires three *Quavers* to fill the bar, and the *Quaver* has the value of the eighth part of the *Semibreve*; therefore between these two ternary times there are eight degrees of speed of which one has more than the other. Not only is it necessary to know how to dance in the above-mentioned times, but to know how to divide and to distinguish the above-mentioned beats with the various kinds of steps and *caprioles*. There is no step which does not begin on the fall of the beat; there is no jump which does not land on the beat whatever the time might be, although it is permitted to the excellent Masters to dance in *intercadenza*. What this is will be explained in its place.

We moderns do not measure the cadence with the steps as did the ancients, for whom each step occupied one bar. We run more beats into one step, and we put more steps into one bar. One *ambuettè* used to be done in one bar of ternary time; in our time there is nobody who does not repeat two or three in one bar. In two bars, also of ternary time in *chaconne* tempo, one *jeté*, three *battements* and an *assemblé sur place*, were done; now in the same time with the sequence of the same steps, up to eight or ten *battements* are repeated; thus in other combinations of steps they are repeated and joined together in various ways.

They are wrong who dance and jump *staccato*[14] over a *fugato* tempo where they require a *two-four larghetto* tempo as is claimed by the *ballerini groteschi sbalzante*;[15] as also those who, to a *tamburino* tune, two-four *andante*, or in a *three-eight* time called *taice*[16] tempo, dance with *staccati* jumps such as a *contretemps*, a beaten or flying *capriole*, a *brisé*, a jump *sur place*, which are unsuitable and unbecoming. And so there are many variations of time signatures in order that the dancing will be uniform and the jumping will be with the pace of the tempi because, although there are only two times, binary and ternary as already stated, they embrace many variations. And thus each character can find the time of the Music suited to his dance. In *chaconne* tempo, which has very many changes, the *Ballerino* should not change simply because he has started together with the Music in a *staccato* style, if the Music changes theme from *languido* to *fugato*, from *sostenuto* to *andante*, where only the notes change but the time is always the same; therefore, as I said, the *ballante* must not vary the sequences of steps from *staccati* to *fugati* to *attitudini*, nor according to how the Music is marked.[17]

If in a *grave*, the pace of the Music is *sostenuto*, and if from time to time certain repeated bars of notes were to appear, the *Ballerino* would also repeat. In the *fugues* these sudden changes are often seen: from the *furioso* one passes to the *staccato*, to the *pause*, where the *attitudes* and *Tableaux* are employed. Let us imagine Boreas in love with Flora, who disdains him because she is in love with Zephyr; she flees and Boreas follows her; this requires Music which is very wild, and the good *Ballerino* will fill it with a multitude of varied steps and actions expressing the character, and which

61

perfectly match the quality of the Music; he catches up with her, and Flora, exhausted, falls to the ground: the Flowers languish, wherever Boreas passes the little Zephyrs placed in various *Tableaux* are stunned; Boreas reaches Flora, stops, and stays in *attitude:* here the Music must *pause* or be *syncopated;* thus the multitude of steps has no place, but the cadence must be filled with more poses than steps. The chase is again taken up, the *furioso* must be repeated, and so alternately the steps are adapted to the light and shade of the music, and the dance will be done according to the art, full of action, rich in variety, and it cannot fail to obtain the audience's applause.

Let us return to the differences between the diverse times, the *Minor Triple* time or the *three-two* needs three *Minims* in its bar; one *Minim* is worth half a *Semibreve;* therefore the *three-two* is twice the speed of the *Major Triple.* In order to make a bar in *three-four* time, three *Crotchets* are required; the *Crotchet* has the value of one quarter of the *Semibreve,* and half of the *Minim,* so that it is four times the speed of the *Major Triple,* and twice as fast as the *Minor Triple,* and so much for the ternary times. Let us turn to the *Binary.*

The *Medium* time, that is *two-four,* takes two *Crotchets* to the bar, one of which equals a *Sospiro.*[18] The *six-eight* time takes six *Quavers* to the bar, and one *Quaver* is equal to half a *Sospiro,* which is the same as half a *Crotchet,* so that it is one third slower than *Medium* time.[19] The time *a capella*[20] takes eight *Quavers* and is one *Sospiro* slower than six-eight. The *twelve-eight* time takes twelve *Quavers* to its bar, and is twice as slow as three-eight and, although it is also in binary time, it is one third slower than the *Major Triple.* With this distinction of times and proportion of speed a good *Ballerino* should contrive to match his steps; and before dealing with these, we shall discuss the positions.

7

Of the Positions of the Feet

§1. Of the true positions   §2. Of the false
§3. Of those in the air   §4. Of the forced
§5. Of those in the Spanish manner

As well as the five positions accepted by all, I will add to them others, and they are the false, others in the air, others forced, that is enlarged, and others in the Spanish manner.

§1

The *true* positions are five. I do not deem it necessary to speak of the parts of the foot; it is well known which is the toe, which the anklebone and which the heel. In all these five positions the body will always be balanced in the first mode. (Ch. 4, No. I)

The *first* of the true positions is formed by well placing the feet flat on the ground, the toes well turned out opposite each other, and the heels together, forming an obtuse angle.

We will make a geometrical explanation which will be necessary during the whole course of this Treatise. A *right* angle is formed by two straight lines, one lying flat, the other falling perpendicular to it; every angle greater than a right is called *obtuse*, and this is the angle which forms the *first* position; less than a right angle is called *acute*; the *perpendicular* is that straight line falling upon another forming two right angles, one on either side. All the right angles are necessarily equal to each other.

The *second* will be when the feet are separated at a distance of one foot between the heels along the same line, the toes well turned out, and the heels facing each other in such a way that, if a perpendicular line were drawn from the point of the intercostals to one between the feet, the two heels would remain equidistant from it so that the said perpendicular would divide that space into two equal parts.[21]

The *fourth* will keep the distance of a foot between one foot and the other, not laterally, as in second, but in front and behind. This means that the heel of the foot in front will be on a straight line with the anklebone of that behind.

The *fifth* is formed by placing the heel of one foot touching the toe of the other in such a way that a right angle is formed between the toe of one and the heel of the other.

§2

The *false* positions are also five and are necessary to know since they are employed in the Theatre by *ballanti Groteschi* in almost all the characters, and particularly in dancing the steps in the English manner, but according to Italian usage, because in their [English] national dancing they do not use either true or false positions, but their dancing is rendered pretty and light by reason of the great freedom with which it is practised.

The *false first* position is quite opposite to the true one. The toes are turned in, touching each other at the tips.

The *second* is also done with the toes turned in; the only difference from the first, in which the toes are touching each other, is that in this one there is a distance of one foot between them.

The *third*: where in the true position the heel of one foot is placed beside the anklebone of the other, here the toe of one touches the anklebone of the other.

The *fourth* keeps the toe of one foot on the same line as the anklebone of the other at a distance of one foot.

The *fifth* turns the toes of one foot inwards, touching the back of the heel of the other foot, which has its toes turned towards the heel of the other, forming an acute angle.

§3

The positions *in the air* have not been considered by anyone but I judge them to be no less necessary than the others and in this our Treatise we will often speak of them. In so many steps I see that one foot must pass through, or pause in, or end in one of these positions, and therefore if they are indeed employed, why not speak of them? It does not seem to me enough to say that a foot remains in the air without saying in what situation. Having given to this mature reflection, I would like to give them their place and a principal place. To say then position in the air, I mean to say that one foot is in the air and one firm on the ground. There are five then, in which the body will always be balanced in the fourth manner (Ch. 4, No. IV).

The *first* will be when one foot is placed completely flat on the ground, the other completely raised, the toes well turned out as in the true position (§1) and the heels not perfectly joined together because one is up and the other is down and this does not permit it.

The *second*, when one foot at a distance, and on the line as described in the true position (§1), is in the air instead of remaining on the ground.

The *third* is when the foot, which in the true position touches the anklebone of the other with its heel, instead of remaining on the ground, is raised from it.

The *fourth* does not differ from the true position except that the foot which is now in the air should keep its heel on a line with the anklebone of the other.

In the *fifth*, the foot in the air will have its corresponding heel to the toe of that on the ground at the same distance as in the true position. Thus these positions in the air are no different from the true positions except that the foot which is lifted from the ground governs the position.

<h1 style="text-align:center">§4</h1>

The need we have to know these positions in the air, I feel also applies to the *forced* positions, numbering three, excluding the first and the third, which should not be accepted as forced at all, and we will speak of them.

Of the *second*, there remains nothing more for me to say except that, where in the true position the distance to be kept between heel and heel must be of one foot, in this forced position, not having any determined distance, it will be greater, as required.

The *fourth* is related to the true position, giving the distance of more than one foot between the heel of the one and the anklebone of the other, as much as the step demands, not having even this distance assigned.

The *fifth*, as in the true position the heel of the one touches the toes of the other foot, here the heel will be at any required distance, but on the same lateral line as the toes of the other. Therefore there is no other difference than a greater distance between these and the true positions.

<h1 style="text-align:center">§5</h1>

The *First* Spanish position is formed with the feet parallel to each other, the insides touching at all parts, the legs, the knees, and all will be naturally stretched.

In the *second* the right foot will be carried behind the left at a distance of one foot, and the toes will be in a straight line with the heel of the other.

The *third* will be done by carrying the right foot to a position so that its instep is resting against the lateral part of the heel of the left foot.

The *fourth* is taken from the same place as the third, enlarged by a distance of one foot, so that the feet will be parallel.

In the *fifth* the heel of the right will be carried to the toes of the left with both feet forming a straight line. And these are all the positions acknowledged by me, and necessary for an understanding of the whole of this Treatise. That being said, we can start on the explanation and formation of all the steps.

8

Of the Steps

Everything hitherto explained is employed in the good formation of the steps, which are the soul of this fine art, and as this is the principal aim, it needs some attention. I will endeavour to explain myself with the greatest clarity I can, even though the task is somewhat arduous since the path I have to tread is a stony one where hitherto nobody has set foot except for Signor Dufort, who has spoken only about *noble steps*, but too discordantly, and far removed from modern taste. I do not speak of Maestro Fabrizio Caroso da Sermonetta: he is so remote from our new style that he seems to know about everything but the Dance, although we believe that he had attained merit and applause in his century.

One cannot begin any step except from one of the positions explained and without the body being placed in one of the set equilibriums. Each step is composed of its requisite movements, either simple or compound. We shall speak of them one by one in detail, and we shall give them those names by which they are ordinarily known, most of them being in French.

I will not use choreographic signs but I will make a broad explanation without putting many signs before your eyes, which in fact would cause more confusion rather than not; not that these signs are enough to indicate all the movements which are made in a step, but they only tell you from which position they begin and in which they end. This I will do by means of explanations and I hope to achieve from this the desired end.

9

§1. Of the simple or natural step, *Simple ou naturel*
§2. To walk well

§1

From the name itself, it is understood that this step is without artifice, pure and simple, as nature teaches everyone. Those steps that are made in walking are the *natural* and *simple* steps. Each may begin and end in any position. The movement which composes it, is stepping at a moderate pace.[22] I will not enlarge upon this and on its diversity backwards, sideways, turning, because these are things that nature herself teaches to all and that everyone, I think, knows how to walk. The distance that will be taken from foot to foot is not determined; the stature of the *Ballante* will decide how the step is to be adapted; not too short if tall, not too long if short, for the one and the other would be faulty.

§2

There are very many who walk in a blameworthy manner, and since the Dance is the lathe upon which the human body is refined, this should remedy the defects; therefore, I will suggest how to make this step more pleasing. The knee curves naturally, extending the instep gracefully, and placing first the point and then the rest of the foot. The feet may be turned out but not too much; and to remedy any defects there are, either through being spoilt in youth or through having some imperfect joint, constant practice walking about the room in the prescribed manner will remedy every defect.

10

---

§1

I would not really give the name of step to this which is called *plié* and *rise*, because telling one to do a step means to advance at least one foot from where one is standing, which is not the case in this *plié* and *rise*, as it always stays on the same place: and since here names are not in question let the world do as it pleases, for nothing usurps the essence of the thing. This *plié* and *rise* is nothing more than, placed in any position and in any equilibrium, you bend the knees smoothly, and smoothly you rise;[23] this done, the body is balanced on one foot only, with the toe of the other just touching the ground, or else raised in the air. It consists of two movements of the body, one the *plié* and the other the *rise*.

§2

Let us establish as a firm and general rule, that in bending, the feet must always be turned out and the knees also face outward and not towards the front.

11

Of the *Passo Staccato*, called *Dégagé*

The *dégagé*, although it has no set form, being a simple detachment of one foot from the other in the combining of steps, is nevertheless more necessary than the others. The end of a step does not necessarily serve as the beginning of another to be joined to it, so that it is necessary to detach one foot from the other; that is, to take it from that position which ended the preceding step, to that position from which the subsequent step must begin; that is the use of the *dégagé*. For example, having done a *glissade forwards* which ends in fifth, should you wish to attach a *contretemps*, how do you do it, if this begins from the fourth? Then it is necessary to detach the foot from the fifth to the true or forced fourth, depending on your need and how you will use the *contretemps*; should you desire to do another *turning* in order to come back to the same place, the detachment of the foot is necessary as much to prepare for the turn as to get out of the upright position where you found yourself in the preceding *contretemps*; for if you desired to take it from the same position, you could not really travel, but all will be attainable using the *dégagé*. It also serves as a preparation for any *capriole* which in such a case is done with impetus, and strength.

Besides this it serves to fill out the time. For example, if we were in binary time, which begins on the up beat, and the step or jump or *capriole*, or whatever it might be, is taken on the down beat, how can the rest[24] be filled which is taken in the air? If the *dégagé* is not used, you must stand still and wait to re-enter in cadence; but it is more difficult to come in on the beat from this standing still than using the *dégagé* to fill it out. A blind man who walks with an escort is not as likely to stumble as one would be without a guide. Thus, the detachment of the foot helps you to keep in time. I also admit that you can let this rest pass and await the cadence but only once or a few times, and this is reserved for those *Ballerini* who know how to do it: not only can you use these entrances in *legato* tempos but also with the *contratempi* and with the *intercadenza*, as we noted in Chapter 6.

Dancing in *contratempo* is when you let two or three beats pass and then begin the movement. And this is what dancing in *contratempo* involves.

The *intercadenza*[25] are such movements that you do by ending one step off the beat, and the beginning of the other is joined to the following beat, and not because the entrance is out of time, which would mean you are not dancing in cadence. This is how it is usually employed: a *capriole* lands in *intercadenza*, a step is linked to the entrance of the next beat, as long as there is no delay and one is joined to the other; this often occurs and chiefly it falls to the lot of those *Ballerini* who are versed in the art, because to remain calm in this *genre*, it is necessary to be a thorough *Ballerino*, for only such a one can succeed in carrying off this style attractively.

Not only is he well used to this but he also needs to cover ground; sometimes he will have to cross the Stage in two steps, but the tune does not allow it, not giving enough time, so then the real strength of the *Ballante* stimulates him to cover the necessary ground, without remaining short of time. In beating, you cannot make use of the *dégagé* unless you want to dance in *contratempo* or *intercadenza*; but this I never agree to at the beginning or the end of the dance.

One movement only is considered in this step, and it is the walk. From these things which seem of slight importance, one recognises who has a fundamental knowledge of the Art, and who has only a superficial one.

12

Of the *Passo Marciato, Pas Marché*

Since we have begun with the simplest things, let us follow our method; by following this, things of greater importance will seem easier. The walking step, called *pas marché*, resembles the natural step and in effect is the same. The only difference is that the natural step is not done in any other way except that which is naturally demanded in the step quoted, as we described (Ch. 9). However, the *pas marché* is done as recorded here. Imagine that the right is in front in any position, you raise this foot and, arching the instep well, carry it to forced fourth in front, where it is gently placed on the ground; you raise and carry it forwards either behind the right to fourth, or to second, as the action that you wish to express will necessitate: but the toe of the foot must only just touch the ground, keeping the heel raised, while giving to the whole body a grand air.

This is useful in the Theatre, either to walk across the stage with majesty, or for acts of surprise and admiration, or to impose some order; and in such a case it should be accompanied by some gesture of the arm and head, to indicate whatever is commanded. It is also useful when genuflecting to kiss the hand of one who is taking the part of the Monarch, and in other similar situations.

13

Of the *Passo di Marseglia, Pas de Mareseilles*

The *pas de mareseilles* is easy to do and beautiful to look at. This step took its name from the same *Ballerino* called *Monsieur de Mareseilles* who introduced it into dancing. This celebrated *Danzatore* had great suppleness in the insteps, which enabled him to form and embellish this step. It consists of nothing else, than three pliant movements of the insteps. For example, wishing to do it from one of the positions on the ground, for it can be done not only from all five of these but equally well from those positions in the air, the Body is balanced in the first manner if from a position on the ground, in the third if from a position in the air (Ch. 7, §1 and 3); placed in fifth on the ground, rise on the balls of the feet and return the full foot to the ground, and rising once again come down as before, and having done this three times, the *pas de mareseilles* will have been done.

In placing the full foot on the ground for the first time the knees may also be bent, and this adds value to the step, but certainly not the other two times, otherwise it would simply mean bending and rising.

14

Of the Beating of the Foot, the *Battements*

§1. *Basso piegato* §2. *Disteso*
§3. *On the instep* §4. *Alto staccato*

The beating of the foot is a step so fundamental in the dance that I would go so far as to say that by using this step alone one can be a perfect *Ballerino*. It is beneficial to a *Danzatore* because it makes him free and nimble in our beautiful Art. It is necessarily used in most steps and can be used for all adornments and embellishments. It is frequently used in almost all the cadences as padding or to join the steps, and here a touch of brilliance is introduced to gratify the eye of the spectator. Whoever has not perfect use of the *battements* cannot be a *Ballerino*, because this, besides producing lightness of leg, looseness of sinews, and flexibility of the joints, gives a great softness and facility to any kind of detachment of the leg, whether you wish to do it in the air or with flexion, rendering the tendons and the muscles supple and tractable; furthermore it lightens the feet and strengthens them; in short it facilitates everything. Experience has proved to me that when I had to dance, if first I practised the *Battement* it succeeded well: on the contrary, without practising it my legs were heavy, and I ran the risk of straining the nerves, or fibres of the muscles.

There are various kinds of *Battements*. First the *basso piegato*,[26] which is of great benefit for making the knee pliant, and its long exercise is chiefly useful for strengthening the thigh muscles. Those who are accustomed to do a violent and forced movement need continual exercise of such movement, not experiencing any obvious discomfort: but if they cease using it, then wishing to start again everything feels painful. Thus the beating of the foot being in itself no ordinary movement, using it constantly causes no discomfort, but if out of practice, it produces an uncomfortable sensation. In order to do it, a beginner is supported by a chair with the body well placed in fifth position with the right foot, for

73

instance, in front of the left; thus placed the right foot is raised and carried to second in the air; then, from this same position lightly drawing it along the ground, it is carried behind the left in fifth position with the toe low, and the instep arched; the knee is bent, remaining in the same situation of the fifth position in such a way as to form an obtuse angled triangle, with the leg and the thigh being the two lines which form the obtuse angle at the inside point of the knee, and the whole of the left leg and thigh, without bending, will make the hypotenuse.* Then returning once more to second in the air, keeping the knee in the same second position, carrying the toe of the right in front of the toe of the left, always arching the instep, a second beat will be done; and thus by way of repeating it as many times as you can and with the greatest possible rapidity, you will become solicitous and free in using it in the dance. As has been said for the right, should be likewise done with the left, so that it should be practised with first the one, then the other foot.

This step only has two movements done by the foot itself. The first, carrying it in the air, the second to the fifth behind, or in front. In the old days it was only repeated twice, to end a step or fill in a bar; we repeat it as many times as possible, and thus it is rendered more brilliant.

§2

The second kind of beating of the feet called *battement disteso*[27] is used to acquire velocity in the leg for doing interwoven *caprioles*. It also begins from fifth, and the raised leg which must do the beating passes through first in the air and goes to fifth in front, if begun from behind, keeping both knees stretched. It is repeated as many times as possible, and done with one then the other leg and above all you must try to do them with the utmost speed in order to acquire the quality and the ease which the *capriole* requires. In doing them, the ball of the foot that beats stays so low that it just skims along the ground.

The movement in this is considered as only one because it does not stop in first in the air but passes speedily through it.

§3

The beating *on the instep* is also begun from fifth, in which the knee of the leg that is going to beat is bent, with the toe very low, and passing it through second in the air, it is carried to fifth behind in the air and from this will go to beat in front of the instep of the supporting foot; thus it is repeated as many times as you can with the greatest possible speed, for the quicker it is, the more beautiful. This beat against the instep can be done jumped, by taking a little spring accompanied by two beats but with the rule that the first is done with a little spring and the second when the foot is on the ground, whereas if it is desired to do more of them, this is left to the *Ballerino's* judgement.

§4

We have another kind of *battement*, which is called *alto staccato*.[28] Placed as usual in fifth, the right leg, for example, is raised with the knee well stretched and turned out, with the instep arched, and the leg is detached at least as high as the shoulder, then it lands behind the left, and it is important not to let it pass the supporting leg, otherwise the body will be seen to twist, and raising it again to the same height as the first, it is again lowered to the front, and having done the second with the same care, thus as many as possible are repeated.

It will seem difficult not to pass the supporting leg by the impetus produced when lowering but this has to be done carefully, restraining the impetus of the lowering: easy to achieve if one proceeds with caution.

Here two movements are considered, the first lifting the leg and the other lowering it. These are also done as fast as possible, in order to obtain the desired benefit, and to acquire a fine detachment of the thigh.

I myself have tried the said beat and have gone higher than the head: indeed I put my left hand up high, lifting it to the perpendicular, and with the right foot, and more exactly the instep, I touched the palm of the aforementioned left hand, an obvious sign of having detached the leg well.

Mind then not to take the exercise of these beats too furiously, and do them after rendering the sinews soft and pliable; and do not forget to keep the supporting leg very steady because I, in the exercise of them, heated by poetic fervour, let the leg which was beating knock the other that was on the ground from underneath me and, landing flat on my face, broke my nose; and with the same carelessness Cesarini had the misfortune to break an arm.

---

*An *obtuse-angled triangle* is one which has an obtuse angle. The *Hypotenuse* is the line opposite the greatest angle and consequently the said line is the longest.

15

Of the *Tordichamp*[29]

The practise of the *tordichamp* also contributes to the loosening of the sinews. To do it, balance the body on both feet (Ch. 4, No. I), start in the first position in the air, bend the knees and carry one foot, the right or the left, skimming to fifth position; then detaching it, the foot itself forms a circle in the air, with a well stretched instep, and carry it once more to first position in the air. Be warned, that when the knee of the leg forming the circle is stretched, the other upon which the body is supported is also stretched; this stretching is done gradually as the circle is begun and while it is being formed.

In this step, when the foot glides, bending while carrying it from first to fifth, it can be brought either to the front, or to the back; and wherever it is carried, the circle will be traced. And this comprises one single, continuous movement from beginning to end.

It is employed by all three categories of *Ballerini*, with the difference, that in the *ballo grave*[30] ordinarily it is done with all composure, in the *mezzo carattere* it is done with great velocity, in the *Grotesco* it is done on a grand scale. And all this according to the nature of the real characters, but then every one must know how to do it in all three variants, as often happens when executing it. It is done jumping in the air, of which we shall speak in the *caprioles*; sometimes it is repeated two and three times in the same jump and in this case it is all done to the side, without carrying it from first to fifth. Then the Music determines its speed or gentleness.

In studying it, start slowly and, having become accustomed to making the exact circling and movement of the leg, gradually increase the speed until it is exercised with the utmost velocity.

16

Of the *Passo Mezzo Tronco, Demi-Coupé*

Ｏne of the principal steps in the Dance is the *demi-coupé*, not only because it is much used in the Dance but, furthermore, because it enters into the formation of various other steps. It is done *forwards, backwards, to the side, turning forwards, turning to the side* and *turning sur place disfatto.*

To do it *forwards*, place yourself in the first equilibrium, and the feet in one of the positions, for example in the first; bend the knees evenly in the prescribed manner (Ch. 10, § 2) and, supporting the body on the left, the right is slowly brought to fourth position in front where, stretching the knees, the left foot is brought to second position, touching the ground only with the ball of the foot and the heel slightly raised (Ch. 4, No. III), and this second is not of the usual distance but is closer to the first, about halfway between one and the other; that is how it is formed but many times the foot stays in the air either at the back, the side or in front, and provided that it is not placed in front on the ground it is always *demi-coupé*, but placed in front it equals the whole, as we shall mention later.

That *backwards* is quite the opposite. Begin from fourth and, after bending, take the foot which is in front to fourth behind and the other foot goes to second, as in that explained above. Some wish in this, as in the former, that the last movement is carried to first. I do not oppose that but long experience has shown that it is easier to end it in second; for the rest, I leave the liberty to end it where it will be easier, and especially if it has to be joined to another step, in which case it ends in that position which may serve for the beginning of the next step to be linked to it.

To do it *to the side* place yourself in the same first position, and wishing to do it to the right, the right foot is lightly carried to second after having bent according to our custom, and again join the feet together in first in the air with the left brought close to the right. In order to repeat another of them, again gently bend the knees and the left, passing behind the right, is brought to fifth position and, stretching the knees, the right is placed in first in the air.

It can also be done *turning forwards*. Placed already in first and with bent knees, as described above, the right goes out to fourth very smoothly and with the left you make a half turn, at the same time lifting the right heel, fixing the ball of the foot on the ground, turning on the axis, and join the feet in the above-mentioned position. If you then wish to end the turn with another *demi-coupé*, bend the left behind in fourth, and doing another half turn with the right, the feet are joined together in first, and you find yourself turned towards where you began.

There is some divergence between this and the *turn sideways*. The first task is to aim towards turning on a straight line, which is from the side, for if you do not proceed with this prudence and anticipation, you travel crosswise, as will be seen if tried, therefore in order not to fall into this fault it is worth observing and exercising well. Let us explain the step in order to have a more complete idea. Placed as you would be in first, and the knees bent, the right foot is carried to second position and in stretching, making a half turn with the left and turning on the ball of the right, both feet are brought to second; and to follow it with another, the left bends behind, and the right with another half turn joins in first, and you return to face the direction from where you began.

That *turning sur place disfatto* is the complete opposite from that explained above, where one turns toward that side of the leg which is the first to move, and here the *disfatto* will turn on the contrary to the side opposite the leg doing the first movement: that is to say, if turning to the right side, the left will begin the step, if to the left the contrary; for the rest, everything refers to that explained above.

Every *demi-coupé* contains two movements and both are compound. The first is the *plié* walking, and the rise carrying is the second.

17

Of the *Coupé* or *Passo Tronco*

§1. *Of two movements* §2. *Of three movements*

A large part and almost all of the *coupé* is explained in the *demi-coupé*, where, without repeating the description, we shall mention what has to be added. In all the diverse manners that the *demi* is done, so is the full except that this can be done in two and in three movements.

§1

The beginning of the *coupé of two movements* is similar to that of the *demi-coupé*, and then instead of the leg which does the second movement remaining close to first position, it is carried in a half circle to fourth position in front, being *forwards*, behind in that *backwards*, to the second in that *to the side*, and to the fourth wherever the front is in those *turning*; and in all these the foot must be firmly supported on the ground. And this is the full *coupé of two movements*, which are the same as those explained for the *demi*.

§2

In that *of three movements*, having done the whole *demi-coupé* and having arrived at a position between first and second with only the toe touching the ground, again you bend naturally, and in rising detach one leg to second in the air and, while lowering it, carry it to true fourth.

18

Of the *Passo Gettato, Pas Jeté*

§1. *Simple*   §2. *Beaten*

The *pas jeté* can begin from all of the positions on the ground but it is always best to start it from the fourth, being the most comfortable, and it may begin with the one, or the other foot. It is done *simple* and *beaten*; in the one and in the other manner you can do it *forwards, backwards, sideways, turning,* and *turning disfatto* and *doublé,* that is, repeated. Let us start with the *simple.*

§1

To do it *forwards,* place yourself in fourth with for example the right in front, gently bend the knees and lift the same right to fourth in front in the air, stretching the knee, keeping the instep well arched; the other will remain bent, and the same leg returns to the fourth as at first, as though throwing it; the knees are immediately stretched and at the same time, having done this, the left leg is lifted behind to fourth in the air; and this lifting of the back leg is done with such skill that when it reaches fourth in the air, although resembling a little spring, you definitely do not jump but you only rise. Dufort is misled, in declaring that a little spring is absolutely essential; what is more, his Treatise is only concerned with Ballroom Dancing, where on no account does one jump. It is permitted in the Theatre, doing in effect rather a little spring not in the nature of the *jeté* but with theatrical licence where it is allowed; indeed it is often necessary to exaggerate the positions themselves many times and to do steps that would be reprehensible, and this is done either to make an impression or to cover the ground which the *Ballanti's* action demands.

To do it *backwards* nothing is changed except, in bending, raise the back leg to fourth behind in the air, as that in front was raised, and the same is then again lowered and immediately placed on the ground as the other is raised to fourth in front in the air with the same swiftness as explained above.

Having to do it *sideways*, the beginning will be the same, and after the *plié* the leg is taken to second in the air, from where it is lowered to the true second, raising the other immediately to second in the air, and so it will be completed.

In that *turning*, after having placed yourself in the said position, made a *plié* and lifted one leg in the air, in the same time as the already raised leg is lowered the whole body makes a quarter turn immediately raising the other leg.

To turn *disfatto*, turn to the side opposite the foot which is the first to be detached. Having made a *plié* and lifted one foot into the air, this detached foot in the air is thrown behind the leg which is on the ground, making a quarter turn of the body, immediately lifting the other leg in the air.

Each kind of these *jetés* can be repeated, called *doublé*; the said *doublé* means that if two of them are done with the same leg, making them simple, that foot which in beginning was behind can go in front, and that in front, behind. If the turn *disfatto* is repeated, it turns towards the same place from where it began; if, however, it is wished to end the full turn, one will be done *fatto* and the other *disfatto*.

§2

The other kind of *jeté*, called *beaten*, consists of one beat and one *jeté*.

Forwards, it begins from fourth in the first equilibrium; after having bent both knees, detach the front foot, for example the right, to second in the air and, in lowering it, make it beat on the calf of the left leg and carry it again to second in the air; then, without pausing, immediately throw it to fourth in front, lifting the other to second in the air. Note that, having beaten one foot on the calf of the other and made it return to second in the air, you should jump a little in the manner of a *demi-contretemps*. What this *demi-contretemps* is will shortly be learnt.

That *beaten backwards* is different only in that, as the above explained was beaten in front, in this it is beaten behind; as, for example, placed with the right in fourth in front and after having made a *plié*, detach the same to second in the air; without stopping there, it beats behind on the calf of the left and is immediately lifted to second in the air, from where it is at once thrown to fifth behind and the left is raised in the air.

The *beaten sideways* differs from these only in that the throwing is done in second, as we explained in §1.

The *beaten turning fatto* and *disfatto* is related to the simple, doing the turn after the beat.

Each of these *beaten jetés* can also be repeated as many times as is wished:

one beaten in front and one behind, also all in front or all behind but, however, one with one leg, and the other with the other; for should you wish to do them with the same leg, a *temps de cuisse* and not a *jeté* would be done, for whichever way it is done, it must always change legs except in the *demi*, which can be done with the same leg. It is true, however, that sometimes they can be done with the same leg but then one needs to have recourse to the *dégagé*, which means placing the leg that finished in the air on the ground.

There are two movements in the *simple*, the first of which is the bend detaching, and the second the rise stepping. The beat increases the number of movements.

19

Of the *Mezzo Gettato, Demi-Jeté*

Once the full *jeté* is understood, the *demi* is easy. This has the same divisions, that is the ways of doing it. It begins like the other, and differs in that, having thrown the leg that was detached in the air, instead of lifting the other you stretch the knees, rising on the balls of both feet.

It contains the same movements as those in the *simple jeté*.

20

Of the *Pistoletta a Terra*

The *pistoletta* is a very brilliant step, suited to every kind of *Ballerino* and to all characters. It can be done equally with one, or the other leg, *forwards, backwards, sideways, turning*. There is no difference, except in covering the ground. Its intrinsic value is that of a beat, although a skilful *Ballerino*, if he wishes, increases the number of beats by more than one. It is taken from fifth position, in which we take the example *forwards* with the right foot behind; bend the knees and detach the aforesaid foot to second in the air, then it will go to beat on the calf of the other leg, covering ground forwards with a little light spring done on the left, which hardly rises from the ground, and, on landing from this, the right is carried to fifth in front.

To do it *backwards*, take out the front foot and beat it in front of the other leg, covering ground backwards, and the foot which in the beginning was in front, is carried to fifth behind.

Sideways, it may be beaten in front as well as behind, and equally all the beats may be repeated either all in front or all behind, or one in front and one behind, thus changing legs, or all on one leg; all that remains to be noted is that ground is covered to the side of the leg which is beaten.

Turning, the circular motion is added, and you turn in the direction of the foot that beats, and these are the *pistolette a terra*; there are also those in the air, which will be spoken about when dealing with the *caprioles*.

21

Of the *Tortigliè*

Only the *Ballerini Groteschi* use the step known as the *tortigliè*. The Italians introduced it into English dancing and in other national dances, although those nations do not use it themselves. The false and the Spanish positions occur in this step; it begins from the true third position and in this it ends; but that foot which was in front at the beginning is behind at the end. It is done *forwards, sideways,* and *turning,* and we shall speak of them all separately.

To do it *forwards,* place yourself with the right in true third position in front, then turn lifting[31] the heels; the feet are placed in third Spanish position (Ch. 7, §5) and, turning again lifting the heels, the toes are turned out, the left leg should be in front in true third lightly touching the other.

To do it *sideways*: also placed with the right in front in the said position, with this foot raise only the heel turning it outwards, then lift the toe of the left, turning it inwards to form the false first (Ch. 7, §2); afterwards, turn the toe of the right foot outwards, keeping the heel on the ground, and immediately turn the heel of the other, the toe of which is fixed on the ground, making it move in front of the right; you are in true third with the left in front. Thus each foot makes two movements, neither leaving the ground when the toe is turned inwards and the heel outwards. If the heel is turned out fix the toe, if the toe, fix the heel on the ground; and the first foot turns the heel then the toe, and the second foot first the toe inwards then the heel, but alternately. If you wish to do another, it is not done to the same side but to the other, and it is begun with the left that is in front, which will do the same as the right did, and this does the same as the other.

Similarly you do those *turning.* You do nothing more than turn toe and heel, which makes the body turn. When the step is begun on the right, it is turned to the right, and if on the left, to the left. It can be repeated many times but one does not make more than a quarter turn. When they are repeated, the first one begins with the foot in front, the second however with that behind and so alternately they are repeated because, being in succession, all must begin with the same leg.

Its movements are four, two for each foot. The first turning out the heel of the right foot, the second the toe of the left inwards, the third the toe of the former turned out, the fourth the heel of the latter turned in.

22

Of the *Passo Bilanciato, Pas Balancé*

The *bilanciato*, called *balancé*, very much resembles the *demi-coupé*, adding an inclining movement of the body to the side of the supporting foot. When more than one of this step is repeated, one is done on one leg, the other on the other, and the inclining movements are done opposite, first to the side of the supporting foot, then the other to the corresponding foot. From this alternating movement, which gives a swaying motion like that of a pair of scales, it takes its name of *balancé*. In all the ways that the *demi-coupé* can be done (fully described in Ch. 16), so can the *balancé* by adding an inclination from the waist, as was said. They misunderstand, who think it can only be done sideways as likewise Dufort foolishly insists. The inclination can be done forwards or backwards, seeing that it can be distinguished by the movement of the body.

This step was much in use decades ago because in that era there was more variety in the Ballroom Dances. It was customary in the *Sarabande*, the *Amabile*, the *Passepied*, the *Follia*, and in others like them. Nowadays similar kinds of Dances have fallen into disuse and at Ballroom assemblies nothing other than *Contredances* and *Minuets* are seen, principally a *Minuet Ecossais*, rarely a *Taice*. Improvised things are quickly learnt. For which reason one cannot see in them the gracefulness of such things well done and studied. The disparity is always observable, irregularity is never lacking; the use of composed, regulated dances cannot prevail because to be rid of such defects too much would be required from the dilettante. But why so? Because they want to learn everything in a couple of months although six months at least would be necessary to master the figure of a *Minuet*, and with another six months of continuous practice it might be possible to dance it with mediocrity provided however that one is the right age, quick and teachable.

The intolerance of Pupils these days does not allow time: they neither strengthen themselves nor exercise even in the equilibriums, the principal foundations of the Dance. How necessary it is to have this equilibrium which is neglected by them will be understood when we speak about it.

23

Of the *Passo Cadente, Pas Tombé*

In this chapter we shall describe the *passo cadente*, that is *pas tombé*. This is the only step in which the body is out of equilibrium; it is very similar to the beginning of a fall. It may be done *forwards, backwards, sideways, turning*, not only *sideways* as Signor Dufort thinks, and beginning from a position on the ground, as well as in the air.

To do it *forwards* then, begin from second position, and whether on the ground or in the air, the carriage is the same, the leg, if on the ground skimming, if in the air, lowering, until it reaches the proper position. Placed already in second, slipping one leg imperceptibly out of equilibrium, carry the said leg into the forced fourth position in front, at the same time bending both knees; then rising with the body evenly balanced again, finally bring the other leg to true second, or to that position that will be called for by the beginning of the next step to be joined to it. From this, any sort of step may be begun again, whether the repeat is jumped or on a *plié*, walked or chased.

Wishing to do it *backwards*, there is nothing different to add, except that, whereas in that forwards the leg slid until it reached forced fourth in front, here it is carried to fourth behind, also forced, bending in the same way and, on rising, the supporting leg is carried to the position as above.

The *sideways* is taken from this same second and, being out of equilibrium, you fall onto the foot which skims to the forced fifth, passing it through first, inclining the body to the side of the foot which was fixed on the ground and, on rising after the usual bend of the knees, the leg is detached to second, and at times to another [position], when however another step has to be joined to it. Only in inclining the body does this differ from that *backwards*.

That *turning* merits more attention. The beginning is the same as the others; the fall differs, and is that, when falling, the leg slips into forced fifth position behind, turning the body one quarter; the other leg is carried to an arbitrary position, making the front where the side was. All these kinds each contain two movements: the first is the glide falling, the second is the rise moving to the position.

24

Of the *Mezzo Cadente, Demi-Tombé*

Let us also admit the *demi-tombé*, although nobody else considers it, and without further explanation, I would say that it ends at the second movement, which is the rise from the *tombé*, without carrying but only stretching the knees, keeping the toes in their place.

Diverse as the ways of doing the full can be, so they are in the *demi* only excluding the last carrying of the leg. *Turning*, the body remains turned by one quarter called foreshortened.[32] Practice then, and especially the Theatre, will teach some things which here I cannot explain and demonstrate; now I do not pretend to give more than the first rudiments, in order to be able to reason fundamentally when the occasion arises.

25

Of the *Pas Grave* or *Courante*

§1.   With one *plié*, that is in three movements
§2.   With two *pliés* or four movements

From the name itself one can understand that the quality of the *pas grave* is serious and majestic. It is used in the Theatre and the Ballroom; it enters into all kinds of dance and especially in dancing the *serio*,[33] the beauty of which is increased when done with grandeur. It was very much used in the ancient dances and particularly in the heroic and the *gravi*.[34] In the *Minuet* it looks sublime, this being one of the most noble and serious kinds of dance. It appears often in the *Amabile*, a gentle dance very much in use not so long ago. The celebrated Dancing Master Monsieur de Beauchamp, who had the honour of giving lessons to Louis le Grand,[35] was its inventor. It was used in his time in the dance called *Courante*, as this step was also called, now known as *grave*. It can be done *forwards*, *backwards*, *sideways*, *turning*, *a pie fermo*[36], *sur place*, *in the air*, and in these manners it is done with one or two *pliés*. Let us speak first of that with one *plié*, that is in three movements. It is taken from all the five positions.

§1

To do it *forwards* with the right in front, for example, in the said position the body is balanced in the first manner; bend the knees equally and, stretching them, the right foot, with arched instep and the toes only just touching the ground, is carried to forced fourth, and on the said foot the full weight of the body is sustained; then carry the left leg to true fourth in front of the right.

Although this step does not often occur *backwards*, nevertheless it must not be overlooked. It is begun from the same fourth position, and in bending and stretching, the foot with only the toe on the ground is carried to the back, and the other also goes to fourth behind.

That *sideways* is taken from fourth and, for example, wishing to do it to the right, place the right leg in front in fourth as was said; after the *plié* and the rise, bring it to second and the left in fourth behind, or in front, as required by the step, which has to be joined to it; as, for example, having to accompany it with another to the other side, it cannot end behind because the other *pas grave* to the side cannot begin from this position.

In the *pas grave turning*, nothing more is added except for the turn of the body, and this must not be more than one quarter, for, being *grave*, by turning more it would lose its dignity, and the person would run the risk of visibly losing his composure.

We have the *pas grave a pie fermo* which in truth is nothing more than a *plié* and a rise. Placed in fourth or in second, bend the knees with all composure; in rising, the foot which is in front is lifted from the ground, resting only on the pointed toe and stretching the instep. In each kind of this step an air of stateliness befitting its gravity should always be assumed.

There are other kinds of *pas grave*, one of which is called *sur place*. This step is different, in that it ends with the same leg with which it began. It is taken in quite the opposite way from that explained above, and it begins, for example, with the right in fourth behind the left; bend, and stretch sliding the toe of the same, hardly touching the ground, carrying it to second position, and, after skimming and bringing it almost into first, place the same in the natural fourth.

That *in the air* is also done with the leg behind, for example, the right: bend and lift the same leg into the air; carry the same leg which is already in the air, stretching the knee little by little until it arrives at second in the air from where it is carried, thus stretched as it is, to the fourth, still in the air. This is a movement entirely done from the hip joint, and the French call it *tems d'ancora*.[37]

Every step of this kind contains three movements, which are the *plié* the first, the second the rise and carrying, and the walk the third.

§2

In addition, there is the *pas grave* in four movements, that is with two *pliés*: it begins as usual with the *plié* and, bringing the back leg to second, stretching at the same time, again bend both knees equally, letting the body fall perpendicularly and this is the second *plié*, and the added movement; then stretching again, it is brought to fourth skimming along the ground in one of the manners explained above.

26

Of the *Demi-Pas Graves*

There are the *demi-pas graves* which can be done with the same diversity as the others, the only difference being that these end in the second movement, that is to say after the *plié* and the rise, without adding to them the last walking movement.

27

Of the *Passo Sfuggito, Pas Échappé*

The *passo sfuggito* is not called thus, but by the French term *échappé*. This step is much used by the *ballerini grotteschi*, being a step more accentuated than that which serves for the *ballanti seri*. It consists of two little springs, and a *plié*[38] between two little springs. There are three different ways of doing it: *sur place*, *turning* and *forced*. It may be taken from all positions except from the second.

To do it *sur place*, let us take an example from fifth, assuming that the equilibrium is in the first manner. Rise on the balls of both feet, from where, taking a little spring scarcely rising from the ground, land opening the legs evenly, skimming the feet along the ground; you land, as I said, in second, while at the same time bending both knees. From the same *plié* in second position the knees are stretched, doing another similar little spring to land again in the same position from which they started, but that foot which at the beginning was in front, should now be behind. Most of the time one is obliged to end it with the same leg in front which was in front at the beginning, and that behind which was behind, and sometimes when another step has to be joined, it ends in that position which will serve as the beginning of the step to be joined.

To do it *turning*, start as above; the turning motion of the body is given during the little spring, so that when landing in second position, either a half or a quarter turn will have been done: then in the second little spring, bringing the feet together, do the same amount [of turn] as was done in the first. In such a way, if the first were one quarter, the second would also be one quarter, and the whole step will comprise one half; if it were half in one, in the other it would be again so that in the entire step one full turn would be done.

In that *forced*, instead of landing in true second position, you land in a forced second from which you again join [the feet] as explained above. The forced second position will always take into consideration your stature, which according to the articulation and muscles will determine the distance between one leg and the other. Two are its movements: the rise springing and the joining together.

28

Of the *Mezzo Sfuggito,* *Demi-Échappé*

Hardly anyone admits the *mezzo sfuggito*, which is the *demi-échappé*, but this does not mean that it does not exist. In order not to repeat an explanation, I say that it has the same differences as the full, beginning equally like it, and ending with the first landing in *plié*.

This half step is never executed alone but is used in taking any sort of step which begins from a *plié*. This done, a *capriole* in the Italian manner may be taken without need of another *plié*, using that with which the *demi-échappé* ended.

29

Pas de Bourrée

We shall speak in this chapter of the *bourrée*, in which of all the steps more diversity than in any other is to be found. It consists of three steps: one on a *plié* and two natural. First we will speak of the *simple*, which is done *forwards, backwards, sideways, over and under sideways, under and over sideways, all over sideways, all under sideways, over and under turning, under and over turning, all over turning, all under turning, turning disfatto.*

§1

This step can begin equally well from all the positions, and in order to do it *forwards* we will take an example from the fourth, because this is the position where the body can most comfortably be maintained in equilibrium; thus placed, bending the knees according to our usual rule, carry the right, which was placed behind, to fourth in front, and from here it is stretched; finally you do two natural steps forwards, ending in fourth.

That *backwards* will be similarly placed in fourth, and in the same equilibrium; after having made a *plié*, instead of carrying the foot which is behind to fourth in front, the foot which is in front is carried to fourth behind, and the two natural steps will also be done backwards ending in fourth.

Wishing to do them *sideways*, you do them either to the right or the left; placed in the same equilibrium and in fourth position, after having made a *plié*, carry one leg to second where it is stretched, and sliding, the other leg is carried to fourth under, from whence detach the first to place it in second, with which it is completed. Wishing to follow it with another from second where the first ended, bend again and that leg that was not the last to move is carried to fourth, and the other to second after having stretched, and with one natural step done with the first foot, it ends in fourth as the first [*pas de bourrée*] began. This step is repeated with the same foot as the side to which it is travelling, that is, with the right foot if to the right, with the left if to the left. This step is done in the returning step of the *Minuet*, although it is not recognised in this: but in reflecting on it the truth will be known.

That *over and under sideways*, by the name itself will show that it is a step that begins over and ends under. For a better understanding, let us explain. Placed in fourth, for example, with the right in front and after making a *plié*, the left doing a half circle will pass to fourth in front and, rising, the other will naturally pass through first to be carried to second lightly sliding along the ground, and it ends by carrying the left leg under to fourth.

Quite the opposite is that *under and over*, also *sideways*, which begins under and ends over. Here is how it is done. Placed as usual in fourth in the same equilibrium and, bending, make half a circle with the front foot carrying it to fourth behind, and the other is brought to second making it pass through first skimming; it will end with the first foot being carried to fourth in front. Be warned, that in this step, as in that above, the half circle must be made tightly round the supporting leg, which remains still.

In that *all over* we make no further explanation, but will say that it begins over and ends over.

So also for that *all under*, which begins under and also ends under.

The other kind of simple *bourrée over and under turning* will be done thus. Placed for example with the right in fourth behind, with the usual *plié*, carry the said right sliding to fourth in front of the left tracing half a circle; and stretching, carry the left to second while giving a turning motion, and then the first foot will be carried to fourth behind the other which will make the said turn one quarter, or at the most one half, and not more, otherwise this would be a *crossed bourrée*, as we shall soon mention.

On the contrary, that *under and over turning* starts with the right foot in front in fourth, and sliding, carry it to fourth under, turning to the right, and, stretching, place the left in second, and it will end with the right foot, which is carried to fourth in front of the left, without making more than half a turn as above.

In that *over and under*, turn to the opposite side of the foot which will be the first to move, and the other to the same side as that of the foot which will make the first move.[40]

That *all over turning* begins over and ends over.

Contrariwise, that *all under* begins under and ends under.

That *turning disfatto* is done by carrying the front foot under after having already made a *plié*, and, stretching and beginning to turn, the other foot is brought to second, carrying the first foot to fourth in front will end this step; not more than half a turn should be made, turning to the opposite side of the foot which moves first.

§2

There is also the *open bourrée*, and first that *forwards*. It is begun from the third and, after having made a *plié*, carry the front foot to fourth in front, skimming the ground and, after having stretched, carry the other foot to second, making it pass through first, arching the instep, and it will end with the first foot being carried to third behind the other.

The *open backwards* also begins from the third, and the foot which is behind, let us say the right, is carried to fourth and, after stretching, passing the left through first as above, place it in second, and this step will finish by bringing the right to the front.

Let us pass to the *open sur place*, which is done without travelling either forward or backward. It is also begun from third position, and, in bending, the front foot goes almost to second, then stretching, the other foot is carried to the true second, and the first returns to the third.

§3

Although the *crossed bourrée* called *croucé*[41] resembles that *over and under turning*, it is more refined and needs more dexterity of movement. It has no *plié* at all; it is taken from second in the air, or else from fourth also in the air, and sometimes, as needed, from fourth behind. It turns to the opposite side of the foot with which it is taken. For example, if it is taken with the right foot, it must turn to the left. Placed in fourth with the said right foot behind and making it pass through second in the air, place it in fourth over the left, to face the direction where the back faced; in order to do this, it is necessary to carry the right in the air, which will make almost three-quarters of a circle, and you should turn in the manner of an axis on the left, in order to find yourself with this in fourth under; then carry the left to second and the whole turn will end carrying the right again to fourth under.

§4

To do *two pas de bourrée turning forwards*, it is necessary to begin by placing yourself with the right leg in third in front, and then bending, carry the right to fourth in front turning the body only a quarter of a turn; after that, place the left in fourth, also in front, and the right foot in fourth behind, completing a half turn, and this is the first *bourrée*. From here, bend again and carry the left under the right to fourth turning to the right, and the right to fourth in front and the other will be carried to fourth over this, and thus they are completed.

You can also do the aforesaid *two pas de bourrée turning sideways* and they are taken from the third position. To do them, placed in the said position and wishing to go to the right, after having made a *plié*, carry the left to fourth and rise on the balls of the feet, stretching the knees, having started to turn the body round; then the right will be brought to second, and the first one ends with the left, which will be placed in fourth under. That done, in order to do the second one, the foot which is in front, after another *plié*, will be placed in fourth and, after having stretched, carry the left to second and the right will be brought naturally to fourth over.

§5

The *pas de bourrée fallito* was much used by the celebrated M. de Noverre. With this step he facilitated and embellished the movement of taking a *capriole*, which formerly used to be taken with a *demi-coupé*, with a *demi-sissonne*, or else with a *brisé*. In my opinion, however, the use of this step belongs to the *Ballerini seri*, or the *mezzo carattere*, not having need of much elasticity; but the *Ballerino Grotesco* cannot make any use of it, being that the *pas de bourrée fallito* is extremely dry, and therefore it would not be a very good preparation for a *capriole*; on the contrary then, the *pas brisé* added to a *demi-sissonne* gives another preparation for the jump, and with it much spring is acquired, and it is easier to repeat the jump. We will explain the step, and first.

Let us speak of that *to the front*. To do this it is necessary to be placed in fourth with the right for example behind the left, and, bending, detach the left leg to second position in the air, from where it is carried to third under,[42] the left rising high on the balls of the feet; when coming down again, detach the same right to second in the air and thus it is ended. This step may be done slowly as well as sharply. Besides that we described above, it serves mainly to join on another step, and especially when you wish to do a *pas trusé*: after the detachment of the leg, this step is done as described, then the *trusé* is joined, as also occurs in other circumstances.

It is also done *to the back*, and this is the same as that *to the front* but, whereas that was all done *over*, this is all done *under*; its beginning and ending becomes a dry movement, so that as it gets smaller the change of foot is hardly noticeable. It is begun with the back leg, and being for example the right, which after the *plié* is detached to second in the air, suddenly it is carried behind again, then the left is hardly lifted and comes back to the same place,[43] and with the right again being detached, it is ended.

§6

The *pas de bourrée* is done also with a *jeté*; in other words instead of the first step, it begins with a *demi-jeté* and then the other two ordinary [steps] follow. It is done *open forwards* and *open backwards*.

The *open bourrée jeté forwards* is much used in the *Chaconne*, and in similar tempi, indeed in any tempo, provided that it is slow. It is often used in the

Theatre. Its characteristic is covering ground without detracting in any way from its charm. To do it, after placing yourself in position with its equilibrium, as already stated, the knees are bent, and the front foot is carried to fourth in the air, for example the right, from where the same leg is thrown to second, and the left passing through first is carried to fourth in front and the right follows close to the true third behind, although it would be no error to carry it to fifth behind for these Theatrical steps may be embellished with arbitrary airs and graces which the *ballante* may choose to give them, who, if he desires to cover ground, makes use of the forced fourth if not of the third.

In the *open jeté backwards* nothing else changes, except for the *jeté* in second, and the carrying is the same, which will be done first behind, and the last in true fourth over.

<h2 style="text-align:center">§7</h2>

The *bourrée tombé*, of which we shall speak in this paragraph, begins with a *demi-tombé* which is substituted for the first bending and carrying movement, and is followed by the exaggerated walk and the simple walk.

To do it *forward*, do one *demi-tombé forward* and the last two movements of the *simple bourrée forwards*. To do it *backwards*, do a *demi-tombé back*, and the last two steps of the *simple bourrée backwards*. Thus it is also executed in all the other ways that one might wish, joining the *demi-tombé* in the required manner with the corresponding last steps of the *bourrée*. This step is used in the Theatre in precise gestures, in emphatic actions: as of a personage afflicted by extreme pain, or mortally wounded, gradually falling with the movement of the *demi-tombé*, and to raise himself, driven to the end of natural forces, he uses the two simple movements, with accompanying expressiveness of the arms. It can also serve for one in a fury, wanting to wound another but, prevented by inner remorse, or restrained by circumstances, he stops with the arm raised, in the act of striking the body.

<h2 style="text-align:center">§8</h2>

The *bourrée en l'air* is a compound step as is the *trusé* and the *pas de chaconne*, and others. This step is composed first of two *assemblés* then a *demi-contretemps* but done only in *attitude*.

In order not to disturb the order of things since we are speaking of the *bourrée*, I have said from which group it is composed, which is enough to mention for the moment and it will be better understood when we speak of its components. Here is how it is combined. First do an *assemblé*, or instead a *fourth capriolata*, one leg remaining behind, then do another with the same leg in front, and join on a *demi-contretemps* remaining in attitude in fourth in the air, with the left leg half curved, keeping the foot well stretched.[44]

The *bourrée en l'air legato* exchanges the *demi-contretemps* for an open *pas de bourrée* and that is, after having done the two *assemblés*, one with the right foot behind and the other *sur place*, the said *open bourrée* is joined.

§9

The last kind of this *bourrée* is *of four steps*, and every kind of *bourrée* explained above may be done with four steps; this step which is added to them is almost like a *dégagé* without pausing in between and serves either for filling out the music, or to make it more comfortable to join on another step.

Nothing else remains, than to speak of their movements. All those from §1 to the end of §4 each have three movements. The first of these is the *plié* carrying, the second the exaggerated walk, and the simple walk the third. To those of §5 is added one movement, and they are different from the others. The first is the *plié* detaching, the other the rise, carrying the third, and the last is also detached. Those of §6 have three movements, and they are firstly the *plié jeté*, the exaggerated walk the next and the simple walk last. Those of §7 also have three: the first is the *demi-tombé* and the other two as usual. In §8, the first of these are as many as are contained in the two *assemblés* and the *demi-contretemps*. The other [consists of] those of the aforesaid *assemblés* with those of the *open bourrée*. Those of the last section are increased by the last movement of the *dégagé*.

103

30

Of the *Passo di Sissone,*
Pas de Sissonne

§1. *Simple*   §2. *With a rise*

The *sissonne* is a very different step from the others, which almost all begin with a *plié*; although it needs its *plié*, it is not at the beginning, as we shall explain. It may be started from all positions on the ground as well as in the air, except for the first. It is done *forwards, backwards, sideways, turning, turning disfatto* and repeated *doublé,* and it is done *simple* and *with a rise.* Let us begin with the *simple.*

§1

Placed in one of the positions already mentioned above in the first equilibrium, that is in fourth with the right in front, to do it *forwards,* without a *plié* detach this leg to second in the air, stretch the knee and the instep well, supporting the body on the left. Then moving the left at once, and lowering the right, both are made to meet in fifth on the ground, and the right in front in that space which was between the feet while the right was in the air, and not on the same straight line, but advancing a little forwards; and after, without pausing in between, both knees are equally bent, and with a little spring rising, the left is detached to second in the air, and thus it will be completed.

It is also done *backwards* with the difference that the foot which was behind is detached to second in the air, and in lowering this to fifth together with the other, it covers ground to the back, as the other covered it to the front, and with the same *plié* and with the same jump rising the other is detached to second position in the air.

That *sideways* is not only different from this in that it covers ground to the side but, in the last second position in the air, the same foot is raised which was the first to be detached. If it is begun with the right, end with the right, if with the left, with the same.

Turning fatto, nothing else is added, only the amount of the turn, which is done when the foot is lowered to fifth, and it is turned to the same side as the foot which was first detached.

Then to speak of *disfatto*, the only difference is that it is turned to the opposite side of the foot which first is detached in the air.

Those repeated called *doublé* are the same, doing more than one, with this difference that, being repeated *forwards* or *backwards*, the foot is changed because the second begins with the foot which, in the first, ended in the air; if they are done *sideways*, they are all taken with the same foot, since the first ends with that with which it began. Very often in that *sideways*, two or three of them are repeated with one foot, and then changing it another two or more are done with the other, and they are called *repeated, changé*. *Turning* then, if all are done on one foot they will be *fatti*; if the foot is changed they will be *fatti* and *disfatti*.

The movements of the simple *sissonne* are three: the first is the detachment, the second is the landing in the fifth, and the last is the rise with a spring.

§2

As we said, that *with a rise* can be done in as many different ways; nothing else is added to the first except the bending movement at the beginning; that is, it starts by bending the knees and, in stretching, one leg is detached to second in the air, according to the manner explained above.

It is increased by the first bending movement and thus it contains four [movements].

31

Of the *Demi-Sissonne*

The *sissonne*, whether it be *simple* or *with a rise* and of whatever other category except the *repeated*, may be halved by ending it with a bend of both knees, without rising after the landing. This *demi* will have its place whenever another different step which begins with a *plié* has to be attached, either a jump or a *capriole*, and it is much used especially if you wish to do a *capriole sur place*, because therefore it begins with greater elasticity.

The Italians, as those who make great use of the *capriole*, use them frequently, and the *Groteschi Saltatori*[45] even more so. The *Seri* then add a *pas brisé* to it, join the *demi-sissonne*, and then cut an attractive *caprioletta*.

These *demi* lack the last movement, that is, the *simple* only has two, and that *with a rise*, three.

32

Of the *Galliard Step, Pas de Gaillard*

The *galliard step* was much in use among the ancients, who employed it in *balletti a due* called *balli alla Gagliarda* from which this step took its name. These *balletti* were lively and generally duple times were used. We also employ it in a *carré*, as we shall explain later. This step is only done to the side.

To do it, place yourself, for example, with the right behind the left in one of the three positions excluding the first and the second. Bend the knees and, in stretching, rise on the ball of the left foot, detaching the right to second in the air and, in placing the left flat on the ground, send the right to the first position, which then returns to second; thence skimming along the ground, bring the left to fifth behind and afterwards raise the other to fourth in the air, then immediately bring it back to fifth in front. If this step is done on a grand scale, as was said, a jump is done on the instep, in other words, in rising on the ball of the left foot, and the replacing of this flat when the other is lowered, the said jump is taken travelling to the side.

Its movements are five. The first is the *plié*, the rise stretching with the return to first is the second, the third the walk, the slide the fourth and the fifth the detachment.

33

Saraband Step

N early everyone believes that the *saraband step* and the *galliard step* are the same; indeed, one under two names, but I see a difference in them and in truth it does exist. This is done ordinarily in *chaconne* and slow triple times. If you start from the same three positions, for example with the right behind in fifth, bend, and the said leg is brought to first in the air, and rise on the ball of the left foot as though with a little spring, which is a movement of the instep, but the foot never really leaves the ground, although jumping a little certainly is not wrong; the right is brought to true second, and lastly the left is placed in fifth behind.

It consists of only four movements, and the first is the *plié*, the rising the other and the last two are the walks.

34

Pas Coursé

The *pas coursé* greatly resembles the *fourth Italian capriole* travelling to the side so that, wishing to show one of these without interweaving, this step will be done, which has the same characteristics and the same timing.

If placed in any position other than second, use the *dégagé* to come into this position, and once there, bend both knees and then, stretching them, make a little spring with both feet; the left approaches first position, and lightly beats the heel of the right sending it to second, and this [left] lands where it beat, and at the same time the right lands in second position where it was chased.

They can also be done *turning* in which nothing else is added but the circular motion, and for the rest it is the same as that explained above.

It contains three movements: the *plié*, the rise with the spring and the step.

35

Of the *Passo Scacciato, Pas Chassé*

§1. *Simple*   §2. *Open*   §3. *Beaten*   §4. *Of four steps*

The *pas chassé*, of which much use is made, takes its name from the action inasmuch as one of the feet, in hitting the other, detaches it from its place, and this makes a simple step. There are various kinds, of which we shall speak in separate Paragraphs, and first of the *simple*, which is done *forwards*, *backwards*, *sideways*, *turning* and *turning disfatto*.

§1

The *simple forwards* begins from fourth, and in the first equilibrium: bend the knees and, in stretching, with the back foot beat the front foot and chase it to fourth position in front, and then doing another natural step to fourth in front with that leg which hit the other, it will be completed.

In that *backwards*, the foot in fourth position in front, after the *plié* and the stretch, will beat the other, chasing it to fourth behind and, with that leg which chased, another step is done backwards to fourth behind.

That *sideways* begins from the second position, and if you wish to go to the right, after the *plié* and the stretch, the left foot beats the right foot chasing it to second, and it finishes with the left, which is carried to fourth in front.

To do it *turning*, it also starts from the second; when one leg has chased the other, it goes into second and the body turns immediately, and it ends with the foot that chased, bringing it in front of the other. The amount of the turn remains arbitrary.

Turning disfatto is done contrariwise to that explained above, where if turning to the right the right is chased, in *disfatto* if the right is chased, it turns to the left, and if the left, to the right.

110

Three movements are contained in this step: the first is the *plié*, the rise chasing the second, and the walk the third.

§2

Also given is the *open chassé forwards* and *open backwards*, which we will describe in this second paragraph.

To do the *open forwards*, place yourself in the same fourth position and, for example, with the left chasing the right to fourth in front after the usual *plié* and rise, the left then goes to second, and the right is brought to fourth behind.

In the *open backwards*, after having done the *plié* and stretch, the front foot hits that behind, chasing it to fourth behind, and then that foot which chases goes to second, that chased into fourth in front and thus it will be completed.

To these, besides the three movements explained in the *simple*, another is added, which is the last walk.

§3

In this third paragraph we shall speak of the *beaten chassé*, which is done sideways, and done *beaten on the instep* and *beaten disfatto*, *beaten turning* and *beaten turning disfatto*.

That *beaten sideways* starts from the second position: bend the knees and, wishing to do it to the left, make a little spring, and the right foot will beat the left on the calf, with which beat it is sent to the true second, the right lifting to second in the air at the same time; from there, the right goes to fifth behind, the left to second, and it ends with the right going to fourth in front.

That *beaten on the instep* is done, for example, with the right foot in front: bend, and the same right goes to beat the left foot on the instep, at the same time chasing it a little backwards, and immediately returns to the fourth position; the left will then beat the calf of the right, and will return to fourth again. In the beating which the left will do to the right, it will not chase it nor will it really cover any ground at all, but will hardly touch the calf, and then immediately return to fourth as was said.

The *beaten disfatto* is no different, except that the back foot beats that in front, which again beats the right and returns to the same fourth. To that *beaten on the instep turning*, is added the circular motion to the side of the foot which beat, which, after the beat, returns to the same position and the other foot goes in front, also turning the body, in which even a full turn can be attained.

The *beaten turning disfatto* turns in the same direction as the beaten foot.

These *beaten* ones are increased by the beating movement and contain the others of the *simple*.

111

§4

Every *chassé* as we have explained above may also be done with four steps, adding another simple movement, walking, which, although it resembles a *dégagé*, is not one, as we said of the *bourrée of four steps* (Ch. 29, §9) because this last step must be done consecutively and be closely linked to the others, bringing the leg *forwards*, *backwards*, *to the side*, according to the quality and manner in which the step will be done.

36

Of the *Mezzo Scacciato, Demi-Chassé*

The step just explained may be performed halved, called *demi-chassé*. Speaking first of the *simple*, it is done with all the diversity of the full, which has been fully described, ending it after the chasing movement, omitting from it the last natural step, that is the walking movement which this *demi* lacks; thus it consists of only two movements, which are the *plié* and the stretch chasing.

That *open* is not halved but is always used in full.

Those *beaten* may be halved; indeed they are used too much, by taking away from them the last movement. For the most part, one beat of the foot and one *assemblé* are joined to these, whether *forwards* or *turning*. The *beaten demi-chassé turning* takes no more than a quarter or a half turn at the most, and with the next sequence the full turn may be completed.

The said linked steps occupy the time of two bars of music, either in two-four or in three-four.

37

Of the *Ballonné*

The *Ballerini* highly prize and esteem the *ballonné*. The *ballanti seri* generally use this, dancing with the utmost gravity of which they are capable, because, done with gentleness and giving to it that flexibility which is sought, the majesty and solemnity of the Dance increases.

It can also serve for the *Ballerini Groteschi*, doing it adroitly however, and adding to it the play of the arms, which with contrary positions, makes a fine sight. Doing it *to the front*, *to the back*, *to the side* and *turning* are its diversities but they differ little one from the other. This step has much in common with the *contretemps*, only adding to it the flexing of the knee. For example: balanced on both feet in fourth position, equally bend the knees slightly, and in rising do a little spring on the instep, which means lifting only the heel off the ground, although in fact lifting the whole foot would not be wrong; then the front foot is detached to fourth in the air in front, and therefore it is called *to the front*; *to the back* would be behind, and *to the side* it will be done sideways; the difference lies only in this movement; so, the leg having been lifted in the air, the body firmly poised in equilibrium completely on the other leg, gently bend only the knee of the leg in the air and, by returning it to fourth in the air as it was, the said step is completed. By 'as it was', I mean to say front, if that is where it was, in second if to the side, and if to the back, it is again carried behind.

Turning, we shall say nothing more except that, in springing, the body turns the required amount and for the rest then it is similar to that *to the front*. These however are done in *chaconne* time.

This step can only occupy the time of one bar.

Its movements are three. The first the *plié*, the rise with the spring the second, the third flexing and carrying once more in the air.

38

Of the *Developpé*

The step is called by the French *developpé*, this being an unfolding, we mean to say a group of thigh movements.

§1

Strictly speaking it should begin with the leg in the air but, in order to make an exact explanation, it will be taken from the fourth position on the ground. If you desire to do it with the right, for example, place this behind the left; and with the body well balanced on both legs, open the right lightly to second in the air, where, bending its knee somewhat, it is brought to fifth also in the air and, having reached this, it is stretched, then making a half circle, it is brought behind to fourth in the air, and marking another quarter circle in the air, it is brought once more to second in the air* where it may end, or else continue to be brought to fifth still marking a circle, from where it may return afresh to second in the air. Usually it is danced in duple and triple times; dancing in triple, it is done up to the sign*, in duple time the other two movements are added.

When this step is done slowly it is said to be *sostenuto*, done with speed, it is called *andante*; and there is no other difference between them.

§2

Besides these there is the *jumped, sauté* as it is called in French, in which with that foot on the ground you do many little springs in the manner of ·demi-contretemps*; the other does as many crossings in front and behind in the air.

§3

The *beaten developpé* does not differ from these, except that before marking the circle in the air to bring the leg to the front or to the back, some beats, that are always to first in the air, will be done.

The movements of the step just explained are four up to the appended sign.* The first is that which is done when the foot is taken out to second in the air; the second is in the bending of the knee, taking it to fifth in front in the air, from where it is taken to fourth behind in the air which will be the third, and the fourth to the second; if it follows to fifth in front in the air, the same fourth movement will be continued and going to the same second will be another movement and this would be the fifth.

39

Of the *Glissata*, the *Glissade*

We shall speak of the *glissade* in this chapter, which may be done *forwards, backwards, sideways, turning fatto,* and *turning disfatto.*

Wishing to do it *forwards,* place yourself in fourth position with for example the right in front of the left; the body is balanced on both legs; then bend the knees and, in stretching, take the right to fourth in the air, when, as soon as it is placed on the ground, with the left foot you lightly brush the ground and bring it to the fifth behind, and from this same position you can follow it with another, and as many as you wish, because the foot in front always remains in front and that behind, behind.

That *backwards* is the same with the sole difference, that the back foot is detached to fourth in the air behind, and that in front slides until it reaches the fifth in front.

The *sideways* enjoys the privilege of being able to begin under and end over, also to begin over and end under. It is also begun from the fourth; if to the right, the right [foot], instead of being lifted into fourth in the air, is detached to second in the air and, after being lowered, the left slides to fifth, which equally may be over or under.

To do it *turning fatto,* it is necessary to turn to that same side as the foot which is moved first; this, from the position in the air where it was first lifted, is brought behind to fifth,[46] giving a turning motion to the body, and the other foot is brought skimming also to fifth behind while the body again turns, and the entire circular motion which is made during the *glissade* cannot strictly be more than one half because if the full were made, then the step's appearance would alter, and be more like the shape of an *assemblé.*

Being *disfatto* is quite the opposite, in which, if you wish to turn to the

117

left, first move the right, and it is brought in front while lowering from the position in the air, and the rest follows as above explained.[47]

Three are its movements: the first is the *plié*, the second stretch and carrying in the air, and the walk the third.

40

Of the *Passo Unito*, or the *Assemblé*

The *assemblé* bears much resemblance to a *capriole* and so an *assemblé* is often used instead of this. The *Ballerini* make great use of it, and still more so the *Ballanti*, who, when they have to do a *capriole* to the front, followed by another turning, leave out one, and do an *assemblé* in its place.

For the French it is more customary than for we Italians, because they do not care to make much use of the *caprioles*, preferring to dance *terre à terre*. Some of our Ladies would sooner be French than Italian; in order to avoid fatigue they more willingly do an *assemblé* instead of a *capriole* and from their stupidity, in truth, originates the *assemblé*.

In a figured *pas de deux*, where the Man interweaves the *capriole*, the Lady, in order to reserve all her strength for her solo part, generally joins an *assemblé* and shows her ability when the spectators' eyes are all fixed on her dance, being engrossed in it alone, without having any regard to the whole *ballo*, where the greater part of the spectacle, and the honour of her colleague, lies; but those Ladies who do not mind what the others call personal glory, do not do this because all their skill is applied from the beginning to the end.

But let us leave this invective apart and return to the composition of the step, which may be done *forwards*, *backwards*, *sideways*, *turning fatto*, *turning disfatto*, and *sur place*.

The *assemblé forwards* may be done on either leg, and can begin from any position in front, except from the second [sic]. For example, in fourth with the right in front, balance the body on the left and, bending the knees, raise the right to fourth in the air stretching only this, while the left remains bent all the time, sustaining the equilibrium of the body; and in rising and stretching from this, a supple movement is given to the knee, and still more to the instep, in such a way as to enable you to make a little spring, scarcely rising from the ground and advancing very slightly; you land with both feet on the same spot, carrying the right to one of the positions in front except second and first, although speaking of the simple *assemblé* one lands in fifth, in the other two positions when another step which begins in one of them is joined to it.

In that *backwards*, the beginning is the same in that the foot in front is also lifted to fourth in the air, bending, stretching, and rising as said above; the only difference is that you travel backwards and the right lands behind in one of the three positions mentioned above, as will be called for by the following step which will be joined to it.

The *sideways* begins from the same position and, in lifting the foot in the air, detach it to second, then lowering it, cover ground to the side and land in one of the three positions described, for not even this to the side lands in second.

Turning is the same, adding the required amount of turn while landing, and to do it *fatta* you turn to the side of that foot which is raised to fourth in the air; on the contrary, in order to be *disfatta* you turn to the side of the foot that is on the ground.

That *sur place*, however, takes the shape of a *capriole*. This differs from the others: here you bend both knees equally, then rise again stretching the insteps in order to lift the whole body just off the ground, otherwise it would be a jump and not a step, and you land in fifth position on the same place. It is called *sur place* because no ground is covered in any direction.

All these kinds of *assemblé* are done with the tips of the toes touching the ground, so little must the feet be raised above it.

Two movements are considered in this step: the first is the *plié*, the second is the rise with the spring, for landing is not judged to be a different movement, as noted in Chapter 5 on Movements.

41

Of the *Ballotté*

By the sound, this *ballotté* might be confused with the *ballonné* for the only difference is none other than the alteration of only one letter: but this change of letter gives great variety to the steps. It consists of three *jetés* done on one, then the other leg, and ends with an *assemblé*; the first two *jetés* are done with speed, the third is longer, to which is joined the *assemblé*. It takes two bars of music, the first on the first *jeté*, the second in landing from the *assemblé*. This step is done sometimes in triple time, sometimes in duple; in these times it is done either slower or faster: everything depends on the *ballante*'s ear and experience; and this step can be used by every character.

In as many ways as the *jeté* can be done, so this same step can be done, therefore we do not describe it.

The movements are all those contained in three *jetés* and one *assemblé*.

42

Of the *Ambuettè* [48]

The *ambuettè* is a step which can begin from all positions, but as we said, the fourth is that which is always preferred above all others as being the most comfortable, and it is done either with the one, or the other leg. It is done *forwards*, *backwards*, *sideways*, *turning fatto* and *disfatto*, and repeated, *doublé*.

To do it *forwards*, for example, place the right foot behind the left, and bending both knees, the back foot will then mark a half circle and will be thrown to fourth in front and, as soon as it is placed, with a natural movement the left is carried to fourth in front; the moving of this foot must therefore be immediate on the placing of that which took a little spring, and from this the right passes to the fourth in front, so that this *ambuettè* ends with the same foot with which it began; and it begins indifferently, either with the one, or the other foot, provided that the foot behind ends in front, from which ending it takes the description of *forwards*.

I said that when carrying the first foot from back to front, it will be *thrown*: it was not by chance that I used such a term, because there the motion of a *jeté* is given, and so I distinguished by saying 'with a *natural movement*' when instructing in the carrying of the other.

That *backwards* on the contrary begins in front and ends *behind* and is done thus: say for example that the right is in fourth in front, after the *plié* this same marks a half circle and is thrown to fourth behind, and the left, which remained in front, immediately goes behind to fourth again, and the right also goes to fourth behind. It goes without saying that in the throwing the usual little spring is done.

That *sideways* is done similarly; it differs only at the end, in that it terminates in second with the foot, with which it began, advancing to the side when landing on the ground from the little spring.

122

In *turning*, nothing else is added except the amount of turn, which ought not to be more than one quarter or at the most one half, although sometimes it is turned more but this is out of mere necessity and ends in second. In order to be done *fatto*, turn to the same side as the foot which will be the first to move; and in order to be done *disfatto*, turn towards the opposite side to that of the foot which first moved.

The *repeated* is nothing more than that each *ambuettè* referred to above can be done as many times as you wish with the greatest speed.

This step is the favourite of our valiant Monsieur Carlo Lepicq. He does it with such mastery and vivacity that it looks like an interlacing in the air, a brilliant *capriole*.

Four movements are contained in this step: the first is the *plié*, the second the rise, the third and fourth are the walks.

43

Of the *Fouetté*

The *fouetté* is a very brilliant step which, like the *ballotté*, serves to end a cadence. By its true nature it takes one bar in duple time, but it can also be done very well in triple time if it is wished; but doing it in this time, which is outside the nature of the step, depends on the ability of the *Ballante*. It may be done in two ways: *sur place* and *turning*.

To do it *sur place*, begin for example from the fourth position with the right in front, bend the knees slightly, and in stretching lift the right leg to fourth in the air, from where circling it reaches the second similarly in the air and, having arrived there, bend both knees at once as the right foot is sent behind to fifth in the air, from where, again stretching, the same is taken out to second in the air. During this time the left leg can remain still or it can do two little springs, either on the instep or scarcely lifted from the ground; the first is done with the same movement of bending the knees when the right leg, having arrived at second in the air, goes to fifth bending, and the other is done in extending.

That *turning* begins in the same fashion and is turned to the same side as the foot with which it is done; it is a full turn and ends in second in the air.

Speaking of the step considered by itself, this is how it is used, but when performed in the Theatre two *assemblés* are added to it at the end: the first is taken with the same leg which is in the air, carrying it to fifth in front, and the other will be an *assemblé sur place* (Ch. 40). In this case it would occupy two bars of music whether in the one or in the other time; for the most part it is used either at the beginning of a section or else at the end of a cadence. Whenever it is wished to link it to another step it is done alone.[49]

44

Of the *Demi-Fouetté*

To do a *demi*, it ends at the second movement, which is the *plié* carrying the right leg to fifth in the air, from which *plié* one can take another step, as would be a *brisé* or similar step which begins with a *plié*. This is never employed alone but it serves to link another step to it, as was said of the *demi-échappé*.

45

Of the *Pirola, Pirouettes*

The *pirouette* is a step which is always done turning on the same place. The body may be turned one quarter, one half, three-quarters or a full turn. It is done in many diverse ways, turning *to the right, to the left; disfatta, sur place sustained, forced of indeterminate number, low, in retiré, toe and heel, heel and toe, extended open, crossed*; and usually it is begun from the fourth position.

Wishing to do it *to the right* with a *quarter turn*, with knees extended, carry the right foot, which is in front, to fourth behind marking a half circle in the air until it arrives at fourth position as already stated; and as a general rule this carrying with the said *plié* serves to give a pleasing quality to the *pirouettes*; so, bending the knees, place only the ball of the foot on the ground, raising the heel of the other foot, and rise on the balls of both feet maintaining the equilibrium of the body in the second manner (Ch. 4,); fixing the balls of the feet on the ground, and exactly on the same spot as though it were an axis, turn the body, making the body line parallel to the line which was horizontal to your right side.

If you wish to do a *half turn*, keep to the same method, and the leg is carried to fifth behind and, turning in the same manner, the chest should be where formerly the back was.

To do *three-quarters*, it is carried to forced fifth behind, and you turn until you face that direction where previously your left side was.

To do a *full turn*, take the foot which is carried behind to a position beyond the forced, and in turning come back to the same situation from which you began.

To turn to the left, begin with the left leg in front and then carry it behind, and turn to the left in one of the four degrees.

To be *disfatta* means that instead of carrying the foot from the side to the back, you carry it in front of the foot which is on the ground and turn specifically to the required amount.

To do a *pirouette disfatta on both feet*, place yourself in fourth for example with the right in front; from the same, rise on the balls of both feet and turn to the left, the body turning one quarter; the foot which was in front will now be behind. This *pirouette* cannot make more than a quarter turn, for to do a half it would be necessary to be placed in forced fifth.

The *pirouette* is called *sustained* when speed is not used in the turning but it will be turned with more feeling if the music is *patetico*.

There are the *forced indeterminate pirouettes* which are done on the ball of one foot only, on which you turn quickly, as many times as possible. That is why they are called *indeterminate*,[50] for they do not depend on the will of the *ballante* to turn more or less, but on what his ability and agility will allow. At times the *Ballerini* incorporate *tordichamp* or some beats *fatti* and *disfatti* in this *pirouette*, or some flexing of the knee of the leg which is in the air while turning on the ball of the other foot, and in such a case it is permitted to the *serio* to do it in a sustained manner.

The *low pirouette*, which is also *indeterminate* and *forced*, may be done only by the *Ballerino Grotesco*, and is done with bent knees and turning rapidly on the ball of one foot.

The *pirouette in retiré* is also peculiar to the *Grotesco* and is done while turning on the ball of one foot; the other rests against the knee of the same leg that is turning, or behind the bend of the same knee. This *pirouette* is also numbered among those known as *indeterminate*.

The *toe and heel* is again peculiar to the *Grotesco*, and is, that the toe of the foot which is in the air rests against the heel of the foot on which you turn, and this is also an *indeterminate pirouette*.

Contrariwise is that of *heel and toe*, in which the heel of the foot in the air rests against the toe of the foot on which you turn. It also belongs to the *Grotesco* and is *indeterminate*.

The *open extended pirouette* is done turning on the ball of one foot, keeping the other at a distance of second in the air and extending the knees well. It is one of the *forced indeterminate* and may be done by all characters.

To the *Grotesco* also belongs the *crossed pirouette*, which again is *indeterminate* and is done thus: the foot not touching the ground is placed on the instep of the foot on which you turn.

There are others but because they are related to these, we shall leave them aside.

All these *pirouettes* need great equilibrium, indeed they all depend on it; it is also necessary to do them on a smooth floor in order to do a number of turns. I myself have managed to do nine turns with the advantage of having found a place on the Stage where I could turn without hindrance, and whoever wishes to show off these *pirouettes* should be careful not to do them on an uneven surface where it is easy to lose balance, and accounts for the dubious success of the *pirouette*.

The renowned Florentine Sig. Vestris, at present in the service of the King of France, is so free with these *pirouettes* that he can astonish an entire Theatre with only one. He can change the feet twice or thrice during the same turn without stopping to interrupt the turn: truly something to be eternally admired, but what is most stupefying is that he suddenly stops while turning at the greatest possible speed and remains in *aplomb*, with such particular freedom that he stays immobile in that equilibrium.

With respect to the *aplomb*, nobody can compare with the much loved, incomparable Monsieur Pitrot. He managed to maintain perfect *aplomb* for two minutes, and in this same attitude did every possible sort of beats, *fatti, disfatti, high, low, extended, on the instep* and as many as the skill of an expert *Ballerino* might demand; he also did *tordichamp* in various ways, but not only is this worthy of wonder, for what is more, he does not remain in equilibrium on the ball of one foot as others do but he raises the whole body on the tip of his big toe, and extends all the joints so perfectly, that the whole thigh, leg and foot itself fall into one perpendicular line. At the end of his solo, when everyone else would be breathless and consequently would find it difficult to strike exact equilibrium, he is placed in *aplomb* more firmly and comfortably than a man at ease and fresh stands on his own feet. Things apparently supernatural yet borne out by the testimony of eye-witnesses all over Europe.

46

Of the *Contratempo, Contretemps*

§1.   *Simple*   §2.   *Open*   §3.   *With a flying bound*
§4.   *Contretemps* and *pas de bourrée disfatto*   §5.   *Beaten*

In this chapter we shall speak of the *contretemps*: one of the principal steps, and practised by every kind of *Ballerini*. It is divided into *simple, open, with a flying bound* and *beaten*.

§1

The *simple* is done *forwards, backwards, sideways, turning fatto* and *disfatto*, and is begun with one or the other foot. It can be taken from all the positions, except from the first and from the second; but to do it *forwards* the easiest is from the fourth, for the reason so often quoted. Taking the example from the fourth with the right foot in front, balance the body on this, and only the ball of the left will barely touch the ground; bend the knee, and rise springing to land on the right foot, holding the left in second in the air, from where it is carried to fourth in front, and end with another simple step forwards on the right, ending in fourth position. Please note, that while landing from the little spring which is taken on one foot, the ground is covered a little forwards.

In that *backwards*, not only is the ground covered backwards while landing from the little spring, but the two simple movements, which end in fourth, are also done backwards, and beyond this there is no other difference.

The *contretemps sideways* is distinguished by the two aforesaid movements that are done sideways and the ground that must be covered while landing is to the side.

To *turn fatto*, bend as usual and rise, springing on the front foot which will be the right, if turning to the right, if to the left, the left; while landing on the same foot, turn, and that which was behind will make a circling step, and the other finishes in fourth position in front.

That *disfatto* is done in the opposite way: rise springing on the front foot, let us say the left for example to turn to the right, the right to the left; when landing from the little spring, the leg which was behind in fourth in the air is then carried circling to true fourth; if it is desired to do a half turn, it will be completed with the other in fourth in front; wishing to do the full turn, half is done while landing and it is completed with two simple movements.

§2

The *open to the side*, is taken from the second position: bend and rise springing, for example landing on the right, then carry the left to fifth, and again the right is carried to second. It is called *open* because it ends in second position and serves to join on another step which begins from this position.

§3

All the *contretemps* steps explained may be done *with a flying bound*, and involve a force, a greater impetus, that is given to the body and serves either to take any *capriole*, or to travel any figure. If it is done in preparation for a *capriole*, it is necessary to force it to give greater height to the jump because, should it be taken slowly, the articulation [of the joints] cannot be well controlled, which, not being well controlled, cannot give that necessary elevation to the body to rebound, because a body, speaking of bodies in general, not only of the living one, will have more strength in its resilience when it is more controlled, this resilient force being nothing more than a continuous, violent movement of extension; *vis elastica est continua vis se dilatandi*. In order to go beyond any figure then, it is necessary to give it greater impetus for, if the *contretemps* is done slowly, you might not be able to travel [enough].

Four movements make up each type of these *contretemps*. The first the *plié*, the second the rise with a spring, the third and fourth are two simple walked movements.

§4

The *contretemps* and the *pas de bourrée disfatto* are very much used by the *Ballerini Groteschi* and also by the *mezzo carattere*. Today, however, when good taste has become more refined, this step has almost fallen from use. It served as an expedient for travelling across the stage, as well as enabling the *ballante* to draw breath; but for the past twenty-five years, six or seven famed *ballerini* have brought honour to theatrical Dance, gradually purging it by removing certain rather tasteless and trivial customs where some beautifully graceful combinations have been introduced in exchange for the said step.

130

In order to understand what this step is, already fallen from use, we would say that it was a sequence of *contretemps* and *bourrée disfatto* (Ch. 29) and some other unnamed steps, as there are so many other unmentioned sequences, such as in the *chaconne*, in the *trusé*, in the *flinc flanc*. This sequence was done crossing the stage or also travelling from up to down [stage].

But coming to the formation of this step, if you wish to do it with the left foot, place the right in front, and detaching the left foot, bend, and do one *contretemps* to the side to the left, after which one *pas de bourrée disfatto* with the left foot is joined, with which the step will be completed. Usually one *flinc flanc* and one *assemblé* terminate this step sequence, which will conclude the step and the sequence, not the turn, because it is *fatto* and *disfatto* simultaneously.

<h2 style="text-align:center">§5</h2>

All the forms of *contretemps* [explained in §4] may also be done *beaten*, to which nothing is added except one beat. It frequently begins with a *dégagé*, finding yourself in any position except the second and the fourth, for, being in one of these two, the detachment is omitted. Placed then in position balanced on the soles of both feet, bend the knees, and, in stretching them, spring on the left foot for example, and at the same moment with the right foot beat the calf of the left, whence it is carried to the fourth position, then following it with two simple movements either forwards or backwards, turning or sideways, according to the type of *contretemps*. Thus there is no difference other than the beat, and consequently it is increased by another movement.

47

Of the *Mezzo Contratempo*, the *Demi-Contretemps*

Having explained the full *contretemps*, I have revealed everything pertaining to the *demi*, because this is nothing else than the beginning of those, ending after the landing without adding the two simple steps, but it ends by lifting to second in the air the foot on which you did not jump, so that if you wish to take another, a *dégagé* is done with the same leg that is in the air.

The *beaten* can also be halved by omitting only the above-mentioned simple steps.

The *contretemps* and *bourrée disfatto* cannot be halved however, since it is a combination of steps which in its entirety demands everything described.

Its movements are no more than two: the *plié* and the rise with a spring.

48

Of the *Tempi di Coscia, Temps de Cuisse*

Nothing else is involved in this *tempo di coscia*, or *temps de cuisse* as it is known in French, other than a beat of the thigh and the leg accompanying the beat of the foot. Some desire that after the first *plié* you should beat with the foot and the knee stretched, alleging that in this way it can be executed more brilliantly. Others claim, with more reason, that doing it with a bent knee has a different value and renders it more praiseworthy, and in fact the French use it thus, in which manner it appears more attractive. My opinion is also this, for when you wish to do it in a *grave* the beat of the Music is filled out more with the said bend. It is done in various manners: *forwards, backwards, sideways, turning, repeated.*

Wishing to do it *forwards*, place yourself in fourth position and begin with a slight bend of the knees, then extend to second in the air that leg with which you wish to beat, for example the right; on lowering from the said second, lightly beat with the calf the front of the left leg, at the same time stretching both knees; during the whole step the thigh that accompanies the movement of the leg is brought into play; the same beat that was made will make the leg rebound, sending it to second once more but a little closer, from where, without the slightest pause, it is carried to second in the air, and this with the right leg; with the left, as soon as it is beaten, a light little spring is done, travelling forwards.

Backwards, there is no other difference except that the beat is done behind, that is with the front of one leg beating the calf of the other leg which, with a little spring, travels backwards, and the leg which beat also goes to second in the air.

Sideways, after the beat, the left leg, with a little spring, will travel further to the side and the other will go to second in the air as usual.

Those *turning*, whether to the right or to the left, always have the same movements which we have now explained, adding only a turn which is done during the jump and cannot be more than one quarter for each *temps de cuisse*; it is usually turned to the right if done with the right and doing it with the left, it is turned to the left.

Repeated forwards they are all done with the same leg and, instead of ending with the leg which beats in second in the air, it is carried gliding to fourth in front. In repeating, having done the first backwards, the second is done forwards with the other leg and they also end by gliding to fourth. Those to the side do not change legs but are all done with the same and end in the proper second in the air as we said.

It consists of three movements: the first is the *plié* extending, the second the rise, and the third the beat.

49

Of the *Fioretto, Fleuret*

§1.   *Simple*   §2.   *With a chassé*   §3.   *With a jeté*
                   §4.   *Jumped, sauté*

In this chapter we shall speak of the *fleuret*, which is so necessary in dancing that there is scarcely one Dance into which it does not enter. It can be danced to any Musical time whether *binary* or *ternary*, but its true time would be the *three-four*. It is done *simple, with a chassé, with a jeté* and *jumped*, and we will start with the *simple*, as the most easily understood.

§1

The *simple* is done *forwards, backwards, sideways, turning*. To do it *forwards*, place yourself in fourth for example with the right leg behind and, without a *plié*, detach it to second in the air, and, without stopping, just skimming the ground, carry it bending to a slightly forced fourth, and the left, which remained behind, is carried to third behind the right where, rising on the balls of both feet and with a natural step done with the right to fourth in front, it will be completed.

That *backwards* begins with the front leg, making it pass from second by carrying it with a bend, gliding to fourth behind: if this is done with the right leg, the left, which remained in front, is carried to third in front, and rise as before, and the right, which was behind, is carried to fourth behind with one simple step.

That *sideways* also begins from fourth, and for example the right is carried gliding into second and then the left closes in third behind, and rising on the balls of both feet, the right once more goes to second position.

Turning, the movement of a turn is added, which is done by the first leg marking a quarter circle and, bending, it is carried in a transverse line to the side and, rising, the other is placed in third behind while turning the body.[51]

Four movements are contained in each of these *fleurets*. The first is the carrying gliding, the *plié* the second, the third the rise, and the walk the fourth.

§2

The *fleuret chassé* may also be done *forwards*, *backwards*, *sideways*, *turning*; wishing to do this *forwards*, after placing yourself in position and having done the first step forward and the same *plié* which was done at the end of the first step, the foot which is behind goes to strike with the anklebone the heel of the other foot chasing it to fourth in front and thus it will be completed.

In that *backwards*, the foot which started in front is chased to fourth behind after the first step which is used in the others.

That *sideways*, if not done with some care, can be confused with the *demi-chassé sideways*, which is closely related to it but, however, it has its own distinctive features. This, as was said of the *simple to the side* (§1), begins from fourth, and after extending to second, [the foot] is chased to the second in the air, whence it is immediately placed in second on the ground.

In that *turning*, the chasing is also done in the second movement with the addition of the circling as described in the *simple*.

The movements are also four because the chasing is not added, but is in place of the rise on the balls of both feet.

§3

The *thrown fioretto*, that is the *fleuret jeté*, can also be done in all the described ways, adding to them the *jeté* movement, or more precisely by changing the second movement and the third.

We will show an example *forwards* by detaching the right from fourth in front[52] or behind to second in the air; continually sliding, the same leg is carried to fourth in front; the left foot which remained behind is thrown behind the right, chasing this to fourth in the air, from where this is also thrown in front of the left, which is thrown to second in the air where it stops, thus completing the step.

In that *backwards*, you use the same *jeté* movements backwards.

Sideways, if you wish to do it to the right, carry the right foot to second position and, in rising, it is lightly struck with the other foot behind and goes to second in the air, and again is thrown in front of the other which is also lifted to second in the air.

In *turning* the amount of the turn is added and thus it will be completed.

Four movements are also contained in this, changing the second and the third to *jetés* and the fourth to a detachment in the air.

§4

The *fleuret sauté* is done with a little spring in the manner of a *demi-contretemps* which is employed before the start of the *simple fleuret*, because the landing from the spring is joined to the beginning of the *fleuret*, having the same movement as if it were carried, and then follows the *fleuret*, which should be in one of the variants as described in the *simple*.

This is increased by one movement more than the others, and it is the spring.

50

Of the *Brisé*

The *brisé* done in its true form has nothing in common with the *capriole*; indeed an *assemblé to the side* is more like a *capriole* than a *brisé*. This step is greatly used by the French, and although it might be a little thing in itself, none the less it appears to have more value by being a brilliant step, as it makes more effect done by those *ballanti* with supremely lively footwork than a *capriole* done by another. In truth then, referring to the subject of the *capriole*, it is executed as though it were a *fourth capriolata to the side*, but since it is done on the ground it becomes a step and not a *capriole*, whence in calling it a *capriole* the teachers of the art commit an error, showing that they cannot distinguish this from the step. It may be done *forwards, backwards, sideways, turning, repeated*, or *doublé*.

To do it *forwards*, if you wish to take it with the right leg, place yourself in any position except the first and the second, but the best is always the fourth; placed then in this with the right behind, bending, extend the foot to second in the air from where, with the calf of the same leg, beat in front of the instep[53] of the other, which by the same strike is chased to fourth in front.

To do it *backwards*, instead of beating in front with the calf of one leg the instep of the other, beat with the instep of the right for example the calf of the left, which, being chased, forms a semicircle and goes to fourth behind.

Sideways, it is begun like that *forwards* and the beaten foot travels to the side and ends in a forced fifth.

In *turning*, the circular [movement] is added to it, turning to the left if it is done with the left, and if with the right, turn to the right.

Each kind of these *brisé* can be *repeated* and this equals *doublé*. You can repeat with the same foot doing as many of them as you wish; they can also be done changing feet, in which case first you extend one and then the other.

This step has three movements: the *plié* extending, the stretch beating, and the carrying.

51

Of the *Passo di Rigodone,* the *Rigaudon*

This *rigaudon* consists of nothing more than an arrangement of a *contre-temps* and an *assemblé*, but the *contretemps* is slightly different from the usual. This *contretemps* may be taken from the four positions excluding the second when used in a *rigaudon*; we take the example from fourth, and in stretching you spring, and landing for instance on the right leg, lift the left leg in the air, then at once return it to the ground in first position, and immediately lift the other to second position in the air, placing it again in the same fourth; that equals the *contretemps*. Then in order to do the *assemblé*, bend the knees and, barely rising into the air, do an *assemblé sur place* with which the *rigaudon* will be completed.

This is a step which is always done *sur place*. With the French it is very fashionable, and especially in their *Contredances* also called *Rigaudon*, and these are danced in binary time; *Quadrille Contredances* are not only filled with this, but also with other Theatrical steps, such as the *chassé, fleuret, ballonné des contretemps* and similar little steps.

The movements of this are six: four for the *contretemps* and two for the *assemblé*.

52

Of the *Pas Trusé*

The *trusé* is also a combined step, composed of many others. It contains four movements, consisting of three steps and one jump. The first step employed in the composition *trusé* is a *demi-contretemps turning*, the next is a *demi-coupé*, the third a *beat behind*, and the jump will be an *assemblé sur place*. This is a step always done turning.

Counting its movements, join all those which are contained in the steps of which it is composed.

53

Of the *Pas de Chaconne*

§1.   *Simple*   §2.   *Jumped*

The *pas de chaconne* is also one of the compound steps, so called because it takes the name from the Time in which it is danced, which is triple: *sonata spiritosa* and with many variations of the tempi contained therein, passing from *allegro* to *armonioso*, to *dolce*, to *fugato*: and in all of its variations it always maintains the same metre. This is done *simple*, and *jumped*, each with its own diversity.

§1

The *simple* is done *sur place turning fatto* and *disfatto*. It takes two bars of Music, composed of three different steps. I say three, and not four, because one step is repeated. It consists then of one *jeté*, of one *ballonné*, of another *jeté*, and of one *assemblé sideways*. The first *jeté* is done with the right foot to the left with a quarter turn; with the *ballonné* another quarter is done landing on the right leg; with the other *jeté* three-quarters is arrived at, and the full turn is completed with the *assemblé*. Wishing to do it *disfatto* detach the back leg to fourth and if, for example, the detachment to fourth is with the right, then bending do the *jeté* backwards and the left leg remains in the air, then spring taking the *ballonné*. The first *jeté* will land on the right foot slightly turning to the left, then with the turn of the leg[54] and the other *jeté* three-quarters of a turn will be done, and with the *assemblé* the full turn *disfatto* will be done.

§2

The *jumped* is also *sur place turning fatto* and *disfatto*. This, instead of being taken with a *jeté*, is taken with a *demi-contretemps turning*, then the *ballonné* is done, immediately followed by the *jeté* and the *assemblé*. *Disfatto*, it is taken with a *demi-contretemps* turning to the left with the left leg,[55] landing with the said leg behind in fourth in the air, from where the *ballonné disfatto* is taken also with the left,[56] and then the *jeté* is done, and the *assemblé sideways*, with which the turn *disfatto* of the said step is completed.

It is not given to all the *Ballerini seri* to dance the *Chaconne*[57] because they dance on their own and, for the most part, all the solos are danced impromptu, and if the *ballerino* is not accustomed to dancing in a group, he cannot do this because of the groups of steps, now free, now linked, now held, now violent, now languid, which are in it.

The airs of these are to be compared to the furies, to the role of Boreas,[58] to the *Grande Vitesse*,[59] which is now violent, now interspersed with so many moderations, rendering this style the most difficult of all, and its execution becomes as difficult for the *Ballerino* as for the composers of the dance, because of the great diversity of the variations in the tunes; this applies to the *corps de ballet* as well as to the principal characters.

They require a group of supernumeraries, for the equal balance of the figures[60] is a very necessary thing, since it is from these that the *corps de ballet* of the *Chaconne* will begin. After the said supers have danced twenty-four bars, more or less, the *Ballerino* comes out with a *Solo*, or with a *Duet*, and dances as many bars again, at most thirty-two. A *Ballerino* or *Ballerina* cannot dance more than this and if some are to be found who dance any more, they are those who do not specialise in a similar kind of Dance; they keep doing the *aplomb*, the *attitudes*, things which use much music but no dance: in this form one might freely dance more than twenty-four or thirty-two bars, but if the *aplombs* were adapted to the amount of the Music, it would be certain that one would not be able to dance more than the already stated bars.

54

Of the *Flinc Flanc*[61]

This step is used for moving from one place to another, and for taking a *capriole*. It is composed of three steps, and the whole compound step takes two bars of music: it goes to *Gigue* time, as also to *two-four Sbalzante*.[62] It can be done *sideways* and *turning*.

In order to do it *sideways*, wishing to do it to the left side, place the left foot in front; then bending the knee of the right leg, detach this in the air making a half circle and let it fall in front of the left, which is the *jeté* movement; instead of this *jeté* one can sometimes join an *interwoven fifth*, changing feet; after the thrown movement lift the left immediately, carrying it to second position, bending, at the same time doing a *chassé*, and then an *assemblé sideways* with which this step *sideways* will be completed.

That *turning* begins as we have already explained, but with the steps done on a turn, and then instead of a *chassé* one *demi* will be done with a quarter turn to the same left, and with the *assemblé* done with the right leg the turn is ended, thus completing it.

The reason why in this turning a full *chassé* is not done but only a half is that, if you were to do a full, and then join the *assemblé*, or instead of this a *capriole*, which might very well be attached, you would not be able to make a turn; it begins thus but, wishing to continue it, it would be reversed instead of being completed, and whoever puts it to the test will see that I tell the truth.

55

Of the *Soubresaut*

The term called by the French *soubresant* signifies a jump done in *contratempo*[63] by a horse in order to escape and throw whoever it is carrying; from this action the name of this step is taken, which is employed in the *andanti* tempi, in the furies, and in all two-four tempi. It is composed of one *demi-contretemps* and one *pas de bourrée* either *forwards*, *sideways*, *backwards*, *turning*, according to what is desired to be done. If wishing to do it *turning* travelling over the stage when, for example, the left leg is in fourth in front, detach the same left in front of the right foot, making a quarter turn to the right side, then spring on the left leg, extending the right to second in the air, bending both knees, carry this right to fifth in front, and consecutively, first the left and then the right, both turning in fourth, will make the usual two simple movements, which will form another quarter turn, and thus one half will be made; wishing to do one full circle it can be done very well by making the turns bigger, as necessitated by the other step to be joined to it, and thus the above-mentioned step is completed. It may be done from either foot, turning either to one or to the other side. It may be turned to the left, if you spring on the right, and to the right, springing on the left, just as it can be turned to that same side as the foot on which you spring.

The other variants are combined in a similar way, joining the *demi-contretemps* with the *bourrée*, according to the ways described.

It is composed of four movements: the first is the *plié* and spring, the second the *plié* and travel, the third and fourth the walks. It is not like the other linked steps that are made up of the movements of the steps which comprise them, because the spring of the *demi-contretemps* and the beginning of the *bourrée* are done at the same time.

56

Of the *Carré*

Before giving an explanation of the *carré* we shall make a little geometrical digression about the *Squared Parallelogram*, on which shape this step is based: it must be squared in order for this to be in the said parallelogram shape, not oblong, rhombic, or rhomboid.

The squared Parallelogram consists of four straight lines equal to one another, forming a right angled square, whose said opposite lines will be parallel to one another. Parallel lines are two straight lines lying on a flat surface, which, drawn to infinity, maintain the same distance.

Let us return to the step which is used by all three kinds of *Ballerini*: *Seri*, *mezzo Carattere* and *Grotesco*, as in *Oltramontano*[64] and *Maschere*[65] characters. This Step must necessarily be done by two People, each forming their own squared Parallelogram. It may be done with *jeté, chassé, glissade* and *galliard* steps and we will take the example of a *chassé*. The two *Ballanti* are placed opposite one another, and each does a *chassé sideways* to the right in a straight line, and then detaching the leg turning back to back, each does another *chassé* to the left, also *sideways* in a straight line, forming a right angle; afterwards, another *dégagé* is done and, turning face to face, they do the third *chassé* each to the right on a straight line parallel to the first, and thus a second right angle is formed; once more the *dégagé* is made, with which they turn back to back, and with their *chassé sideways*, each to the left in a straight line parallel to the second, they form the other two right angles and each will have closed his Parallelogram; but the *carré* is not finished, for another *dégagé* has to be added, and again facing front, each is where he started. It can be performed with the other steps as it was done with the *chassé*.

57

Of the *Rondeau*

The *rondo* is not the formation of a new step but if any sequence of steps is done turning and then repeated it is called a *rondeau*. For instance, if a *pas de bourrée under* were done, and following that a *ballonné* and a *jeté* were linked, returning to the beginning of the *bourrée* with the other steps mentioned, this sequence and repetition of steps makes what is called *rondo*, and this is ordinarily formed of *bourrée, chassé, glissade, jeté* and similar little steps, which, being repeated, are a *rondo*.

58

Of the *Attitude*

The *attitude* is a movement of any part of our body, and it is not solely restricted, as others believe, only to the movement of the arms, but it may be expressed by the head, the eyes, the legs, and by everything else capable of making gestures. The true Theatrical *attitude* does not consist of a single and simple gesture, but is a union of several poses, being an accompaniment of the arms, the legs, the head, the eyes, which must express in which emotional state the person is found.

In his fifth letter, Monsieur Noverre states that if the *ballerino* knows nothing about drawing, he will never know how to arrange in equity the members of the body [to place them] in *attitudes*: the head will not be agreeably placed and will contrast badly with the opposition of the body, the arms will no longer be placed in easy *attitudes*, everything will be cumbersome, pitiable, and all will be devoid of uniformity and of harmony.

Just as the Dancing Masters who do not practise Music are ill fitted to arrange the classify the airs, and are never able to capture the spirit and the character, so those who know nothing about design will not know how to arrange the *attitudes* in just proportion.

The *attitudes* may be done *sur place, to the front, to the back, turning* and *forced.*

In order to do this Theatrical *attitude sur place,* it is necessary to be placed in one of the positions, and you begin by bending the knees and, in stretching, rise only on that leg which remains on the ground and on which the whole body will be supported in equilibrium, and the other leg is lifted in the air, curving it at the knee, and the arm on the same side is lifted in a half circle with the palm of the hand facing towards the chest; the body is turned in an oblique line to the side opposite that leg, which is in the air, with the head turned to the corresponding side, where the eloquence of the eyes express the state of the *Ballante.*

After placing yourself in position to do it *to the front,* and wishing to begin with the right, place this leg in fourth in front, then in rising naturally lift it to fourth in front in the air, bending it slightly, holding the body facing completely forwards while raising the left arm in a half-circle, as above, and for the body, the head and the eyes, observe the aforesaid.

That *to the back* only differs in that, instead of lifting the leg in the air to the front, it will be lifted to the back, and the corresponding arm will be lifted on the same side; so that the *attitudes,* whether *to the front* or *to the back,* differ in that, being *to the front,* the leg will be carried forward and the opposite arm will make the pose; that *to the back* is distinguished only by the leg being lifted to the back and the arm on the same side will be lifted to the front.

To the side, the body is balanced on one leg, lifting the other to second in the air, keeping the knees stretched, and the arms may be equally lifted, allowing them to be carried to any kind of pose called for by the action.

Turning, only a quarter turn and nothing more is added.

Those *forced* will have more exaggerated poses than usual, denoted by the term itself. These are beyond the [normal] position, and belong to the furies, who go beyond the norm in everything. They are also used in dances characterising the *Oltramontani* as well as *Coviello,*[66] or *Scaramuccia,* dances full of diverse kinds of *forced attitudes.* To do an *attitude* in the manner of a fury, the same arm as the leg which is in the air will be lifted high beyond measure with the fingers held with the said irregularity, expressing the kind of rage which makes all the limbs of the body rigid, with scintillating eyes, gnashing teeth, like mastiff dogs, and everything else which can characterise their embittered, vicious and spiteful character; for regularity should never be observed in them but only a skilful speed in gesturing.

Note well, that despite their unseemliness and disorder, nonetheless they merit all attention: more indeed than all other characters they need to be expressed and performed with bodily agility, swiftness of legs, with grand and free gestures of the arms. What then shall I say about the ear? It should be acute and attentive because, in their dances, the tunes are marked and violent, and from this it comes to pass that rare are the *Ballanti* who succeed in such characters.

These are danced in *Ternary* time, very *scaggiosi,* [67] with equally fast musical accompaniment. Sometimes the furies have burning torches in their hands and in waving these, in making *tableaux* of groups of many intertwined furies, it is necessary to be very agile and experienced in the Art.

Do you wish to know why in our Italian Theatres characters of this kind do not succeed? Usually because many times they take a *serio ballerino,* accustomed to gentle and manly *attitudes,* versed in the pathos of his languid impassioned gestures, and give him the task of portraying the violent character of a fury. How can this be done, if great vivacity and fire is needed in the Action? If he is accustomed to soft gestures, how can he adapt himself to violent ones? This is trying to make him contradict his character, to take him away from his system and to put him in another where, so to speak, he is out of place.

This is the truth of my reflection. In the French Theatres, where the dances are complemented by the perspective scenes by the most renowned Artists, the *Ballerini* only exercise that character of which their ability is known to be capable. They do not attempt to undertake everything; they do not waste time where they know they could not succeed. A poor *Ballante* is not sacrificed by dragging him into that character for which he has no capacity. Whoever is capable of being a *serio* gives everything of himself to that *genre.* The *Grotesco* will concentrate on his speciality and does not put on buskins.[68] The *mezzo carattere* puts all his effort there: the *gavottine,* the *tempi brillanti* are always his constant exercise; and thus they are all done to perfection. Their aim is: *Plurimi intentus minor erit ad singula sensus.* Whoever is suited to the furies always performs these, or else a symbol of the wind, which is similarly danced. Those of this character dance the *grande Vitesse,* so called by the French. This is not the character of the fury or of the wind but it is full of the same *attitudes.*

59

Of the Use of the Arms

§1.   In Opposition.   §2.   Rounded

The use of arm movements is so necessary, that upon it depends good or bad dancing, so much so that without it the *Ballante's* body would be reduced to a walking statue without expression and without grace. All three kinds of *Ballerini* can move the arms in four manners, *low*, *half-height*,[69] *high* and *exaggerated*, this last kind called by the French *les grands bras*.

§1

We begin with the *low*. We have already said on other occasions that the arms in opposition move by carrying forwards that arm opposite the foot which is also in front, that is, if the right foot is front, the left arm will move; the fingers must be neither clenched nor open, but moderate, the thumb and the index curved towards each other and keeping a distance of one finger between the tips, the same space between the index and the middle, and thus with all the others. The arms should not be too open, too stretched or too bent, but they fall naturally at the sides. For example, if you wish to move the right arm, both wrists begin to turn slowly inwards, the left remains at the side, and you begin to extend the right outwards with poise, keeping the distance of one palm from the body and, after turning the wrists again, they stop with the palm of that hand which is in front, the right, as we said, facing the heel of the opposite foot, which will be the left, and when you begin to extend the right leg forwards, the left arm will begin to move with the same grace as we said for the other, and this [the right] will return to its side with both wrists moving in the same manner and thus it continues with each change of leg.

Those at *half-height* begin to curve at the elbows and, lifting both equally, when they reach halfway, neither high nor low, they begin to move with the same opposition described above and with the same turns of the wrists and of the arms.

Those *high* are carried to shoulder level, from where the movement is begun. Let it be affirmed, that if you wish to carry them high from where they were held naturally at the sides, the elbows begin to bend softly, then lifting, always keeping the palms of the hands turned towards the thighs, the wrists turn to the point where the flat of the hand is in view and the arms remain extended in a straight line with the chest, so that if a thread were held from one hand to the other, this would touch the clavicles; from here they begin to move with alternating motion as we explained above, and the eyes look at the hand in front.

Les grands bras, exaggerated arms, are, as we said, those employed in the *tableaux*, in the *attitudes*, in the Furies, and in other similar actions. These cannot have a determinate measure, an exact distance, but may be lifted as much as desired above the others according to the character, the expression, the spirit, the ability that is demanded from the performer.

With such arms one can thus proceed with or without opposition, and this depends on the good taste of the *Ballerino* without being attributed a mistake.

In the turning [of the wrists and arms] this opposition is not always done but frequently the arm movement is on the same side as the foot which is first carried, and in truth there is no exact rule for this, for many times one begins with corresponding arm and leg and ends in opposition.

It should not be thought a fault if from time to time in the *exaggerated* arms, they pass over the head; in this case it is permitted but in others it would be an error.

The *Groteschi* make great use of these *exaggerated* arms, as much in comic characters as in the *Oltramontani*.

§2

The *rounded arms* may be *low, half-height, high* and *exaggerated*. In whatever mode, their movement is the same, that is they are carried forwards at the same time and together they are carried back again.

The *low rounded* are those that move away from their sides hardly by one palm, and as one is moved so is the other, carrying them both forwards and both back.

The *half-height rounded* go to the height of those of *half-height* in opposition, and move evenly as in those described above.

The *high rounded* are the arms that are completely open, gradually carried forwards, almost as though they would be joined, but they do not cross beyond the sight of the shoulders[70] and, reaching the line of vision almost in a semicircle, they are carried back to their place. The *Ballerino's* eyes do not need to follow this even movement of the arms because they, like the head, must remain neutral, not as formerly in the arms in opposition. Whenever this even movement of the arms is used, it is accompanied by an inclination from the waist, carrying it forward with the accompaniment of the arms and, in straightening up from the waist, these also extend until they are back where they started and the body is upright. For the most part the *Ballerini seri* make use of them in a finale, in a solo, in retiring, and such like; and they are also used in taking a jump: for example, wishing to do a *capriole sur place*, it is taken with a *brisé forwards*, and the arms *high rounded*. The *Groteschi* however take the *capriole* with *low rounded* arms, which gives greater force and impetus to the jump.

The use of the arms is the *Ballerino*'s greatest asset most of the time, and especially for the *Serio,* who can be recognised as an expert by this quality alone; and, in truth, with experience one sees that whoever possesses a fine carriage of the arms, a soft flexibility of the knees, remedies and counter-balances some other defects, since these [*Serio* dancers] have little strength in the legs and almost no breath. Because to render the *serio* style pleasing, it is necessary to dance languidly and one is so accustomed to this kind of softness that, as the French say, the machine is always *languissant*; for which reason whoever dances the *Serio* does not find it easy to dance other characters but they dance with grace the *Gravi,* the *Lurnie [Loure]*, the *Passacaglie,* and some the *Chaconne,* although, as we said in the relevant chapter, the dancing of these is not for all *Ballerini seri*.

The *exaggerated rounded* arms are used by the *Groteschi* in *Scaramuccia,* in Masked Characters, and in *Truffaldino.* These are Characters danced in the same *chaconne* tempo and are well expressed by Fabris, Francesco Lucchesi, Gennarello Bimbi, and Lenzi, with his celebrated *Tagliavene.*[71]

The true *Ballerini,* whether *Seri* or *Comici* must equally be in general possession of everything pertaining to dancing; no real distinction can be made between one Character and another, for if it is difficult to dance the *serio* it is no easier to dance the truly light comic. Should the *Grotesco* be less skilled in the art of expressing through gestures the Pantomime and comic Action than the *Serio* to express the same in Tragedy? In the light comic as in the comic[72] *Serio,*the Action must be lively, loquacious, expressive and natural. A *Serio* who plays the part of Hercules impassioned by Iole, a tormented Orpheus, frenzied by the loss of Euridice, should he not show the state of his heart, just as a light Comic shows his in the character of the enamoured Mirtillo? Is not the language of the enamoured the same? Are not the Heroes subject to the amorous longings with the same anguish as are the Shepherds? The Pastoral dancing, like that of the Artisans, has always been the *Grotesco*'s speciality and why should it not be in the future? Those who are biased and full of prejudice are mistaken in making distinctions between the merit of the one and the other character.

Each one is worthy of applause, each is skilful if he expresses his Action well, if he portrays his Character well.

Far be it for me to speak ill of the *Serio* but experience shows certain people's fanaticism, some who declaim against the *Grotesco* and declare themselves partisans of the *Serio*. These go to a performance of a Tragic Event performed by a famous *Ballante Serio*. These his partisans soon become bored, begin to yawn, to show their boredom and inertia; and becoming inattentive, and forgetting that they are on his side, they would rather see something cheerful, something ridiculous; complaining about what they like is a little strange. The prudent Man, the wise Man, despises neither the former nor the latter and is only interested in whoever performs his duties well.

Tullio Cicerone did not make any distinction between the Tragedian Roscius, and the Comedian Aesop, celebrated and famous Histrions of their times: but wearing his consular purple, he honoured them equally with his friendship and familiarity. That illustrious Man, so knowledge-able, lover of merit, did not differentiate between the one who performed heroic characters well, and consequently wore the royal mantle, and the other who presented comedy, performing a satirical role, who was clothed in rustic and peasant wool; but he recognised that in their respective styles, both played their own parts excellently, and equally he included both in his friendship. This is the judgement of the judicious, not that of one who allows himself to be carried away by his own fanaticism.

60

Of the *Caprioles*

There are various kinds of *caprioles*, and before we begin to speak of their diversity, we will show how the cuts[73] are counted. To count those of a *capriole in the French manner*, place yourself in fifth position, then detach the right [foot] to second in the air, which will be the first cut, then carry it to fifth behind the other foot and this will count as the second cut, from where, returning to second in the air, the third cut will have been made. The fourth is made carrying it once more to fifth in front, and thus a *fourth capriole in the French manner* will have been interwoven, and of this we shall proceed to speak.[74]

§1

The *caprioles in the French manner* are taken from third and also fifth, and end in one of the same positions. Their cuts are always even in number, as in the example of the *fourth* demonstrated above, so that, if adding another cut by detaching to second in the air, which will have the movement of a *fifth*, it would no longer be completely in the French manner because it ends open, but begun in the French manner and ended in the Italian. A *sixth* would be in the French manner and would be made by adding another cut, carrying it to fifth behind. In a *seventh* another is added by detaching to second in the air, and this too will have started in the French and ended in the Italian. In an *eighth*, the same foot would be brought to fifth in front, which would be

155

wholly in the French. In the *ninth* in the second, in the *tenth* in fifth behind; the latter would be done wholly in the French manner but the former is begun in the French and ended in the Italian. The *eleventh* cannot be attained except by a faulty interweaving, and, however much elasticity and speed in the feet one might have, if it is reached, besides upsetting the whole body, the whole *capriole* will always be forced and unsuccessful in the eyes of the spectators. The *caprioles* must be natural, and they must be done only as far as you are capable without disturbing or forcing yourself.

§2

Those *in the Italian manner* are taken only from second, excluding all others, and in this they end; and they are extended as often as they are bent.[75] The cuts of these are the same as in the French, the only difference being in their beginning and their ending. There have been some *Ballerini* who have had great strength in the said position and not in the other.

To begin counting the cuts according to the Italian usage, the first will begin from second to fifth, and thus it will proceed. If it remains closed, the *capriole* will have been taken in the Italian manner and ended in the French, in opposition to that taken in the French and ended in the Italian.

§3

The cuts of the *capriole in the Spanish manner* are also marked in two movements. These begin with the feet parallel, that is in Spanish position. For example, place the right foot behind the left in Spanish second and count the first cut carrying the right to Spanish first, the second will be the carrying of the right to Spanish second in front, the third with returning it again to first, the fourth to second behind also Spanish, and you would follow this order in counting all the cuts.

Signor Viganò introduced another usage by taking the *caprioles* in the French manner and ending them in the Spanish. He made great use of them and aroused common approval, [these caprioles] being something new and difficult. Unlike so many who, wishing to imitate him, did a *fourth* in the French and then a sixth [cut] in the Spanish manner, he, Viganò, did a *sixth* taken with the left in front for example and, after having interwoven it, which obliged him to finish with the right in front, he turned in the air to the right, cutting the sixth in the Spanish manner with the left in front in Spanish second position. Whoever does not distinguish wherein lies the difficulty of these two transmuted cuts cannot judge their merit. Not only is the difficulty in cutting at the end from the French to the Spanish but still more in the movement of turning the body.

To do a *broken Spanish sixth*, take it for example from Spanish second with the right foot in front in the air and, in rising, the left goes to rejoin the other and you interweave the Spanish *sixth*, which ends landing with the left foot in front. If you wish to do it with greater elevation, it then needs to be taken with a *contretemps* and is jumped on the back foot,[76] thrusting it forwards, and then the interweaving follows as above, and then this has the movement of an *eighth*, because in my opinion, that leg, which is carried from behind to the front, counts as two cuts, and you must not count it in the same way as when it is taken from the front.

The interweavings of these *caprioles* must be done closer together, contrary to those in the French and Italian manners, wherein the wider the interweavings are, the more brilliant they appear, but in these, too much widening and detaching diminishes their worth.

The same may be done *to the back*, in which the leg which is in front is thrown high to the back, and the other, in the process of joining it, interweaves its passage.[77]

Those *sur place* are taken from second position: the *Ballerino* bends and jumps perpendicularly, interweaving as many cuts as his ability permits. I myself have attained the *sixteenth*. These may be taken from both feet on the ground and ended in the same way, or with one foot in the air, or start thus and end with both on the ground, or with the same in the air which was there when beginning it, or changing the one on the ground for that in the air.

Without doubt, the most difficult of these three varieties of interweaving the *caprioles* is the Italian. Its great difficulty is found in opening the legs while interweaving over and under; the contrary motion, which is made in order to land in second, presents such difficulties in the Italian *caprioles* that the *eleventh* is easier taken in the Italian and ended in the French than the *tenth* terminated in the Italian. And these are the interwoven *caprioles*.

§4

The *beaten caprioles* are those which always beat on the same place without interweaving the feet.[78] For instance, if you wish to do a *capriole beaten in front* and count its cuts, place yourself in fifth with, for example, the right in front, then detach it to second in the air and this is the first cut, carry it again to fifth in front and a second will be done, once more detach it to second in the air and a third will have been done, then carry it to a fifth in front and a fourth beat will be done; and thus continuing to count the cuts, the *capriole* will be named by as many as are done, which will always be an odd number, landing on one foot, landing on both together will make the number even.

That *beaten behind* is counted similarly, always beating the leg behind.

§5

All these kinds of extended[79] *caprioles* can be done in a similar way, *ritirate*,[80] be they French, Italian or Spanish, interwoven or beaten; there is no difference, other than drawing up the legs and doing them *rancignate.*[81]

§6

We said in Chapter 15 that the *tordichamp jumped in the air* is numbered among the *caprioles*, and this is the place to speak about it. Nothing is added, but it is varied by taking a jump, and during the time spent in the air you do one or more *tordichamp*, as we shall better describe below.

I was the inventor of one kind of *tordichamp sur place*. I jumped drawing up the legs together in the air, and at the height of the jump, detaching both legs into a forced second in the air, I did two *tordichamp* with both legs at the same time: with that foot which had been front I did the *tordichamp* outwards, with that which had been behind I did one inwards, and on landing I found myself with the foot in front which in jumping had been behind. To this *capriole* I gave the name of *gran gorgugliè.*[82] It was so very difficult to do these opposite circles with the legs that whoever puts it to the test will recognise the value of this type of *tordichamp* but the custom was to do both either inwards or outwards.

These kinds of Jumps cannot be taken from both feet, but must be preceded by a *sissonne*, which will give the elastic impetus to the jump. Similarly they may be done with one leg in *retiré* keeping the other stretched, and they are also taken with a *sissonne*; these with one leg may be done equally outwards or inwards; in the same jump two may be made but the circles of the leg are smaller. Doing one of them, a large circle is made with a wide detachment of the leg. If you wish to repeat it with the same leg, it is anticipated by another *sissonne* with the leg which was extended and on which you land. Wishing to change legs, the *sissonne* is done with the leg which did the first *tordichamp*, and with the other leg, which is drawn up, the other *tordichamp* will be done and thus changing reciprocally they can be repeated as many times as the *Ballerino*'s ability will permit.

In a similar *capriole* I have landed on the same leg which did the *tordichamp*, adding the turn to it and also doing two *tordichamp* with the turn and landing on the same leg; that became a *tordichamp ribaltato.*[83] The difficulty of this *capriole* is not easily understood by whoever does not know the real strength in the art of jumping.

Equally, they are done *with a bound, turning* or *to the side*, and these are usually taken with a *bounding contretemps* or with a *dégagé*.

§7

The *gorgugliè* is an ancient *capriole* which is taken with a *dégagé* turning, and then in the jump the body is held straight and perpendicular, the legs and thighs in a horizontal line parallel to the ground; one will remain firmly extended, and the other will do the *tordichamp*; on coming down, land on that leg which remained extended, and the other, with which the *tordichamp* was done, stays in the air, and a full turn will be done between the *dégagé* and the jump. In order to have greater elasticity, the jump is taken with the leg that is detached, which will give greater impetus to the jump. In a jump of this kind, it is not possible to repeat more than one *tordichamp* but more *gorgugliè* can be repeated, either with the same leg or changing.

I also introduced a *gorgugliè with a bound*. I was in the habit of taking it with a *flinc flanc* and it could also be taken with a *contretemps* turning, and when I had my back to the audience I took the jump keeping the left leg still and high, not completely stretched, but slightly curved, and with the other I did the *tordichamp*, at the same time turning to face the audience and, landing on the left leg, the other remained in the air. This *capriole* served me in *Grotesco* characters or in the *Oltramontani*, which, with awkward and clumsy dress, made a good impression. Not only did I do it in the described manner but I also landed from the said *capriole* on the leg which had done the *tordichamp*, this being almost a *tordichamp ribaltato* as I said at the beginning.

There is another sort of *gorgugliè*, in which in the same jump two *tordichamp* are done, the first, for example, with the right foot outward, and the other with the left inward, and they are done *just off the ground*.[84] The French use them thus when doing *caprioles* in their *Serie* dances. They can be done in a variety of other ways, *just off the ground*, *low*, *in the air*, and in as many others as all noteworthy *Ballerini* have done them, or in as many as the skilful ones of our own time may wish to do of their own invention. I have only described those which are more common and more practised.

The *salto del fiocco*[85] has the movement of a *third* interwoven in the Spanish manner; it is done *to the front* and *to the side*. That *to the front* is taken with the legs parallel in the Spanish manner. It is preceded by a *dégagé* or a *contretemps*: jump on the left leg, raising the right parallel to a certain height and then the left must go well over the right and you land again on the same. This is the true *salto del fiocco to the front*, and not as some do it, hardly or not at all passing the left over the right.

That *to the side* is done with the legs turned out in a true position: jumping on the left, raise first the right and then the left, which also must go well above the right, and land on the same left; but this cannot attain even half the height of that *to the front*, with which it is possible to remove the hat from the hand of a very tall man standing on a chair with his hand stretched up high.

Another variety of this jump can be done from Spanish first: bend and, in jumping, one of the legs, either the right or left, is sent high; you land again on the same, keeping the other leg stretched throughout, but with this the same height cannot be reached as in that explained at first.

§9

This *salto ribaltato*[86] is usually done *just off the ground* or *high*: this last needs greater detachment of the thigh.

To do it *just off the ground*, place the left foot, for example, in second in the air, and on the straight right balance the body in the fourth manner (Ch. 4, No. 4); bend the knee and, stretching it, jump passing it over the other, which is always kept stretched, landing on the same leg on which the body was first supported, giving a full turn to the body in the jump, and the same leg always remains in second in the air.

That *high* cannot be taken from both feet but needs to be preceded by another movement, which might be a *dégagé* and a *jeté* turning, not done as usual but with greater vehemence to give great elevation to the jump: being in the air with for example the left extended, the right, with great detachment of the thigh in such a way that the knee passes close to the face with the leg pointing upwards, the foot going higher than the head, makes a big circle in the air, giving to the body the movement of a full turn; the right then, as I said, passes over the left, and you land on the same right, keeping the other in second in the air.

This *salto ribaltato* was invented by Monsieur Michel, the best *Ballerino grotesco* that France has produced.

Those *just off the ground* may also be beaten but are more difficult. In taking the Jump, the foot which is extended does two beats on the instep of the other foot and then rebounds over the other, as explained above.

To render this jump more difficult, I took it from both feet on the ground, preceding it first by a *grand brisé* or by a *grande sissonne*; in taking the jump, I carried the right, marking a wide circle with a very great detachment of the thigh, although not more than half a turn could be given to the body. Thus such great elevation was reached in this jump that the heads of the tallest men could pass under the back of my knee; furthermore, the second time that I danced in Turin, S.A.R. the Duke of Savoy, the present King of Sardinia, *Felice Regnante*, made a Grenadier much taller than the supernumeraries come onto the Stage attired as he was in Theatrical dress, and with my said jump even he could pass under the back of my knees.

They can also be done *rancignati*, that is, that the leg which passes over is bent.

§10

This *capriole* called *spazza campagna*[87] is taken from fifth position: bend both knees and, in rising into the air, without detaching the feet from the same fifth, draw the legs up under the body, as much as possible, then extend them equally held together in fifth to the front, level with the head, which is bent so that it is hidden behind the legs; from here extend both legs to the sides, opening and extending them as far as possible, raising the head, and at the same time straightening up from the waist and, on beginning to come down, the legs start to come together until on landing they are once again in fifth, but with that foot which began behind, in front.

To take this *capriole* it is necessary to precede it with a *grand brisé* or *grande sissonne*, which can give vehemence to the jump, and generally the fifths from which it is taken and in which it ends are forced, for where the greatest impetus for elevation is required an exact position is not sought but that which will give most strength to the jump.

Those *sideways* are taken with a *contretemps sideways*; wishing for example to do it to the right, the *contretemps* is done with the same leg, and, taking the jump drawing up the legs, the right is thrown against the left, the head is concealed as above, and in the opening observe that which has been explained.

Turning with a bound employs the same method.

§11

The *capriole royale* is taken from fifth and ends in the same. Placed then in the said position, bend the knees equally and, in stretching them, jump detaching the legs to second in the air, keeping the whole body and knees extended and the feet stretched, then join them in first and once more extend them to second, but forced, opening the legs as much as possible; in coming down, begin to bring them together so that on landing they are in fifth as before but with that foot which began in front, behind.

They can be done *beaten* by bringing the legs together two or three times in first, and similarly the said beats can be done closed, that is in fifth position.

§12

The *salto tondo*[88] can be done in various ways, *sur place, to the side, bounding, interwoven,* and *on one leg,* called *di sbalzo*.

That *sur place* is taken from second position, the body is perfectly balanced in the first mode, the arms at half-height, which gives equal weight to the body, the knees are bent, and the body is turned a quarter from the waist upwards to the side opposite that to which you will jump turning, and in extending, the impetus is given to the body for the jump and the turning motion with the accompaniment of the arms. If you wish to do one turn, the impetus for the jump will not be too vigorous, if two turns, it will be done with vehemence; only Cesarini has ever done all three turns easily and perfectly and this was the *capriole* reserved for him.

The *salto tondo di fianco secco* [89] is taken from the fifth position and begins with a *dégagé* to the second and, if the left, then jumping on this same, the turning motion is given to the body by the right foot, doing one or two turns as we described above and, on coming down, you land in second position with first the toes and then going through the foot, as care must be taken in all landings from the *caprioles*.

The sight of the *Ballerini* so often falling in this jump, as also others, comes not of course from the difficulty of the jump but from lack of technique. Foresight is needed, so that at the end of the jump the machine is rendered free from force and thus will be perpendicular to where it lands, for if the limbs remain full of vigour and rigidity they will spring up again on landing, which will make the body lose the upright balance and will lead to falling to the ground. Like an inflated leather ball thrust into the air, if punctured it loses the enclosed air that had kept it buoyant, and in falling it will stay on the same ground, but if it remains full of the selfsame air, it does not stay on its own ground but will bounce up again.

The *salto tondo di sbalzo* [90] is taken with a *contretemps sideways bounding*, and in rising for the *capriole*, the legs are carried sideways in an oblique line, always keeping the distance of second position, giving the turning motion; when coming down, the body straightens and you land in the same second.

The *interwoven capriole tonde* are taken from different *salti tondi* so that, instead of the legs being kept extended at a distance of second position, they are interwoven; how often depends on the *Ballerino*'s skill.

I specialised in similar *caprioles* interweaving a *tenth* during two turns, just as Viganò was singular in doing a *twelfth sur place* in one turn and taking the *salti tondi* in Spanish fifth.

The *salto tondo on one leg* taken from the true fifth serves for the character of *Pulcinella* or the *Mulinaro*; if turning to the right, the right foot is placed front; this foot is drawn up in jumping and goes to beat behind the thigh of the left; on coming down, you land on the leg which remained stretched and the other is immediately placed on the ground, and in this jump two turns can be repeated.

This *on one leg* is also done *with a bound*; you take the *contretemps* right in the middle of the Stage, then jump with the legs together, and the body upright; when you have made half a turn, so that the feet are towards the audience, they move to Spanish fourth keeping the knees close together and, while you do the other half of the turn, they come together to land in first.

If this *capriole* is not done in the centre of the Stage, it will never be effective to look at since all the *caprioles* have their own mathematical point and its counterlight and, should they not be caught together in that, they will never make their special impact, and if they are not taken from this point, it often happens that some jumps end without applause. An experience shared by two *Ballerini* each of whom took a *capriole* of equal value: one aroused applause and the other was regarded with indifference. Did one not perhaps do as much as the other? Yes, but not both knew how to make use of the same point.

All the *salti tondi* which we have explained can be done extended; they can also be done by drawing up the legs under the body.

§13

The *beaten turning* is always taken with a *contretemps* or with a *dégagé*; if it is done *with a bound*, it is preceded by a *flying contretemps turning* and, for example, jumping on the left, open the right leg to second, then beat it in first position; once more detach it as widely as possible, then land on the same leg, lifting the other into the air. In order to do this *capriole* perfectly, the body must be held in the air in a horizontal line parallel to the ground, landing obliquely; this makes no more than half a turn, and you complete the whole turn on the foot that is on the ground in the time it takes to straighten the body, and thus it is done, wishing to do it *with a bound*. If *just off the ground*, it is taken with a *contretemps*, but not *flying*, or with a *dégagé*, and then the above-explained *capriole* is added, which does not have great height, so the Body is not carried in a horizontal line in the air, but somewhat obliquely. Doing it with a *dégagé*, it takes one bar of Music; with the *contretemps*, it takes two in *Gigue* time.

The *interwoven seventh* is the same, and where in the former it is beaten, in this a *seventh* is interwoven, resembling the other in all else.

§14

The *beaten sissonne* is numbered among the *caprioles*. Taken as if you are going to do a *sissonne* (Ch. 30), after the *plié* you take a jump, and with one leg, for example the right, beat the other, doing one or more beats, although one only is dull, and then landing on the left, raise the right to second in the air. This beat can be done either *forwards* or *backwards* as well as *sideways*. But take heed: when repeating these *sissonne*, if done *forwards* or *backwards*, they are done one with one leg, and the other with the other, if *sideways* you always beat with the same leg.

There are also *flying beats* which may be taken from a *sissonne* but because they need greater elevation they are usually preceded by a *bourrée* and then the *beaten sissonne*, in which the body is thrust into the air in an oblique line and the beat is in one of the described manners, landing as explained above, and this last movement of detaching to second is done much higher, in which form it will be the most effective.

All these *sissonne*, as we have explained them extended, similarly we say, may be done *ritirate*.

§15

In speaking of the *pistolette*[91] *a terra* (Ch. 20) we said that besides these, there were others *in the air*, which are numbered among the *caprioles*, and now is the time to describe them.

The *pistolette in the air* have the movement of an interwoven *fourth*, and this *capriole* is numbered among these. Begin it with one leg in second in the air and for example, if this is the right, you jump on the left, interweave and land on the other leg, or even on the same from which you jumped, and one remains detached in second in the air.

These *pistolette* are done by expert *Ballerini* as *sixths*, and all depends upon the speed of the *Ballante* who, the quicker he interweaves, the more acclaim he earns.

§16

L'ale di piccione[92] resembles the *pistoletta*, beginning and ending as we explained above, the only difference is in the beating: in the former the beats were interwoven, in these the feet beat in first near the heels.

These *caprioles* may be repeated as many times as you wish, whether with one leg or changing.

§17

The *beaten jeté in the air* is also numbered among the *caprioles*. It is nothing more than that explained in Chapter 18: the only difference is that the former was done *a terra* and this is taken in the air with the beats being done on the instep; if you wish to repeat them refer to the description of the same (Ch. 18, §2 to the end).

§18

From the title itself these *Turkish caprioles* are meant to be used in Turkish characters: they are done *sur place* with the legs drawn up and, instead of beating as usual or interweaving, beat the soles of the feet together, and this beat can be done twice or at the most three times.

They are likewise done *to the side*, holding the body as usual obliquely in the air, and in these you land on one leg.

§19

The *caprioles* called *galletti*[93] are taken with the legs together, that is from the Spanish first: after the *plié*, which will be done with the knees together, in jumping, draw up the legs – still together – and extend them again, then the heels return to do one beat against the thighs; and in landing you land on both feet, keeping them together.

There is also a different and more difficult way of doing them: after the first drawing up of the legs, stretch them, lifting them forwards as far as possible, curving the body as if lying on the legs themselves, and starting to land, straighten out the legs downwards, and the body straightens up normally.

They may be done in another manner, and that is, in jumping the legs are also together without being drawn up, but right from the beginning you lift them in front, lowering the body over them, and in landing observe the same as we have explained above.

Because they need great height, all these *caprioles* are preceded either by a *brisé* or a *sissonne*. They are called *galletti* because they resemble the jumps of a cockerel; when he jumps to fly, observe that the legs are drawn up as in the first one; if in some fight, in order to attack some other animal, he jumps with the legs straight in front as we have demonstrated in the last two manners.

§20

The *salto dell'impiccato*[94] called *saut empendu* is performed by the characters of *Pulcinella* or a Drunkard or other Dullard, and sometimes it is done for eccentricity, this being a difficult jump. It too is taken with legs and knees together: bend, and in taking the jump, straighten the whole body with the legs together, let the extended arms fall with the hands touching the thighs, and the head lolling towards one side, then coming down, just before touching the ground, detach one leg well into the air as much as possible, landing obliquely on the other foot.

The difficulty of this jump consists in the great height that it needs to draw the spectators' attention to this figure, otherwise it would be reduced to nothing, and he who has no ability to reach this height must on no account do this *capriole*.

§21

The *salto morto*[95] is taken from the true fifth position and can be done *sur place* and *sideways*. To do it in the first manner, it is taken with a *brisé* and a *demi-sissonne*: bend in the said fifth and, in rising, take a big jump extending the thighs to the sides as widely as you can, and you must remain in the air for a time in that position; when it is impossible to hold it any longer, bring the legs together in one movement while landing in fifth; if while descending you wish to beat, its value will be increased.

That *sideways* is taken with a *contretemps sideways*, and it is the same as the other with the usual hold in the air, and it differs in that it is done travelling sideways and the legs are extended to the side.

Remaining poised in the air is very difficult and it needs great skill to do it; the body is suspended in the air with great lightness, the knees are stretched, [the legs] widely extended so that you can remain thus as long as possible.

This step was a speciality of Sig. Cesarini, who remained suspended in the air longer than anyone else.

§22

The *forbice*[96] is a *capriole* used in the character of *Pulcinella*; it is taken from the Spanish first position and in this it is cut; take the jump and, being in the air with knees joined as if nailed together, separate the feet, it making no difference whether the right or the left is carried forwards and, on landing, bring the legs together again in the same first, in which you land perpendicularly; this *capriole* does not require great height.

There is another variety of these *caprioles* which needs greater elevation and it is done *completely open*, that is to say, that the knees do not stay together but are extended with the legs which open with the articulation of the thigh sending one forwards and one backwards.

In the first manner, after the first opening, I closed the legs once more to Spanish fifth and opened them again in the same jump. In the second form, starting to come down, I gave a circular motion to the body, making it do a half turn.

All these *caprioles* belonging to the character of *Pulcinella* are accompanied by a movement of the arm on the same side as the foot. In the character of *Praut*, that is the French *Mulinaro*, the *capriole forbice completely open* is much used.

This character of the French *Mulinaro* is distinct from the Italian; the latter dresses in a tucked up tunic finishing at the knee, with long sleeves, like those of *Pulcinella*; the French dress is close fitting to the body with tight sleeves finishing at the wrists, and he wears his buttons. The colour of the one, as of the other, is white, even a white hat, and sprinkled with powder.

This type of *capriole* may also be done with the movement of the *royale*, that is to say, in the jump with the knees together, [the feet] open to Spanish fourth and then return to first and finally they move apart to more than the fourth, then land in first. In the character of the French *Pulcinella* with two humps, as is customary in that nation, I made the landing with the legs in Spanish fourth and the knees close together and bent, half a palm's breadth from the ground, and in a similar fashion I continued to walk, ending the walk with a *salto tondo* taken from the same position.

§23

The *salto del Basco*[97] is done *sideways*: you start from the closed position, or else from any other, and, for example, if the right is in front, do a *dégagé* to second with this, then a *jeté* with the left behind, then lift the right foot in the air,[98] raise the left and let it go as much as it can in the air; the force of this jump is such that, the more it extends to the side, the better it looks. It can be done with bent or straight knees: if the *jeté* is done with the right, you land on the left, if with the left, on the right foot. From this originated the *salto ribaltato*, already adapted to the form described in §9.

These are the principal *caprioles* to which may be added a prodigious quantity, and even these can be varied as their intrinsic value will suggest to the *Ballanti virtuosi* skilled in diverse forms.

Generally speaking, all these are the steps which, being Theatrical, are then performed on the Stage with some differences, not as we have minutely demonstrated, because they differ one from another and change measure according to the variation of the speed; nevertheless they are the same steps as described but they may be done in tempi *larghi, presti, andanti, fugati*, so that the same step is done in various ways and is adapted to the kind of tempo, for if to each tempo a different step were to be linked, an infinity of steps would be required.

All these *caprioles* and jumps defined are the most exceptional, and few of them can be joined together with another or with others, the reason being that the big jumps require preparation, especially if you wish to do them beyond the normal measure. Furthermore, joining them together, your breath would not withstand the vehemence of doing such jumps and *caprioles* for which the leg must be rested and not exhausted in order to do them well; otherwise the machine would be agitated in such a way that instead of satisfying they would bore the spectator. A breathless *Ballerino*, utterly exhausted, can never land lightly or lift himself gracefully but he needs strength to give impetus for the elevation or to support himself in coming down from high to low on the ball of that foot on which he lands. Moreover, the *ballerino* who wishes to jump must not labour with the legs nor need to dance on the ground, otherwise the joints would be too tired and then they would not be strong enough to lift him; therefore it is necessary that the character must be all jumped or else all in mid-air or entirely on the ground, thus is there the division of the three characters and therefore no properly equipped theatre should lack the *Ballante serio* or that of *mezzo Carattere* or the *Grotesco* for the Heroic, the Comic and the Burlesque characters which ordinarily enter into the dances.

Not only is the taste of Nations diverse one from the other but even within the same City there is disagreement. The Theatres are populated by various ranks and diverse peoples and each longs to be satisfied. The lover of surprises enjoys boisterous leaps, the high spirited wants to see jocosity, the man of sensibility is interested in the portrayal of the passions, but it would be better for me to speak of these in another Treatise devoted entirely to the execution of Theatrical Dancing and the duties of the Composers, with a selection of Programmes appended, both by myself and by various Authors.

In many Parts of the world I have seen the same dances in a Theatre of another City, with the same Music and the same Costumes, rejected, which caused amazement. The reason for differing tastes in diverse Cities and that in the Theatres is attributed to the structure and size of the same, where a different echo does not give the same resonance to the harmony; if the Music is strident, it will perhaps sound unpleasant in a small Theatre, and in a big one, will be no more than harsh. That dance air, which may give pleasure in a big Theatre, will offend the ear when transferred to a small one, the same strength of the instruments detracts from the enjoyment of the Music; it will seem noisy, like dissonant organs. Therefore a knowledge of Music is beneficial to the *Ballerino*, as was noted in the Third Chapter; those knowing the shape of the Theatre would provide some suitable music, or if it has to be newly composed, the Composer should be given the lathe upon which to work with pleasure and not left disappointed. How many Music Masters have found their Works come to grief through not paying attention to this and through not being furnished with these principles; the same applies to Singers, where in one Theatre an *aria* has brought universal applause, whilst in another the public groans with weariness. I hope to make this truth known by means of physical and practical reasons in my other *Treatise* already cited, and how much the power of the Theatre counts, and the qualities the *Danzatori* must have in order to reach the summit of their desires, and to obtain the reward for their labours.

I flatter myself to have been of some use to those beginners who, for their own profit, avail themselves of this my Treatise. Those who, following the fashion of the Young, will criticise the sentences and the manner of presentation, will remain without the advantage which otherwise they might obtain from it. Oh! would to Heaven I could return to the days of my early youth, but with the discernment which by God's grace I now possess, I would become the Wisest Person in the World and would give miraculous portent to this our beautiful Art. But thus it is: the Young lack sense, and by the time that this is acquired, it is vain to regret the wasted years.

END OF PART ONE

THEORETICAL AND PRACTICAL TREATISE ON DANCING

BY

GENNARO MAGRI
NEAPOLITAN

SECOND PART

NAPLES 1779

PRINTED BY VINCENZO ORSINO
BY ROYAL LICENCE

The Author to the Reader

The Best entertainments that can amuse and lift the spirits of men above the tedious occupations are the fine Arts. Music and Dance are pleasing faculties that have great dominion over our minds and are destined to rouse the passions, as is well noted and distinguished by the most learned Cavalier Planelli in his *Trattato dell'Opera in Musica*. Taking place in the splendours of a magnificent Court, they occur in royal weddings and solemnise every other kind of happiness customarily celebrated in Majestic Palaces. But, leaving apart all discussion of the other fine Arts, here I shall only make mention of the Dance, and specifically of the *Contredance*, which forms the object of the present Treatise; and to invent these [*Contredances*] has been my task in the recurring royal festivals for my most amiable Sovereign Ferdinando IV (D.G.), King of the two Sicilies, whose Royal Clemency has had the goodness during six years to bear them with indulgence from the first memorable Encampment settled in Portici, where he gave eight most splendid banquets with regal treatment; similarly in the festivities on the arrival of The Most Serene Princes and Princesses related to the Blood royal, in the festivities celebrating the most happy births of our most Clement Sovereign Lady, it has been my honour to direct and invent the *Contredances*. Therefore, encouraged by royal approval it came to my mind to publish the *Contredances*, recording them with various signs all invented by me, and I have studied the way in which the private individual might benefit, whereby with this variety of Dances he can adorn his own private banquets without need of a Master and Dance Director, who would show them and give the details for dancing them. At length, after racking my brains and after serious reflections, it seemed to me that I had hit the mark and come to a conclusion; I believe I have found

171

a method to bring to light my *Contredances*, and, without any need of word of mouth, to render them clear to the Lovers of them; that the signs might explain them, having first made the Tables of the figures, the signs for the walks, for the places, for the turns, for the *balletti* and for everything else, clearly described so that everyone might study them at leisure, and easily learn them, even though there may be nobody to make the explanations to them.

With this serious reflection of mine I hope to place in our Italy a good system for the dances, introducing the *Contredances à quadrille* working on the lines of the French, among whom good taste in the Dance truly reigns; proof of this is provided by so many illustrious men who have refined this fine Art in all types of Dances.

France has the great advantage, not only in the fine Arts but also in the sciences, of the Academies. These are such, that they bring every art to perfection.

As each one is anxious to show his talent at the Assemblies, he does not avoid sitting up all night, reflecting in order to open the mind to the production of something new, in order to overcome the difficulties, to prepare and to solve them as they are presented to him. From this is born the competition between *Virtuosi* and the noble ambition not to show oneself inferior to another. Thus from this emulation comes the advantage of the sciences, the progress of the Arts. Furthermore, how much enlightenment, how much knowledge one receives from so many new thoughts, from so many problems posed, from so many difficulties unravelled. That which is rendered most profitable, then, is that everyone decides which is the best of all these new thoughts, and the best sets the rule. From here comes the pre-eminence held by France in the fine Arts, as well as in the sciences.

Similarly I hope in this our Country that the virtuous Nobility is now introducing the Academies in order purposely to kindle a virtuous ambition in them and not to envy the good taste of the French Nation.

This my Work, such as it is, is not only beneficial to the Dilettanti of the Dance who, by themselves, without a Master can make use of these marked *Contredances*, but also to the same Masters who, by availing themselves of these signs, can note down their own *Contredances* and prepare them for themselves. Not because they have need of my rules or that they must take ideas from me – I know that they are all able – but so that certain tedious occasions might be avoided; since when composing impromptu it can happen that the figures do not match at the end, thus it is necessary to go back to the beginning, change the figurations and repeat the piece, and this can cause more than a little annoyance. Moreover, some *Contredances*, however beautiful they may be, so often have the misfortune not to please the Noble Dancers and it is necessary to substitute another;

thus a Dancing Master who, in an Assembly, must offer four or five *Contredances*, has to go supplied with ten or twelve; and however good his memory, it is easy for some forgetfulness to arise in such a mob, amid so much tumult, with so many diverse tastes which agree and disagree on the same thing. From all this is born a confusion of ideas, a confused disorder of the things to prepare, and with the duty of satisfying so many and contending with so much, he reaches the state of not knowing where he is. Not so if the dances will be noted down in writing. Argue who will, criticise or applaud: with the written plan the slightest disgression will be amended. A flash of memory does not always rest with us, but the script cannot fail.

For greater benefit I have placed the Music under the *Contredances*, and there are some of those same which I have had the honour to make use of on the occasions of the Royal Festivals; and since they have been benignly regarded by His Majesty the aforementioned Monarch, truly qualified judge of good taste, therefore I hope that they will be applauded by the public. If any one of these should not please, it can be replaced by another, provided that both be of the same length. The above-mentioned Music is not all mine, but from various composers whose names I have included.

If these, as I flatter myself, will accept my efforts in demonstration of my commitment, besides being obliged to them, I promise them a new volume every year of more numerous and intricate *Contredances*, because in this first I have published the easiest, in order not to embarrass beginners with complicated figures, plus the publication of another Book, on which I am working, which deals with the execution of Theatrical dances and the handling of the plot. *Vivi felice*.

SECOND PART

1

Duties of a Dancing Master and How to Behave towards a Beginner

Inasmuch as the Dance removes certain little defects which are in our bodies either by nature or because of contracted bad habits (Part I, Ch. 1), the Dancing Master is first obliged to observe whence they originate and immediately remedy them, this being his primary duty; and since these days one sees those who would like to be Dancing Masters without knowing their craft, to them I direct the precautions noted here, and I do not submit them to those who have come to know the substance of this fine Art, who abound in this Sovereign City.

It is certain that a worthy Master will correct and dispose of the negligence or the defects of Nature, and it is also very certain that a bad Master can spoil that which is good. The first laziness of one of these who understands the Art poorly, from whom instead of composure one learns notably bad habits, is that in the first exercises he takes the Pupil by the hands, gripping them firmly in his own, forcing him to bend and rise, himself accompanying him with the movement of the hands. The result of this is that the Scholar, if young in years, is in consequence delicate and unsteady because of the weakness of the nerves and of the bones; because of his stupidity he leans strongly on the Master who acts as a support. Behold the bad effect. In that effort which he makes to support himself, he lifts the elbows outwards, thrusts out the shoulders, and the chest goes in; by becoming accustomed to this posture it happens that, freed from the

Master's hands, he continues in this ill-composed attitude. If he is a little older and has a rather stiff body, unable to bend well, to stretch it better he presses on the hands of the Master and thus also acquires the same bad habit indicated. Therefore, I will advise here below how to deal with giving the first rudiments. First of all place the Pupil in fourth position, the knees well stretched and turned out; then with a noble and gentle air he should prepare his body with the head high, the chest forward, shoulders down, the stomach and the abdomen held in, the waist inclined forwards, the arms falling naturally with the elbows a little behind, and take care to do everything without over-emphasis because too much affectation leads to impropriety. Then the Master must gently lift his hands with palms upward and have those of the Pupil placed on top of them, just lightly touching without leaning, but only to steady him; the Master should keep his elbows close to the body, because if he widens them a little, out of necessity the Student must move his own away from his body in order to find those of the Teacher, and thus the posture will be upset, which will not happen if the Master holds him as I have described. Therefore the Pupil must not be supported by the Master when rising, nor pressed when bending, but must have a gentle, subtle guide, and thus becoming accustomed to being without support when he is released from the slight support of the hands, he will be elegant and well composed.

The Master should also observe whether some are weak in the knees and the insteps or in one of these two said parts. For this he should use a remedy and make them do a long daily exercise practising walking round the room only on the balls of their feet, keeping the knee and instep stretched without any bend whatsoever and, thus exercising for a few hours daily, the weak parts will be fortified.

To make him acquire a fine pliability of the knees, he will lightly lean against a chair and, placed in first position, he will make a *plié* and rise with that method explained in Part One (Ch. 10, §§1 and 2), and when he understands this it can be done without support; then he [the Master] places the hands as described above and teaches him the positions. Knowing how to do these perfectly and without the guidance of the Master, he proceeds once more with the assistance of the [Master's] hands to help him do the *révérence* of the *Minuet*, of which we will speak fully when dealing with the *Minuet* (Ch. 2, §2). Released from holding both hands he [the Master] will make him do the *révérence* again, guiding him with one, and at the same time he will begin the *forward step*, about which we shall speak soon (*ibid*, §4), with both hands. Having reached this stage, the Master supports him with one hand and in the *révérence* does not give him any more assistance with the hands; at this stage he may begin the *sideways step* with the support of both hands: what this step is will be told in Chapter 2, §5. When he has reached a certain level, he will release one hand, in the *forward step* he will take away both hands, and in the *révérence* will gradually arrive at perfection. From here he will begin the *returning step* with both hands (*ibid*, §6); when he reaches the stage of releasing one hand in this, he releases both hands for the *sideways step*, polishing and perfecting the others. Having left him on his own also for the *returning step*, so that he is doing them all by himself, the Master starts him on the figure of the *Minuet* (*ibid*, §8) steadying him with the hands, and calling the steps in the places where they are to be done. He can also be instructed on how to lift and move the arms with the accompaniment of both his hands, first the right, then the left and then both together, which we shall describe (*ibid*, §7). With this gradual method one may also be sure that he will learn well and quickly and not be bewildered by everything; believe me, I have made this observation through experience.

I conclude this Chapter with another warning, and it is that when the Student is in a position to do the *forward step* supported by one hand, then he should practise to the Music, in order that he learns the beat and begins to know the timing and to divide it as must be, wherein consists the whole fine Art of knowing how to dance well. Indeed the Student must be made to keep the beat, which will render him a perfect connoisseur. I would say that the Accompanist, who must play for a beginner, should also be expert in the Dance in order to accompany him in time with every step and make the beat fall at the exact point required, which we shall also discuss (*ibid*, §10), or at least if he does not know the dance through practice, he should let it be known at which stage of the step the beat must fall, and how the timing is divided. Am I reproached for being too sophistical? No I am not. I speak about what I have proved, and furthermore add that the Accompanist who does not have this knowledge will contribute to the crippling of the Student, because if he does not accompany the Beginner's movements precisely, stop where he stops, pick up where he picks up, play slowly if he goes slowly, speed up if he accelerates, in short accompany him in each detail of his movements, he will thus impede the Dancing Master who minds only the execution of the step, regulating its movement and correcting it in all the details by observing all the small errors that the Pupil commits. What more? The student becomes so accustomed to the measure which at that point divides the step, that the eardrum is always struck by that sound at that precise moment of the step; it is so perfectly impressed on him that, even if he wished, he could not do otherwise than be in time with that sound. On the contrary, if the Player does not accompany according to this principle, the Dancing Master, instead of only paying attention to the Pupil by directing his steps, must trouble himself with the Musician to make him quicken or slow down the tempo; and if about to correct a mistake in the step, he hears the music go on, then he forces, dragging the Beginner by the hands, or stops him in suspense and pushes him back to await the beat; if this goes slowly, thus the step follows with its fault, the Pupil is agitated, bewildered, learns nothing and the defects become second nature. Thus if my remarks seem pedantic, they are necessary requisites in helping the Beginner.

2

Of the Minuet

§1

This *Minuet*, which today occupies almost first place amongst the Noble Dances, is of Rustic origin. It was born among the Peasants of Anjou, a Province of France. They danced it artlessly but with a natural simplicity, just as the Rustics of today dance the regional and national dances. Hence little by little it was improved and under Louis the Great met with approbation and a happy fate: it was put into better order and, by degrees perfected, it came to occupy the principal place among Ballroom Dances. Its step was modified to a determined number and its measure to a prescribed phrase; and here we shall speak precisely of how its step is composed, of the form, and of the cadence which usually goes with it.

§2

In beginning the *Minuet* the Lady places herself at the right of the Gentleman and, accordingly to the rule cited many times, the *révérence* of the *Minuet* starts from the fourth position, although it would not be an error to begin from the third as some do; the Dancers' heads must be turned towards each other, and this, as well as being graceful, serves to let the Gentleman know when the Lady begins to do the *révérence*. The Gentleman must not raise his hand to take that of the Lady unless she raises hers first, so that his does not remain unmet if ever the Lady should wish to begin without giving the hand, this being an arbitrary thing. Thus placed in position, the heel is raised just off the ground and, with the knee slightly curved, the right for the Gentleman, left for the Lady (this difference applies only to the *révérence*, for the rest they will do everything with the same foot), the said feet are carried lightly gliding to second position, placing the full foot on the ground, on which the body is balanced; and raising the left heel, sliding it in the same manner, it joins the right in first, bending the body from the waist to a prescribed degree, neither high nor low; the body is straightened in carrying the left foot to fourth behind the right, and from this straightening the heel is carried to forced fourth, extending the instep, and the left is brought to the right of the toes of the other, keeping more than one foot distance; then turn the right on the ball of the foot, to join this in first;[1] then the left is detached to second, to which again the right approaches in first, repeating the inclination as described in the first *révérence*, and slowly rising, the right foot is carried to fourth behind the left.

If the Gentleman has a Hat on his head, he takes it off with the left hand in beginning the *révérence* and extends the arm naturally; the inside of the above-mentioned Hat should be turned towards the thigh. Then at the first step he puts it on again, just when passing the Lady, when she cannot notice it.

At masked balls, the Hat must not be removed when dancing the *Minuet*; sometimes the mask remains on the face the whole time, but if they are entertainments at which the mask is removed, placing it on the Hat, in this case the Hat is taken off when dancing the *Minuet*.

§3

The *minuet step* consists of a *demi-coupé* and a *pas de bourrée*, but since it is usual to speak of the *minuet step*, we will call it thus for greater facility, in order not to introduce anything new, without making the distinction of teaching the *demi-coupé* separately and then the *bourrée*, since neither of the said two steps change feet, but each will always be done with the same where it is taught as used in the *Minuet*; and be advised that whatever sort of *minuet step* it might be, it always begins with the right foot.

§4

When the *révérence* is completed, the *forward step* is learnt as follows. From the fourth position, bend the knees equally to do the *forward step*; balance the body on the left leg and, keeping both bent, carry the right to first in the air, moving just off the ground; from this begin to extend, keeping the foot well arched; first place the ball of the foot on the ground, and then the full foot in fourth position, balancing the body on this and stretching the knee completely; the left, which remained bent, is also stretched and raised so that only the ball of the foot touches the ground; and this equals the *demi-coupé*. Bend both knees again, and, supporting the body on the same right, carry the left to forced fourth in front with the same symmetry as the other, and both are equally stretched; then do two walking steps, the first with the right, the second with the left ending in fourth. The *pas de bourrée* is begun from the second *plié*. This *forward step*, besides being done straight forwards, is done turning to the right and to the left, in which form it is also executed in the figure of the *Minuet* as we shall observe in §8.

§5

The *forward step* being completed, the *sideways step* is taught in the following manner. Bend the knees, keeping them well turned out and, sliding the right, passing it through first, from where it begins to stretch, it goes to second; having arrived there, the other is also stretched little by little, and you rise with only the ball of the foot touching the ground and if anything the said second might be a little forced; slide the left, taking it near to first,[2] go to fifth behind rising on the toes, stretching the knees, as well as the insteps, from where two other simple movements are made, the first to second with the right, the second to fifth with the left.

§6

The *returning step* is the third step of the *Minuet*. This is begun from fourth with the right in front. Bend the knees equally in the same position and, in stretching them, carry the right to fourth in front with its instep arched; placed there, the body is balanced on it, and the left remains with only the ball of the foot touching the ground, and that will be the *demi-coupé*. Bend the knees again and the *pas de bourrée* begins: balancing on the same right, the left passes through first and goes to second position, then the right goes to fifth behind the other; rise on the toes and, without lowering the heels, carry the left to second, with which the said *returning step* is completed. In the *Minuet* figure, this, like all the steps, will be repeated. The beginning of the second *returning step* is different from the first: from the second rise, with which the first [step] ended, bend and bring the right to fifth behind, where you rise again on the toes, then place the right with the full foot on the ground, and the left remains raised; bend again, and carry this to second, the rest continuing as was described for the first.

These are the three steps which make up the whole of the *Minuet*; each step, as has been seen, consists of a *demi-coupé* which always begins from the first *plié* carrying the right, and a *bourrée* which begins from the second *plié* carrying the left leg.

§7

The movement of the arms should never depart from the natural, but the skill which is employed serves to give grace to nature, therefore we shall speak of their motion as I see it. In the beginning the Lady will hold the arms at her sides, falling naturally, and she holds her gown with three fingers, that is with the thumb, with the index and with the middle; and the other two held naturally without being forced should fall equally balanced at the sides; otherwise holding them more forward than by the sides, the shoulders would hang forwards, the chest would sink in, and the seat would protrude. But placing yourself as I say, the shoulders will be back, the chest out, the head held perpendicular to the body and the waist held erect over the feet. But to return to the movement of the arms, we would say that to the beginning of each *minuet step*, which would be the *demi-coupé*, the forward movement of the arms in opposition to the foot is added; and beginning the *bourrée* in which you change the foot, the arms also change, which will last until the end of the *bourrée*. You must not make the opposition of the arm in all the changes of the step, for this would be too ungainly, even if done in exact harmony, but restrict yourself to do only two in the places indicated, which will be pleasing and in good taste. Besides this movement of opposition, you can also use the *low rounded*, as explained in Part One (Ch. 59, §2), carrying them forwards on the first bar and back on the second. This carriage of the arms consists of only two movements. The first is affected, that is, done by gradually lowering and turning the tips of the fingers towards the thighs, then you immediately return them to the natural, which makes the second movement which comes from the natural carriage itself, and would be taking the hand to the side where it falls naturally, all in one movement, until it is turned towards the heel of the opposite foot at a distance of half a palm from the thigh without bending the elbows.

What has been given is a general rule. Let us now proceed to the particular movement, or better said, to the particular opposition. In the *sideways step* to the right, first the right [arm] is carried forward because in the *demi-coupé* the left is in front, then the left arm, because the feet change in the *bourrée*. In the *returning step*, first the left arm is in front because the right foot is in front for the *demi-coupé*, in the *bourrée* the right [arm], which will stay there to the end, and since the second *returning step* begins with carrying the right [foot] behind, thus the same right arm remains in front until the beginning of the *forward step*, in which the left [arm] is carried forward in the *demi-coupé*, and in the *bourrée* the right.

§8

As was said in §2, the Lady is placed on the right of the Gentleman and they are looking at each other, keeping a distance of two arms between them, and the centre of this distance should be that of the dancing space with the Gentleman being the same distance from it on his side as the Lady is on hers. At the beginning of the *révérence*, in order to take hands, the

Gentleman raises his right, the Lady her left, with the elbows slightly bent, and the whole arm is lifted to shoulder height, well extended; they take hands, with the Lady placing hers on top of that of the Gentleman, who will turn his palm upwards. In the first bow, in which the *révérence* is made to the spectators, the Gentleman will take his eyes from the Lady for only a moment, as she does hers from him, and they look away[3] in an act of submission, then lifting their eyes again to look at each other, they will proceed to do the second *révérence*, lowering their eyes to the ground, raising them after the second bow; the Gentleman will do one *sideways step* to the right and the Lady does one *returning*, with which they return to the first place from where they offer the same hands in the same style, taking two *forward steps* facing the front. After that the Gentleman takes two *sideways steps* marking a semicircle, and the Lady two *forward* but marking a big circle,[4] and they meet facing each other, the Lady on the side where she began and the Gentleman opposite. They release hands and both take two *sideways steps* to the right; from here the figure of the *Minuet* will begin by taking two *returning steps* in a straight line, then joining two *forward steps* in a semicircular figure; having done the first step they will meet obliquely and, having done the other semicircular, they remain opposite each other, from where with two *sideways steps* to the right they will move into each other's place, and once more the *returning step* will be done, the rest following; thus the whole *Minuet* figure consists of two *returning steps* travelling in a straight line, two *forward steps* done in a serpentine, two *sideways* done to the side. In the whole dance they will always turn their heads towards whoever they are dancing with, along whichever line they follow, and the less they can take their eyes from each other, the more grace will be added.

In France, in other parts of Europe and in our Italy too, if three *forward steps* crossing are done, in truth the *Minuet* increases in grandeur: the *pas graves forwards* are still used in the cantons, and especially in giving the second hand and in giving both. For me there could not be a better ornament than the *pas grave* that is of more worth to the Minuet. But in order to dance it in this fashion a vaster Dancing Space would be needed, then perhaps our Dilettanti would be able to do it in that style; but since in our dance festivals these spaces for dancing are too narrow for the great multitude of people, therefore it must be restricted as transcribed above.

§9

The *Minuet*, like that which has no variations of figure, must be brief in order to avoid tedium. After three repetitions of the figure, the right hand is given; and in this also, the Lady must begin to raise the arm before the Gentleman, and whoever does the opposite is at fault and shows a lack of propriety, because by forestalling the Lady, it may seem that he regrets dancing with her and appears to wish to force her against her will to finish the dance. However, the Noble Lady should be warned not to give her hand just at the moment of coming forward, for that would be unseemly and would be as if she wanted to take the Gentleman suddenly by surprise and betray the fine sense of union which should exist between the two dancers; but in ending the *sideways step*, she should prepare to raise the arm, starting at the beginning of the second *returning step*, and look to see whether the Gentleman has his attention directed towards her, as indeed necessarily it ought to be, but at times there are some involuntary distractions, and in this case the Lady should do another turn[5] to avoid showing up the Gentleman's carelessness.

The mode of raising the arm to give the hand in the *Minuet* begins as said with a slight curve of the elbow raising the arm to shoulder height, at which point it will be carried fully extended, but in a sideways direction. This raising should occupy the space of two bars of Music, within the time of one *returning step*. In beginning to do the *forward step*, the arm is bent from the elbow, carrying the forearm forwards, and the upper arm remains in the same place; the wrist, moving the hand, turns towards the ground without the hand bending backwards, and all this takes place in the time of two more bars, and from the first *forward step* they exchange a gracious glance. Then begins the second *forward step*: after the *demi-coupé* the hands lightly touch, that of the Gentleman being underneath and the Lady rests hers on top, and the *bourrée* is done completely circling, which makes a full turn; and each one will end in the same place where they began the turn but right in the centre of the dancing space. The *sideways steps* are repeated, lowering the arm little by little in the course of four bars and the two *sideways steps*. After the first two bars and one *sideways step*, while the right arm is being lowered the left will be raised, and at the end of the other two bars the right will be completely lowered and the left completely in the air, which will bring into play the same movements as was said for the right; and immediately the two *forward steps* are done circling, and the left hands united with the same harmony described for the others, but the turn is done to the left side.[6] Forming then the two *sideways steps* to the right, the arm is gradually lowered to the side in the space of four bars. The figure having been repeated three times, both hands are given in the same way carrying them as was shown for the one. If the Lady gives them contrariwise from where she began to dance, then only two *forward steps* will be done, the first without touching hands and in the second only one hand will be given, which will be the right for the Lady and the left for the Gentleman. If however she gives them from the place where she began, two or three *forward steps* are done circling to the right, and in this case the hands are taken in the second step, and in the act of taking the third the Gentleman releases his right, and the Lady her left, and they end in the same place where each began, but face to face. Be warned that in the course of the last step the hand is gradually lowered so that at the beginning of the final *révérence* it may be lifted to half-height and in the course of the first *révérence* with which the *Minuet* ends, similar to the one at the beginning, the hands which were taken are gradually lowered, and the others lifted to be given at the start of the second *révérence*, in the course of which they are released and again lowered with all the usual grace.

In olden times, frivolities were used both at the beginning of the *révérence* and after, both in the giving of the first and the second hands, first passing back to back, and afterwards giving the hand, and other similar trifles and things which more often than not were tiresome. But our Moderns, full of good taste, have cut out all the trifling gimmicks and have replaced them with natural and brilliant graces; they have removed the bad figuration which was almost always one directly opposite the other in a parallel line, without giving any action to the body;[7] the head remained immobile from the beginning, the eyes expressed nothing at all but passed over all with a fine lack of concern displaying anything but affection for dancing. The hands were exaggerated, and their movement was far removed from the natural: in carrying them forward and taking them back they displaced them almost a palm's distance from the body. They were given two movements, one with bending the elbows raising them from the side, the other extending them and throwing them back, and other indecencies and vulgar trivialities. At the end of the step they went skipping about. Formerly a certain step was in use called *à la Bohemienne*, which lasted for a long space of time; it was composed of a *demi-coupé* done with the right foot, then gliding the left, the right made another simple step and the step ended with a *jeté* done with the left foot; then this fell into disuse and the *Minuet* step called a *fleuret* became fashionable, which consisted of a *demi-coupé* done with the right, and a *fleuret* done with the left. This too was abolished and it was then danced in another fashion, and it is as follows. The *forward step* began with a *demi-coupé* carrying the right foot forwards to fourth position where it made a momentary pause, and again slightly bending the right knee, the left was carried sliding to forced fourth, then with the right foot a simple step to fourth in front, and the step ended with a *jeté* done with the left foot into fourth position. The *sideways step* started with a *demi-coupé sideways*, in which the right was carried to second position, then rising again the left was carried to the side stretching the knees, and then bending them again, the left glided behind the right in third position and, rising, two simple steps were done, the first with the right to second, the other with the left to third behind. The *returning step* also began from the *demi-coupé* from the third position, carrying the right foot to the fifth in front if behind, and if in third in front, it then went to third behind, or else substituting a step bending and rising done in the same

185

third position instead of the *demi-coupé*, the left foot was carried to second, and with the right a simple step to third position was done, ending with a *jeté* done by the left to second position. Certain people also employ some of these steps but use them as embellishment and flourishes, and this may be done by those who manage to dance with ease, for it may be adorned by various graces and one movement substituted by another, provided that this does not detract from its nature and does not alter its dignity.

Dufort, with further lack of taste, wants to embellish the *Minuet*, and after doing the *demi-coupé* he attaches one *pas grave*, substituting it for the *bourrée*, and while he does the said *pas grave*, he wishes the arms to be raised, and the head lowered towards the right, casting the eyes down to the toes of the foot which does the step, regarding it until halfway through the walk, returning the head to its natural equilibrium; this is one of his embellishments which would provoke nothing but derision if done in our Salons.

§10

The time to which the *Minuet* is danced is a three-four triple time, and means that whereas in binary time four *Crotchets* are required for a bar, in this three are needed. Its beating is done in three movements: two on the ground and one in the air. But in the dance of the *Minuet*, one is beaten on the ground, and two are lost in the air. Its cadence is harmoniously united with the steps in the following manner; and first of the *révérence*, which until today has not had any determined measure but has remained at the discretion of the Lady, who filled as many bars as suited her, not being bound to start from the beginning of the Music, but as she pleased. Today, when taste has become more refined and every attempt is made to match the harmony of the Dance with that of the Music, the *révérence* starts with the beginning of one section of the tune and may occupy six bars of music in all: two for the first *révérence*, the first in carrying the foot to second, the other in placing the other foot behind, the other two bars for those two movements forwards and the last two for the final *révérence*, so that each movement of the leg takes its own bar; and this generally applies to dancing *andante*. If you wish to dance with more composure and to give a beautiful flexibility with a sustained bend, as some do with attractive grace, then the six bars will not suffice, but eight are needed: three for the first *révérence*, two for the turning steps, and three others for the second *révérence*. The other three steps then which form the *Minuet* are measured by two bars each, the first bar falls at the beginning of the *demi-coupé*, the second as the first movement of the *bourrée* happens. The ancients ill understood when they compressed two bars into only one and with them Sig. Dufort talks nonsense when he says that to be good, and to dance the *Minuet* well and precisely, it is necessary that both the measures which it contains should not be beaten but one alone is beaten and the other remains in the air, and only the first must be beaten in order not to confuse those who are dancing, or make them mistake one measure for another. I say that this is the manner of confusing them rather than that of beating it twice, in which the measure will be divided between the two steps which form the *Minuet*. Is not Dufort the one who wants all the steps occupying one bar of music? How then does he persuade himself to compound together those steps which make up that of the *Minuet* into one bar, where all the component steps are sustained and clearly defined?

The Composers of *Minuet* music commit a grave error when they compose by putting *nine Quavers* or *twelve Semiquavers* into one bar. This multiplicity of notes is ill suited to a sustained dance such as the *Minuet;* thus there cannot be any correlative agreement between them. This mass of notes needs a padding of connected walking steps. Perhaps in the *Minuet* a theatrical sequence would be wanted to accompany the music? This would be a betrayal of the nature of the Dance. Therefore these Composers should take care when writing their *Minuet* music that the *three Crotchets* or *one dotted Minim* be correlative, that it may be agreeably sweet, reach the pathos of the heart, and not be stuffed with notes which animate the spirits, otherwise the music will never adapt to the dance. If they want to introduce any *andante* note into it, they could do so in the second bar, since in the step corresponding to this there are walking movements, but they could not do it in the first [bar].

§11

The *Minuet* needs hidden control which corresponds to the gracefulness which is sought in it in order to make a good presentation. It needs a languid eye, a smiling mouth, splendid body, unaffected hands, ambitious feet.

The languid eye displays humility, which in the *Minuet* must be preserved; for if the eyes are fixed too much on the person with whom you are dancing, it seems as though you are beside yourself with so much concentration; if they are laughing somewhat, it might be suspected that there was some secret amorous understanding between the dancers; to keep them melancholy would be against the nature of the dance; therefore it suits them to be rather languid, in which case no suspicion can arise.

The smiling mouth must be maintained so that it does not register indignation either through pursing it too much, or appearing sulky or other nasty emotions such as I have observed in some; but to show it smiling expresses and characterises the essence of the dance, which indicates a cheerfulness, a movement of our spirit, which implies the enraptured state of this Faculty. And referring to Sig. Cavalier Planelli, an agitation which is appropriate to gaiety, setting the whole machine in motion, and from these movements the Dance is born.

The body splendid, because with it one maintains a majestic carriage, without which the *Minuet* cannot be said to be good, even if it has all the good qualities and all the possible embellishments. This majestic carriage must inspire an easy air, avoiding above all anything whatsoever false that might savour of caricature.

The unaffected hands, with which the simplicity of the Dance is shown, originate from nature itself; but this natural carriage must be accompanied by a movement which, although it might be artificial, must be such that the artifice appears natural, so that nature is mixed and blended with the art.

The feet ambitious, and this ambition of theirs consists of turning out the toes and keeping them low, in gracefully extending the instep in order to give a good appearance, and this is the ambition.

The *Minuet* thus executed will prove to be in good taste and will be applauded. I have seen these effects on tour in the various nations. I also had the pleasure of admiring our celebrated Monsieur Lepieg [sic] who with graceful figure appeared in it at the Royal Theatre of San Carlo in masquerade costume in the Carnival of the year 1773, in whom the very quintessence of good taste was seen.

§12

If you wish to do the *minuet steps* as they ought to be done, oh how few people there would be who could do them. Oh how much labour it would cost those who manage to do them well! Do not believe that its great difficulty consists in doing the two steps which comprise it; nor because it is composed of two steps, should anyone else presume that he knows how to do the *Minuet* by knowing only the *demi-coupé* and the *bourrée*; more than this is required. The gentle pliancy of the knees, the stretching of the insteps, the pleasing carriage, the precise equilibrium of the body, giving all these now to one leg, now to both, without ever losing composure; the movements of the body, the accompaniment of the hands and of the head, the gravity of walking, are all things which have between them such a close and orderly connection like a golden chain in which, when the first link is moved, immediately they all move; but when a link is broken at the beginning, the rest no longer move, such is the fine union and interaction between the links. Joined to all these qualities is the natural gravity of the *demi-coupé* and of the *bourrée* which follow the proper cadence; then the *Minuet* is well formed. Indeed I would say more, and let who will accuse me of sophistry, that the two dancers must have between them such correlative harmony that one will neither precede nor defer to the other in the smallest action he makes. Is this claiming too much? No, it is not too much. What is too much is the presumption of all those who enter into the dance lacking all these requisites.

Furthermore, the Cadence, which is the indispensable regulator of the

Minuet, is also a rock against which many are dashed. The air of the *Minuet* which, as we said, is in ternary time, must be beaten differently to the airs of the other dances, although they may be in the same time. The *minuet step*, which contains two measures of movement, in order to have the necessary harmony and for the movements to proceed in cadence, to be danced well and with all exactness, requires that both of the measures which it contains should not be beaten (§10 di q.f.);[8] and herein lies the great difficulty which makes one firmly conclude that the *Minuet* is not so easy to do well as others believe. He who dances in public must aim not only at satisfying himself but must consider himself obliged to give pleasure to the Spectators and, in order to please in the *Minuet*, nothing less than perfection is possible because always going over the same figure, repeating the same steps, reduces it to an unfortunate state of inaction unless it is replaced by all that which has been advised.

Something more I would add; that to dance it with ease, you should practise with various people from different Schools. Dancing with one of these, the dancer is at the outset taken by surprise in seeing the other's diverse style. Accustomed as he is only to that of his Master, and having been associated only with that, every new thing bewilders him. If this Student, who has not yet acquired similar practice, undertakes to dance in public, he will often be surprised by others who are not from the same school, when the occasion to dance arises. Therefore he should not lay himself open to this, unless through practice he has been well versed in the various styles.

The dancing Master must inculcate in him the importance of acquiring such practice before he shows himself in public, for the Master may be sure that if he does badly the complaints will be levelled against him.

There are few *dilettanti* whose judgement hits the mark. The great success that these have is not always due to the ability of the Master, nor when they do badly is it due to his stupidity. To judge by these outward appearances is to judge by chance and not by merit. It is necessary to observe if nature has been lavish to one and sparing to another. If one has the good fortune to have limbs well suited to dancing and does not need art to compose them and chances upon a second-rate Master, this man, aided by luck, acquires a good reputation; someone who is badly made and full of ill will may happen upon a Master who knows his duty, might the blame then for the poor success be attributed to him? Why not condemn the pupil's insufficient willingness? It is the Master's task to get rid of bad habits upon which it must be judged whether the Pupil has been well or badly disciplined. A bad figure well placed to dance is the work of the good Master. And only he is good who knows how to execute well what he teaches: he who does not know anything himself can never know how to teach others.

But I feel bitterly reproached by the *Signori Dilettanti*, that I drive them to despair by my producing so many difficulties; and already they want to renounce all the *Minuets* in the World. No, Gentlemen, the case is not desperate. A good choice of Master, continuous exercise, perfect attention to all the qualities required, and the *Minuet* will be danced to perfection.

§13

The Dancing Master must know his Beginner, if he is endowed with a gentle pliancy or if his physique is not adapted to bending well, if he can turn out the legs well or not; thus he instructs him according to his own nature, for if an attempt is made to go against it, he will never learn dancing. If someone has no *plié*, and he is forced into this, he would be trying to do the impossible; the same when on no account can the legs be turned out and all the time spent in trying to do this is wasted. So could not these perhaps learn to dance the *Minuet* well? They could, like the others. It is enough that their natural disposition be accompanied by a lively air, by a noble carriage, and the ability to divide the exact movement correctly in its measures, to follow the cadence well, wherein consists the real substance of the *Minuet*. Is he not able to bend? Let him sustain the step, the foot going out slowly, so that he may fill out that piece of Music which another fills with fine flexibility.

From this lack of knowledge comes the sight of some who grimace while executing any Dance, because the inexpert Master has wished to force them where on no account they should be led. All are capable of dancing well, and the blame should not be laid on him who cannot, but on the Master, for he wanted to guide him along a path which he was incapable of following.

The sympathy and antipathy which sometimes may be encountered between Master and Pupil produces good and bad effects. There being Sympathy between these two can but lead to the happy success of the Pupil. The Master will effectively apply his energies to teach him, and he, in order to learn well, with all diligence will give everything of himself. The Antipathy, on the contrary, renders the one and the other unwilling, although sheer antipathy never predominates in the Master's mind, who, on seeing a very attentive Pupil, cannot help giving all his knowledge to make him succeed very well. Besides, the Student must be utterly obedient and subject to the Master, otherwise he will never learn; if he is inattentive, the temerity will thus irritate the Master so much that he will be left to his own devices and the Master will take no more trouble, and if he continues to give him lessons, he does so for certain reasons which are those that lead to the loss of everything. There is much more I could say on this subject but I shall restrain myself and end in order not to risk referring precisely to some whom I have encountered.

§14

Since at the beginning and the end of the *Minuet*, the giving of hands is at the Lady's discretion and the Gentleman is forced to follow her, as was given to understand, I likewise would also add that, not only is it his duty to attend her in the places described, but in the whole course of the Dance, especially if she makes mistakes. If the Lady who is not very expert should do too few or too many steps, the Gentleman is obliged to omit or to add those steps which the Lady omitted to put in, and immediately take her back again into the figure in order to preserve that harmony explained in §12.

§15[9]

The places[10] for *Minuets* are governed by the number of people who are taking part in the festival: if these are many, then it is necessary to distribute as many places around the Ballroom as it might hold, but not just for the sake of packing so many in so that they are restricted. If however the concourse[11] is not too large, there will be a fewer number of places which, being larger and more convenient, will result in the dances being more successful.

In one place then, it would be better to arrange it so that from the two sides, one opposite the other, the *Minuets* were begun in alternate order, because if the place is divided into two, the crowd will not be all on one side but distributed on two; and also, seeing now the one, now the other Lady dance in turn gives pleasing variety. In such case the order must be this: one Lady must not dance twice in a row, but her *Minuet* ended, the next *Minuet* will begin for her opposite, and thus one *Minuet* for each Lady will follow. The Gentlemen in turn cannot aspire to dance other than that number which they have taken on the dancing space. For example, if the first one who gets up to dance finds four in front of him, he can claim only the fifth place, which he must declare and call for himself, and go out to dance when that number comes up; and if it is this one's turn to enter the dancing space and he does not do it in time in such a way as to make the others wait, so that the sixth enters, he will lose the place altogether, without being able to take the next one, but should go back to the number which is vacant.

If any Gentleman wishes to dance with another Lady and not the one who is in the dancing space, he will go and take the unoccupied place, and notify his Lady of this so that when this number comes up, they may both find themselves available, and in this case the Lady who is in the dancing space, if she finds herself compromised by others, must cede the position to the new one, and return to dance again afterwards.

3

Place Where the *Contredances* Must Begin

Having found the manner to facilitate for the *Sig. Dilettanti* the dancing of the *Contredances* without the need of a Dancing Master, given that they have made themselves masters of my figured rules, it is still necessary to give a fixed rule, according to my knowledge and opinion, on the place for the beginning of the above-mentioned *Contredances*, so that, if my reflections are found to be reasonable, they may be put into performance.

The variations between Countries, the frequency and diversity to be found at Assembly Balls, and my long experience, have made me observe certain inconveniences arising from, and caused by, the false location where the first couple[12] at the head of the *Contredance* place themselves.

I am of the opinion that the *Contredances* should start to be danced at the foot of the Orchestra. The Gentleman, in position so that he is facing the Orchestra, gives his right [hand] to the Lady and not indeed when he turns towards the back because the last couple must be facing the back of the first couple.[13]

I will explain the main reason why the beginning of the *Contredances* must be at the foot of the Orchestra. The Dancing Master must of necessity be in communication with the Leader of the Players, so that he can settle at will the beat of the music, either slower or quicker, to ensure that the instruments are silent when he wishes and start to play when he so desires. If he is at a distance, as he would be if the tail of the *Contredance* is inconsiderately placed below the Orchestra, he must leave, or return to confer with the Leader[14] for every minute detail and thus seek what is needed, abandoning the harmony; and in these interruptions of coming and going the *Contredances* languish, the dancers become bored, and so many other confusions and incongruities are bound to happen. Or should an usher be appointed to report the Dance Director's wishes to the above-mentioned Leader? Or should the Dancing Master's orders be passed by raising the voice until it reaches the Orchestra: poor remedies, and worse than that. Not so when beginning to dance below the Orchestra, where one can easily signal to play, be silent, to slow down, to quicken the tempo according to circumstances. Do not tell me that two violinists should come down from the Orchestra for the accompaniment, for doing so would deprive it of Players, because it is certain that, on the pretext of not inconveniencing and interrupting those who are playing, they will not return to the Orchestra. But why seek to beg all these feeble excuses, if with this rule all can be obviated? Furthermore the Dance floor will be less restricted, because the Orchestra is ordinarily situated at the far end of the Hall, and if the dancers come to start the Dance opposite this, they will be placed near to the entrance of the Hall where there is a great throng coming and going. Therefore from whichever way one looks at it, one can see the necessity and the good order of beginning the *Contredances* below the Orchestra.

4

Diversity in the *Contredances*, and a Good Rule for Dancing Pre-Arranged *Contredances* at Assemblies

The *Contredances* may be done with an indeterminate number of dancers, that is to say, with as many as it is wished to introduce or as many as the Ballroom will hold, or else with a certain determinate number of Dancers.

The *Contredances* of an indeterminate number, where, as was said, as many couples of dancers are introduced as desired, must be placed one after the other in two lines, according to the English style, or in three or four lines and other modes introduced and invented by myself, as we will see in the Chapter on the beginnings of the *Contredances*. *Contredances* of this sort are composed of a few regulated figures, and not of regulated and precise steps. But this does not mean that because the steps are not regulated that all are permitted to dance them, but only those who know what the Dance is can and should. Such *Contredances* are danced with a *marked brisé* which may be adapted to all the figurations and, with its flexibility, it proves more pleasing, for, whether it is done small or big, it never disturbs the Dancer's body, which is not the case in the *demi-contretemps*, which can only be used in the *balletti fermi*,[15] keeping the foot very low. In those *balletti fermi*, if hands are taken, the said *demi-contretemps* or *marked brisé* are always done with the same foot in front as the hand which is held. However, doing similar *balletti* without taking hands, you can change feet as you do in walking. These two steps are done both in *ternary* and in *binary time*; the little spring of the step will be in cadence and in the space[16] will be the *dégagé*, that is, the detachment.

The *Contredances* of determinate number are always done with that number introduced for the first time by the Dancing Master, or by the *Dilettante* who produces them, without being able to decrease them or increase them further. These will be composed of diverse figures, of regulated and obligatory steps, and cannot be danced extemporaneously but they should be studied and prepared, and danced by Ladies and Gentlemen who really know what ballroom dancing is, and know to perfection those steps which should enter into these kinds of *Contredances*. And only thus can all confusion which might arise be avoided, and give delight and not tedium to the spectators.

Very commendable, and worthy of imitation, is the French custom, according to which all the *Contredances* done at Assembly Balls are determinate and prearranged, and one is never proposed unless all know how to dance it; and it is not displayed in public if there is the slightest doubt about some small shortcoming.

Let us consider for a while the impropriety of our use of extemporised *Contredances* which are introduced at Assembly Balls. Never can one see a *Contredance* perfectly danced, either because some of the dancers with poor memory forget the figures that must be taken or, by attending to what must be done, are unable to give that spirit, that free fancy and that brilliant air to the dance that is needed. This would not happen if they were studied and prepared. Something which is perfectly executed always pleases, even if seen and seen again, more than another never before beheld, and full of defects; it is true that novelty always pleases but something new, badly executed, that turns out imperfect, will be censured for its imperfection.

What does it mean, that the greatest entertainment at an Assembly Ball is derived from repeated *Minuets*, seen and seen again, and not likewise with the *Contredances* danced at other Assemblies and similarly in common use? I would not know to what reason to attribute this, if not that it is attributable to a certain prejudice and fanaticism for novelty. Could they not follow our custom in France? Do they perhaps lack subjects and able Masters to make more improvised *Contredances* in an evening? Certainly not. Why not do it then? To avoid the inconvenience which arises from the metamorphosis of converting an Assembly into a dancing school and not to diminish the pleasure of seeing a good *Contredance* by the tedium of first arranging it.

Is proof desired, that the *Contredances* seen many times at other Assemblies will not appear displeasing? Here it is. Ordinarily all Assemblies, if they are to have a happy and gay ending, are concluded with the *Contredance* called *della Regina* introduced by her; this is a *quadrille*, enriched by varied and beautiful figures and all dance it well because everyone often dances it. Is it less pleasing therefore because it is seen over and over again? No. This proves to be so spirited that it closes the Assemblies brilliantly. So if all the *Contredances* are the same as danced at other Assemblies, why should they not similarly please?

Great advantage is taken away from the public's pleasure with this abuse of the always new, extemporised *Contredances*! The Dancing Master cannot interweave intricate, developed and varied figures, but only those few which are simple and easy to execute; doing otherwise, he would run the risk of starting the rehearsal and the music, always going back to the beginning, and the whole evening would pass without being able to do one. Therefore the wise Master will make them flowing and simple, so that it cannot be said that in the Assembly ruled by him, he has not been able to take one *Contredance* to the end. Then an improvised English *Contraddanzina* can be done, danced in binary time, being quick and easy; as also in France it is customary at times.

With this abuse of always dancing new *Contredances* derives the novelty of the Music and it often happens that, by always changing, you meet one of little or no liking, and here lies an air of displeasure at the Assembly where, at once, the discontented souls' resentment is heard. Those which at one time gave pleasure, are thus not established.

Therefore it is not a good thing to want to learn some new *Contredance* extemporaneously at festivals; and for those Gentlemen and Ladies who place themselves in the first figure, it would be advisable, at least, to learn it first before coming to the festivals, so that the others, seeing the figurations of the first ones, can learn and then be able to dance them. And they are misguided who, since they do not know how to dance, insist on putting themselves in the first figure, reasoning that, being in first place, the Dancing Master will see to placing them and under his direction they will learn fast and well. Graciously I admit this. But tell me, will he who has just learned the movements of the first figure, taught to him by the Master, be good enough that in passing to the other figures he will be able to act as the Teacher, who, besides knowing his own part, also knows that of the others whom he must prompt and direct? Certainly not. In fact, wishing to know both [parts], he will know neither one nor the other and cannot avoid disorder and confusion. It is not thus, if the more competent in the Dance are placed in the first figure, and thus successively to the last and least practised, and by the time it is their turn to dance, they will have seen the figurations repeated fifteen or twenty times, so that, when it is their turn, these will no longer be new to them and they will be able to dance them. Where it is a case of showing oneself in public, one must walk with certainty, confident of a good outcome. It is a matter of he who exhibits himself among a notable Assembly appearing ridiculous by badly performing what he is doing. One often finds among the multitude tastes so exquisite and delicate that also place under scrutiny and censure those things which have merited the title of good and even of perfect. What then is to be said of those things which are bad in themselves? Necessarily they deserve derision and scorn.

Let us imagine in a Theatrical performance a good scenic action composed by an excellent Author and presented by good and distinguished Actors, in which all act their roles well, and only he who is entrusted with the principal part does his badly. Please tell me whether he who acts the principal role and performs it badly deserves to be praised just on the ground that he is the main Character and the Protagonist of the work? He deserves rather the blame, and the greater blame because he took upon himself the principal part. Not even the least part, by being least, fails to arouse applause when it has been well performed. Thus it is in the *Contredances*, where merit it not acquired by placing oneself in the first figure but by knowing how to execute it well. Let no one flatter himself with self-love, for this is a veil to Reason, but let him be content to allow himself to be placed by the Dancing Master, who has no other aim but the success of the *Contredance*, without partiality and expectation, which might endanger the good outcome.

5

Advice to the Dancing Master on the Composition of *Contredances*

The best entertainments in the Assembly Balls today are the *Contre-dances*; they arouse jubilation, they awaken the Dancers' aesthetic sense. And in truth the lively dances were in the past the most diverting, the festive dances were sought in Nature herself. Let us observe all the National dances. The *Taice*, the English, the Swiss, our *Tarantella*, the *Tarascone*, the *Furlana*, and so many other dances done by the Peasants in their meadows are all happy and joyful and in those the Villagers take their innocent delights. Our *Contredances* emanated from simple Woodland dances: those turns, those crossing figures, those chains, those passings under and so many other innumerable figurations which are to be observed in them as done in their woods by self-taught Rustics. Therefore the *Contredances* as still preserved today are no more than an imitation of natural instincts expressed in happiness. As the Assembly Balls are an entertainment to divert and relieve us from the serious occupations, it is right then that the *Contredances* should be given pre-eminence in the Assemblies as those which are destined to move our hearts to happiness; and with good reason they open and conclude the Assemblies. Therefore Dancing Masters must direct all serious application to them and, in order to achieve this end, to make sure that they are pleasing, you should observe what will be transcribed here, as practised through long experience.

The first aim in composing *Contredances* is that partners should not always dance together but they should be made to vary, now with a second, now with a third, provided that there are that number, [otherwise] those who begin the *Contredance* would dance more than those who complete it, and those who compose it thus misunderstand; one must always distinguish who dances in the first figure, and then they should not make the second and the third figures too tiring, because whoever completes the *Contredance* expects to begin in the first place, and from this is born the unwillingness to dance it, by which all things done without acquiescence and pleasure soon become tiresome; therefore it is necessary to make the first person dance a little with the second, a little with the third, and even the third with the second, and with such diversity the dancers are not wearied.

The Music for *Contredances* in one whole evening must not be in the same time, but should be varied now in two-four, now in three-eight, now in six-eight. And more than once I myself have introduced in the same *Contredance* the mixing of two times: if for example it begins in two-four, it can end in three-eight. Therefore not only does the harmony vary, which is more charming to the ear, but by changing time the step is changed and thus has our machine more variety. For example, the *Contredance* may begin in two-four with the *pas brisé*; it moves into three-eight and the step changes again into a *Taice step*, that is into *bourrée sur place*, as the *Schiava step*[17] is commonly called. The motion of the Body completely alters because the *brisé* will be sprung and the *Taice step* will be beaten rather than sustained. Often variation beautifies Nature.

Nor do I deem this alone necessary, but also the uniting of the figuration to the time, adapting the figure to the movement of the Music; as for example if the Music were all syncopated, it would be wrong for the Master to insert a round figure, a serpentine, but a chain to which syncopated notes are related, because in this now the hands are released, now taken, and thus calling the figure to the Music or this to the figure with orderly union, the dancer is pleased, and pleases the Spectators. In my experience I have seen its happy effects. I made one piece in two-four, and two pieces also in two-four but used as a *Tarantella*, which completely varied all the melodious harmony although the time is the same. With one piece in six-eight I combined two pieces of *Taice* in three-eight; with that of a three-four *Minuet* time, a *Taice* time or a *Tarantella*. Whoever keeps too much to one piece, and does not want to seem antiquated, needs to vary frequently, introduce new methods and always change form. Everybody will see in the course of my *Contredances* the various styles used by myself. We have reached an era when the taste is too refined and therefore a Dancing Master must have a hundred considerations: firstly the location of the Hall, and of which social rank it is composed; secondly what instruments there are in the Orchestra so that he brings Music which is suited to it. If there are no wind instruments, it will be necessary to go provided with that Music in which such instruments are not necessary. If there are some, he should bring music with wind *obbligati*, but not too many of them. Let them have a solo entrance with *cantabile* accompaniment, but don't do as some Composers of Music, who write a *Contredance* with some solo entrances and then the accompaniment quite the opposite, with difficult leaps and simple accompaniments. These tunes cannot be played without the [appropriate] instruments but if ever they are performed, as I say, they could be used by any Orchestra even if there are no wind instruments. As also the plans of the *Contredances* must be varied, starting them now in two files, now in three, now in four, as have been variously introduced by myself and as seen in their starting positions.

Finding himself at a public masked ball, the Dancing Master, being ordered to distribute the places, must arrange everything according to the size of the Hall and the number of persons who are taking part in the festival, and this rightfully is his task; but when *Cavalieri Direttore*[18] who do not wish the Master to meddle in such arrangements have been appointed for the said festival, then he should not interfere; but if he is enjoined by these same he should do so; and if anybody does not wish to obey him, the *Cavaliere Direttore* must support him and not allow him to remain servile, otherwise he cannot maintain good order, and inevitably confusion will follow. But he must arrange everything with good grace and use all propriety to avoid any strife, and in particular with the maskers who deserve special respect, as if he were the Prince himself or some chief Grandee of his court. However, with regard to the Dances, he must not make any distinction between one masker and another, even if he knows who they are. Nor must he be compromised and take on any obligation to place any masker in the first figure, but in this he must maintain indifference, and let each one take that place which is available to him and then put himself at the beginning of the *Contredance* ensemble when he has seen that the dancers are placed in the figure without any dispute.

In similar festivals the Orchestra is usually placed high up on some sort of temporary platform which will be constructed with either a stairway at the base of the façade or with a space left underneath, capable of holding people. There are the garrulous, who obstinately insist of putting themselves in the first figure and, on finding the space of the dance floor occupied right up to the Orchestra, either mount the above-mentioned stairs or go into the empty space beneath the Orchestra. In such a case, those who have occupied this place are not in the dancing space but those are, who are in that part where the front of the Orchestra falls perpendicular; then the Dancing Master must not decide on his own to begin the ensemble with those who are in the correct place, because those who are on the stairs or under the platform will not want to yield it, believing themselves to have the first place which cannot be assigned to them because it is not possible to dance there. To make the others move back to give them room would give rise to mutterings, but the Directors of the festival must give the right to start to those who are in the proper place, both because in fairness it belongs to them, and because it is to be assumed that they are persons of quality and not those who display a scornful presumption typical of uncouth or base people. Thus when the Director of the festival decides, all are obliged to obey him, and the Dancing Master will not enter into any undertaking which might give the least occasion for disorder to arise on his account.

I have taken the trouble to give this warning because of the various disturbances which have occurred in public festivals caused on occasion by Dancing Masters determined to make some do the first figure, or to act as Judge in determining something not concerning them, so that they ought to behave with indifference and attend to the dance for which they are commissioned.

Being however a dance festival of Ladies and Gentlemen, and although they may be in Masks, then the Dancing Master is not obliged to arrange the places to maintain good order. Firstly, there will be no need for this because all noble People make it their duty to conduct themselves well; secondly, the Dancing Master, taking this task upon himself, might encounter some affront. Wherefore whatever might occur, it must be the Gentlemen who are destined for such direction, one of whom should have the task of supervising the beginning of the *Contredances* and the rest should circulate up and down, so that everyone does not crowd onto one place, and thus the dancers will be at ease, and the Dances may then be seen.

6

Noble Behaviour

§1

As was said in the first Chapter of Part One, how to introduce oneself at a *Conversazione* is learned from the Dance; thus we shall speak of it here. The teaching of this act of gentlemanly propriety belongs to the Dancing Master, who must give the rules to his Pupil, and not wait for the young to learn through practice and from the parents' example; and in order to profit from the said advice he must comport himself according to such method. You enter the salon holding the hat in the left hand, which is also used on the occasions when the hat is raised; the right must be free to pay your respects, either by taking a friend's hand or kissing a Lady's hand. Display a brilliant and sweet air. Taking three paces away from the Person to be greeted, begin the Honours carrying the right foot forward with a natural step and, closing the other in first, incline the body slightly or deeply, according to the rank of the Person who is being greeted, looking him in the face with cheerful mien, if it is a joyful or complimentary visit, if of condolence with grief and, again straightening up, begin to speak in fitting terms and expressions suited to the nature of the visit without being diffuse, which would cause tedium.

The Lady enters with upright body and hands crossed in front of her waist, the right hand being uppermost, in which, if a fan is carried, it is held between the index and middle fingers and, being at a distance of one foot from whoever is to be greeted, she takes the left foot to second position and then again she takes the right to fourth behind and, bending the knees, she will curtsey always carrying the body upright; on straightening, if to a Lady friend or a consort, she will advance that step which kept the distance, but with the front foot, and she will kiss her; thus she will pass to the others distinguishing each by the depth of her curtsey and with various suitable expressions of respect. If it is a dance festival, she will not move around the room but will do the *révérence* on entering, turning her head to acknowledge the entire salon.

§2

Finding oneself standing on both feet and obliged to give and to return a greeting with a *révérence*, it is necessary that, from whichever situation the feet are in, they are carried to first position; the body is inclined to a suitable degree according to the rank of the person who is greeted, letting the arms fall naturally at the sides; if a hat is held, it will be in the left hand, as was said, with the inside turned towards the thigh; then having straightened up, and wishing to give other signs of friendship such as a kiss, advance one step to approach and take right hands.

§3

The Gentleman, wishing to salute someone while walking, should slide the foot forward and incline the body in proportion to the merit of the person he is honouring, looking at him in the face with grace and spirit. Wishing to salute him again, one, two, or more steps are done forward and, again sliding the foot in the manner described, he will do the bow as above explained.

§4

In taking leave of someone, the *révérence* must also be done, going backwards so that, according to what is suitable, one or more are done with inclining the body and sliding one foot after the other backwards.

§5

Should the Gentleman be in a Gallery where there are very many persons who are either all on one side or on both, he will enter so that he stops in first position and will make the first *révérence* to the whole assembly in general, glancing here and there while bowing; and then, having started to walk, and wishing to honour those who are on the right side, before he reaches the nearest person to him, he acknowledges him with a friendly glance and, turning the body somewhat towards him, he slides the right foot forward and makes the bow to him. If he wants to greet another further down on the same side, one, two, or more steps should be done. The same will be applied if they are on the left side; the left foot will glide and, bowing the body, he observes the same as we have said for the right side. Going from side to side, he will change feet accordingly. The Lady will observe the same with her curtsey, and the order just explained.

§6

The Gentleman and the Lady, having entered the assembled company, seat themselves in an act of nobility which characterises the Person. The Gentleman must remain seated comfortably, with his feet placed in fourth or in second position, the body well held, the right arm falling naturally onto the thigh, and the hat will be placed under the left arm. Being in the middle of two persons, he will not turn his back on either side, and speaking with one of them, he will only turn his face and not the whole body towards the one in view. The Ladies will be similarly seated with the hands together on the lap, holding the fan as above, between the index and the middle fingers.

7

Explanation of the Signs and Figures of the *Contredances*

§1. Of the first Table   §2. Of Table II
§3. Of Table III   §4. Of the fourth Table
§5. Of the fifth Table

In order to be able to understand fully the track and figures of these *Contredances*, it is necessary for me to provide an explanation and make known all the signs appended to them, so that the dance lovers may first master all the ciphers that make a plan of each of the following *Contredances*, whereby explaining they may understand well all that is set out before them.

§1

Fig.1 The first figure[20] in the first Table denotes the man's body, marked in the
Tab.I form of a semicircle, the spherical part being the back of the Body; the straight part, that is the Diameter, represents the chest and the two mixtilinear angles are the right and left sides respectively.

Fig.2 That of the man has been shaded to distinguish it from that of the Lady,
Tab.I which will be seen denoted in the second figure of the same Table.

Fig.3 In the third figure, those two curved lines which come out from the sides
Tab.I denote the left and the right arms.

      If from the chest of the Man or Lady, whichever it is, a straight or
Fig.4 curved line is extended without being crossed by another small line, in
Tab.I such case, the dancer will travel according to the direction of the
Contr.I circumscribed line; but without stopping there, he will begin the suc-
fol.1 ceeding figure immediately, as in the second figuration of the first *Contredance* where the firsts pass behind the thirds, entering into the middle of the seconds and without pausing there, straight away join the *mezzo braccio*, as marked in the third figuration.

Fig.5 If however, as in the fifth figure, that line is drawn from the back, then
Tab.I the dancer does not go forwards but travels backwards.

Fig.6
Tab.I   There being however a small bar, that is a small line, at the extremity of that line which extends from the back or from the front of the body, as is seen in the sixth figure, then this denotes that the dancer should stop after having travelled.

Fig.7
Tab.I   The seventh figure, in which at the end of the line a little semicircle is seen, signifies that, after the set steps are done to arrive at the required Contr.
XXII
fol.11 figuration, he turns to face the opposite direction where at first his back had been. For instance in the twenty-second *Contredance*, in the second figuration, the four men are seen having taken hands and all four with the same sign travel until they occupy the place of the four Ladies, while these go in a file holding hands to stop in a lateral line, and all eight form a right angle, as is seen in the third figuration of the same *Contredance*, where one observes the four Men, who, in the second were facing front at the beginning, in the third are facing towards the back, as indicated by the sign explained and shown.

    Extending, however, another line from the little semicircle to the Fig.8 bottom, parallel to the first line, will be the sign to return to the same place Tab.I with the difference, however, of having the chest where before the back Contr.I was. An example of this is to be found in the first *Contredance* in the fifth fol.1 figuration, where the six dancers are seen three by three turned back to back in the fifth figuration and in the sixth they are facing each other.

Fig.9
Tab.I   In the ninth figure the walk forwards is shown, turning to return to the same place, and turning again to face the same way as at the beginning.

Fig.10
Tab.I   One who turns on the same place, and finds himself in the same manner as he was before beginning to turn, is indicated in the tenth figure.

    A tiny line just showing, crossed by another, with the dot above, which Fig.11 is seen in the eleventh figure, is the sign for a *balletto fermo* on the same place, Tab.I which occupies four bars of Music, and then the figuration which is to Contr.
XIX,XX
fol.10
Contr.
VI
fol.3 follow will be interwoven, as it is in the second figuration of *Contredance* XIX and the sixth figuration of XX and in the fifth figuration of VI where four dancers are seen placed in a diagonal line.

Fig.12
Tab.I
Contr.
XVII
fol.9
Contr.
IV
fol.2   In the twelfth figure, there is nothing different to the sixth, except for the dot above. All that is added to that which was explained for the said sixth is that, after the stop, the *balletto fermo* will be done. Thus it is in the fourth figuration of *Contredance* XVII, and in the fourth *Contredance*, in the third and fifth figurations.

Fig.13
Tab.I
Contr.
III
fol.2   The sign of the thirteenth figure, which will never be seen for one person but for two, three and even more together, is of turning a quarter of a circle; as observed in the fifth figuration of the third *Contredance*, the four, who form the ring, will turn one quarter of a circle; and in effect in the subsequent sixth figuration, the first Man is seen in the place of the first Lady, she in the place of the third Man, who is seen to occupy the place of the third Lady, and she that of the first Man.

Fig.14 The sign of the fourteenth figure adds another quarter and makes half a
Tab.I circle, as in the penultimate figuration of the third *Contredance*, where is
Contr.
III seen the above-said sign for two, who are linking arms and turning one
fol.2 semicircle, as in fact in the last figuration they are seen to have changed
places reciprocally.

Fig.15 The sign in the fifteenth figure means three-quarters of a circle. We
Tab.I have an example of it in the second figuration of *Contredance* VI, where the
Contr.
VI two firsts turn three-quarters of a circle, counting one quarter halfway
fol.3 between the two thirds in the third figuration, half when the two change
places and three-quarters where they are seen in the third, that is the Man
in between the two seconds, and the Lady in between the two thirds.[21]

Fig.16 All having to find themselves in their own place, after having turned, a
Tab.I sign will be seen as in the sixteenth figure, which means turning a full
Contr.
I,II circle. Such is the fourth figure of the first *Contredance*, where the persons
fol.1
Contr. find themselves in the same place where they were before turning, such as
IV can be observed in their subsequent figurations.
fol.2

Warning and general rule

Be warned, that much of the time everyone does not make the same
amount of turn, but some more and some less. In order to avoid confusion
they are not all distinguished by the respective sign, but this will be placed
against one only; in order to observe the difference between them, a
glance should be cast upon the figuration which follows to see which place
each one has taken; and this must be a general rule, always to look at the
figuration which follows, especially at the complicated signs of which no
particular explanation has been given and, should there be confusion, with
this rule all doubt will be removed. As also I will say, that at times in a
figuration one figure[22] is found turned one way and, without having
moved, in the following it will be found in another, in such a case I did not
judge it necessary to put the appropriate sign for only turning the body. An
Contr. example of this is found in the First figuration of *Contredance* IV, where in
IV the first the thirds are seen looking at each other and in the second they are
fol.2 face to face with the firsts. Something very natural, for, in order to give
the arm to the firsts they must turn to the right and, without applying a
sign, it is understood that they must do this in order to give the arm.
Examples of other similar things will be found in plenty in the course of the
other *Contredances*.

Fig.17 The seventeenth figure shows the Lady situated at the right of the Man
Tab.I and both taking hands, the Man giving his right, and the Lady her left, thus
there can be even three, four and more, all those in the middle giving both
hands, and the two at each end one only, as are the four seconds of
Cortr. *Contredance* XIX in the sixth figuration who move as explained when
XIX

fol.10 speaking of the eighth figure,[23] all four holding hands. Thus all four
Contr. holding hands do the *balletto fermo* in the third figuration of the twenty-
XXII
fol.11 second *Contredance*.

Fig.18 How to relate the linking arms right and right, or left and left is marked
Tab.I   in the eighteenth figure. If they must turn, the sign and amount of turn will
        be added, as is seen in those eight, but two by two, in the third figuration of
        Contredance XIX, folio 10.   ,

Fig.19 In the nineteenth figure the Man is shown with his right side to the Lady,
Tab.I   and both with arms round each other. The Man holds his right arm straight
        behind the shoulder of the Lady, and his left bent behind his back takes the
        Lady's left hand, whose whole arm will be stretched behind the Man's
        shoulders, and with her right, which is carried behind her back, she takes
        the Man's right. So many times this figure is to be found marked with only
        the two arms, which are round each other, omitting the other two, as in the
Contr. seventh figuration of the fourth *Contredance*, where the sign for the full turn
IV   is also found. To this figure the *balletto fermo* can be added to the travel sign.
fol.2   In the course of the *Contredances* several of these signs will be found.

Fig.20 In the twentieth figure is noted when Man and Lady, both facing the
Tab.I   same way, present right to right and left to left, crossing the two arms of
        the adjoining sides to join the already-mentioned hands in front of the
        chest.

Fig.21 In the twenty-first figure a Man and a Lady are shown facing opposite
Tab.I   directions, and interlacing the arms thus. The Man will have his right hand
        behind the Lady's back, taking her left hand, which she is holding behind
        her back, and the Man's left will be united with the Lady's right, in front of
        the Man's chest.

Fig.22 With the twenty-second figure are indicated a Man and a Lady, placed
Tab.I   side by side, facing the same way, and presenting right to right in front of
        the chest of the latter and left to left behind the back of the former.

Fig.23 Two placed facing each other and both taking right hands will be
Tab.I   marked as in the twenty-third figure, to which, when turning, the sign for
        the amount of the turn is placed in one of the four manners expressed, as in
Contr. the fourth figuration in the fourth *Contredance* where a full turn is made. In
IV   the same situation the left hands can be given, but I did not judge it
fol.2   necessary to add a particular figure, since it is known very well, if the right
        or the left is to be taken.

Fig.24 From the same position both hands can be given, the right with the right,
Tab.I   the left with the left, crossing them, and this is shown in the twenty-fourth
        figure.

Fig.25 Without crossing the hands, standing in the same situation, the twenty-
Tab.I   fifth figure signifies the Man's left joined to the Lady's right and her left to
        the Man's right.

        In the twenty-sixth figure a change of place is noted, namely one

Fig.26 occupies the place of the other, but in the newly occupied place, each one
Tab.I remains facing the same direction as at the beginning.

Fig.27   The two who are shown in the twenty-seventh figure are those who,
Tab.I having moved at the same time as though meeting each other, pass back to
back and return to stop in the same place whence they began.

Fig.28   The twenty-eighth figure refers to the eighth figure for the walk and to
Tab.I the twentieth for the crossing of the arms. This is given only to point out
that the returning will be done with one facing the other, and doing it
otherwise would be an error.

Fig.29   The twenty-ninth is the same as the seventeenth, adding to it the Lady's
Tab.I walk, who, passing under the arm of the Man, returns to stop in her
original place.

Fig.30   The thirtieth, which has three signs adjoined, refers to the linking of the
Tab.I arms in the manner of the nineteenth, with its *balletto fermo*, after which the
Lady, still linked with the Man, will pass from the right side to the left,
thus it can also be done from this to the right.

Fig.31   In the thirty-first is seen the position of the twenty-third figure, where,
Tab.I after the *balletto fermo*, they take hands and make a half turn, with one
passing to the place of the other, thus one full turn, three-quarters, or one
quarter can be done.

Fig.32   In the thirty-second, the Lady and the Man, taking hands, move from
Tab.I the perpendicular to the level plane.[24]

Fig.33   In the thirty-third is a walk done by two, one retreating and the other
Tab.I advancing, and staying in the same relationship, but ground is gained by
the latter and lost by the former.

§2

Fig.1 The first figure describes three persons placed in a triangle, looking at one
Tab.II another, doing the *balletto fermo*; this ended, they immediately place
themselves laterally and give right arms and how they turn will be evident
from the sign placed beside them.

The second figure is the position that the above three will take having
ended the *balletto*; they will find themselves in this second marked pattern
Contr. when the *balletto* is placed in the preceding figure as in the ninth figuration
XXX of the thirtieth *Contredance* because the sign for the *balletto* is placed in the
fol.14 eighth figuration, as we explained in the twelfth figure of the first Table.

Fig.3   In the third figure three Ladies are shown also placed in a triangular
Tab.II figure doing their *balletto fermo*, at the end of which they take each other by
the hands, forming a circle to go round according to the amount marked
for them.

Fig.4   In the fourth figure three persons are noted, the one in the middle giving
Tab.II her right arm to the other who is on her right, who also offers his right
hand, joining it in front of the chest, and her left hand is also joined with

209

the left in front of the person who is on her left, and the two persons who are at the sides take each other by the right and left hand behind the back of the person in the middle: all three walk forwards and, turning, return to the same place, but facing towards the back.

Fig.5 The three persons of the fifth figure have thus interlaced their arms: the
Tab.II one in the middle crossing the arms in front of herself, joins her right hand with the left of whoever is on her left and the left to the right of whoever is on her right and these two at the sides take right and left hands behind the back of whoever is in the middle.

Fig.6 The taking of hands of the two Ladies in the sixth figure refers to the
Tab.II seventeenth figure of the first Table, who walk towards the Man who is facing them and who is coming towards them; he passes under their arms and stops on the spot where the Ladies stood and they continue walking until they arrive at the spot where the Man was and, again turning, all three are face to face.

Fig.7 The seventh figure denotes three interweaving and holding hands.
Tab.II Whoever is on the left side takes with her right the left hand of whoever is on the right side, and her left is joined to the left of whoever is in the middle, who in turn offers his right to whoever is seen on the right side.

Fig.8 The joining of hands of the three in the eighth figure is the same as in the
Tab.II preceding, but where in that the hands were taken in front, in this they are taken behind. That is, that the Lady situated on the right side, passing her right hand behind her back, joins it to the right of the Man who already is in the middle, and her left to the right of the other Lady who is on the other side, passing it behind the back of the Man, and this Lady is on the left side with her left, carrying it behind her back, takes the Man's left hand.

Fig.9 The ninth figure shows a linking of arms of three persons. The Man in
Tab.II the middle extends both arms behind the backs of the two Ladies, and with his right hand takes the left of the Lady on the right side, and with his left takes the right of the other Lady, and they also join hands, the one on the right side giving the right, the other the left: thus both Ladies cross their arms.

Fig.10 Another kind of interweaving of arms can be seen in the tenth figure,
Tab.II which is done by three persons situated in such a way that the Man, who is in the middle, faces the opposite direction to the Ladies. The Man extends his arms in front of the Ladies' chests, offering his right to the left of the Lady on the right side, and his left to the right of the other, and the Ladies join hands under the arms of the Man and behind his back, the Lady on the right giving her right hand, the other Lady her left.

Fig.11 Three persons placed in a triangle and turned back to back form a circle
Tab.II by giving hands, as noted in the eleventh figure.

The twelfth figure indicates three also situated in a triangle taking hands

Fig.12 and doing the *balletto fermo*; the Man gives both hands and the Ladies each
Tab.II give one, keeping the other free.

Fig.13   Three placed on a diagonal line and taking hands are shown in the
Tab.II thirteenth figure, which may be done by four or more Persons, but who
alternately look one in one direction and the other in the opposite.

Fig.14   As in the twenty-ninth figure of the First Table, the Lady passes under
Tab.II the Man's arm and returns to her place; in this where three people are
taking hands, she passes in front of the Man, going under his left arm and
the right arm of the other Lady, and returns to her original place.

Fig.15   This figure differs from the eighth in that, whereas all the hands there
Tab.II were joined behind the backs, here the two Ladies join the two outside
hands in front, that is to say that the one on the right side gives her right
and the one on the left her left, and with the others they circle[25] the Man,
who holds both the Ladies with his two arms.

Fig.16   Three are seen placed on behind the other in a column in the sixteenth
Tab.II figure. The first Lady bends her left arm behind her back, taking the Man's
right hand held in front of his chest; his left, which is behind his shoulder,
he gives to the last Lady, who joins her right in front, and in this manner
they will walk to where the sign finishes.

Fig.17   In the seventeenth figure a *tour moulinet*[26] is described, the Man being the
Tab.II axle, who stands in the middle turning on the spot backwards; as also the
Lady on the left side turns backwards according to the sign explained and
demonstrated in the fifth figure of the first Table, and all three thus turn
one full circle to regain their original places.

Fig.18   Figure eighteen refers to the eighth figure adding to it the walk to show
Tab.II that all three must turn to the same side, and not face to face.

Fig.19   The Chain of three is shown in the nineteenth figure, in which first the
Tab.II Man gives his right hand to a Lady turning one full circle, and in the second
giving the left hands turning another full circle.[27]

Infinite other figures of three are found, but by combining the signs of
these principally explained, all the others can be clearly deciphered.

§3

Fig.1 In the first figure four persons are found in four angles of a parallelogram
Tab.III doing their *balletto fermo*, which ended, they turn to the right and, placed in
profile, they give hands crosswise, turning as far as marked.

Fig.2   The second figure is the position in which the same four mentioned
Tab.III above will be found once the *balletto* is ended; and so many times they are
found thus marked in the *Contredances*, either because in the preceding
Contr. figuration the *balletto* is marked as in the fourth figuration of *Contredance*
VIII VIII, since the *balletto* is marked in the third figuration, or because no *balletto*
fol.4 is done either before or after.

A circle of four is shown in the third figure, which is done once the

Fig.3   *balletto* is ended as many times as marked, and the circle will turn according
Tab.III   to the amount of the appended sign.

Fig.4   The fourth figure, in which are seen two Men one behind the other on
Tab.III   the same perpendicular and two Ladies laterally, shows all hands loosely
held. The Man in front joins his right to the right of the Lady on the right
side and his left to the left of the Lady on the other side, and the Man behind
gives his right to the left of the Lady on the right side and his left to the
right of the other Lady.

Fig.5   The two Men and the Lady are in front in the fifth figure, placed on the
Tab.III   same straight line, the Lady in the middle, behind whose back is the other
Lady, interlacing the arms as follows. The Man on the right side, crossing
his arms in front of himself, joins his right hand to the right of the Lady in
front and his left to the right of the Lady behind, and the other Man,
similarly crossing his arms, joins his right hand with the left of the Lady
behind and his left to the left of the other Lady.

Fig.6   Quite the opposite is the sixth figure where the Men are in the middle,
Tab.III   holding their arms crossed. The Man in front links his right to the left of
the Lady on the left side and his left to the right of the other Lady. The Man
behind joins his right with the right of the Lady on the left side and his left
with the left of the Lady on the other side.

Fig.7   In the seventh figure the two Ladies are seen in a line a little in front of
Tab.III   the Men and nearer to each other than are the Men. The Ladies cross arms:
the one on the right joins her right with the left of the other Lady and her
left with the right of the Man standing on the right side, whose left hand is
linked with the right hand of the other Man; the other Lady links her right
hand to the left of the Man on her left side.

Fig.8   The interlacing of the arms in the eighth figure is the same as that of the
Tab.III   seventh figure of the second Table, with another person added. Likewise
there may be five, six or more.

Fig.9   The ninth figure is like the eighth figure of the second Table with the
Tab.III   addition of another person, and in the interlacing of the arms all this refers
likewise to there being more people.

Fig.10   In the middle of the two Men, standing next to each other, the two
Tab.III   Ladies are seen in the tenth figure, but a little further back. They join hands
between themselves, the one on the right side giving her left and the other
her right. This one links her left arm under the right arm of the Man by her
side and, in front of his chest, they link left to left. The other Lady, also
passing her right arm under the left arm of the Man next to her, links her
right hand to his right in front of the Man's chest; and the Men join their
free hands in front of the Ladies.

Fig.11   In the eleventh figure two Ladies are seen placed in opposite lines,
Tab.III   turned back to back, and two Men opposite each other. The Ladies cross
both their own arms in front of their chests, and the Men, who hold the

212

arms wide apart, take the Ladies' hands. With his right, the one behind takes the left hand of the Lady who is on the right side and with his left the right of the other Lady; and the Man in front, with his right takes the left of the latter and with his left the right of the former.

Fig.12 Two Men are shown in the twelfth figure on the same perpendicular, Tab.III one behind the other, and the two Ladies laterally, looking in the opposite direction to the Men. The Man in front opens his arms and joins his right hand with the left of the Lady on the right side and his left with the right of the other Lady; to this one the Man behind, crossing his arms, presents his right, and she her left, and he joins his left with the other Lady's right.

Fig.13 The thirteenth figure describes all four on the same straight line but Tab.III turned alternately. The Men are in the middle. He on the right side interlaces his left arm with the left of the Lady at his side and joins his hand to the right of the same Lady behind her back, and his right hand is joined to the left of the other Lady in front of the Man on his left side, who links his right to the left of the Lady who is beside the other Man, behind his back, and his left hand with the right of the Lady next to him behind her back.

Fig.14 The fourteenth figure shows another linking of arms by four persons on Tab.III the same straight line, being one Man and one Lady alternately, and the Ladies have turned to face the opposite direction to where the Men face. The Man on the right side links his right hand with the left of the Lady who is on the right side, and behind her back, and his other hand with the right of the other Man. The Lady between them joins her right to the left of the Man on her right, in front of him, and her left to the right of the other Lady in front of the chest of the Man between them.

Fig.15 In the fifteenth figure all four have their arms crossed. The Lady behind Tab.III gives her right to the left of the Man on the left side, and her left to the other Man's right. The Lady in front gives her right to this Man's left, and her left to the other's right.[28]

Fig.16 The sixteenth figure refers to the eleventh figure of the second Table, Tab.III but with one person added.

Fig.17 In the seventeenth figure, they are on the same straight line and facing Tab.III the same way. The Man on the right side presents his right hand to the right of the Lady at his side, in front of her chest, and his left to the right of the other Lady behind the back of the other Man. He, behind the back of the first Man, joins his right hand to the left of the Lady on the right side, and his left to the left of the Lady beside him, in front of her.

Fig.18 One change of place is noted in the eighteenth figure. The first Man Tab.III passes behind the back of the second Lady and places himself on her left Contr. side, and the first Lady passes behind the second Man, remaining on his X right side. Such is the beginning of the tenth *Contredance*.

fol.5 In the half square the first couple occupy the place of the seconds, and

213

Fig.19
Tab.III these that of the firsts. They take hands two by two as described in the twenty-fifth figure of the first Table and, all four moving, the two firsts pass behind the second Lady and occupy the place of the seconds; these pass behind the first Man and thus will occupy the place of the seconds. This passage, continued with three couples, forms a serpentine as half of it is seen in the sixth, seventh and eighth figurations of the third *Contredance*,

Contr.
III
fol.2 which, in order to be complete, must be repeated six times; and then each couple would find themselves back in the place where they began.

Fig.20
Tab.III In the whole square they are found in their own place, but the Ladies in the places of their respective partners; they do everything as explained for the half, with the addition of another passage, and return to their original places.

Fig.21
Tab.III The Figure of Eight outwards round the seconds is shown in the twenty-first figure. The first Man starts walking towards the second Lady, passes behind her back, by her left side halfway between both the seconds and, turning behind the back of the second Man, he stops at his right side and at the same time his partner passes behind the second Man, walking between the seconds and, passing behind the back of the second Lady, stops at her left side.

Fig.22
Tab.III In the Figure of Eight inwards, which is shown in the twenty-second figure, the first Man passes in front of the second Lady and, turning around her, he goes towards the second Man and, passing by his right side and behind his back, he returns to stop in his original place. The first Lady follows the same path but around the second Man and, similarly turning round the other Lady, goes to her place and stands still.

Fig.23
Tab.III The twenty-third figure is given here for nothing else, except to show that, being four, they will do the walk forwards and in turning, each Man turns with the Lady beside him;[29] so it is if there are six or any even number; in odd numbers, however, all turn the same way, as noted in the eighteenth figure of the second Table.

Fig.24
Tab.III The twenty-fourth figure also needs no particular explanation for it is the same as the eighth figure of the first Table, but for four; but it is only shown here in order to see that in similar figurations the person behind must not pass the place of that one in front.

Fig.25
Tab.III In the twenty-fifth figure, the two firsts are shown taking hands, occupying the place of the seconds, passing between them, at the same time as these go to take the place of the firsts.

Contr.
II
fol.1 All the five positions marked with 26 make the figure of a chain of four. In the first all partners take right hands and go halfway round; in the second the first Man and the second Lady take left hands as also do the first Lady and the second Man, doing half a turn again; in the third the firsts find themselves in the place of the seconds and these in the place of the firsts, giving right hands and in the fourth the left hands; in the fifth figure, each

one finds himself in his original place. In the course of the *Contredances*, where a half chain or three-quarters or a whole occurs, not all the passages are written, but for the half there will be the sign of two links, as in the second number 26, three-quarters with three links, a whole with four, and by these distinctions it will be known how long to make the chain, and it will be marked in one of the said manners, as we have seen.

Fig.27
Tab.III
The twenty-seventh figure is also a chain which begins differently, with only the first two giving hands, and for the rest then it follows as in the one above, all four linking hands.

Fig.28
Tab.III
Contr.
XX
fol.10
The twenty-eighth figure serves as a finale, in which no more is shown than turning and unwinding into place, as will be seen marked in the succeeding figurations. Thus are the two circles in the penultimate figuration of the twentieth *Contredance*, and in the last is seen the place each person should take.

Fig.29
Tab.III
The twenty-ninth figure is another change of place in which the only thing observed is that the two holding hands pass inside and the others outside.

Fig.30
Tab.III
In the thirtieth figure, the tenth figure of the first Table is seen in the middle of the three Ladies who are placed in the third figure of the second Table; and the only addition is that if the Ladies turn to the left, the Man in the middle turns to the right and contrariwise if the Ladies do the opposite.

Fig.31
Tab.III
In the thirty-first figure, the four persons, two opposite the other two, form a line; that is they all meet in the same line, side by side.

§4

Fig.1
Tab.IV
The Figure of Eight in the same line round the third couple is shown in the first figure which is done thus: the first Man passes behind the back of the second Lady and places himself between the third and second, he turns around the third and stops in between the second and third and will remain facing the second. At the same time his Partner will follow the same path round the second and third Men, between whom she will stop, turning to face the second Man.

Fig.2
Tab.IV
Another kind of Figure of Eight is shown in the second figure, in which the first Man, after having passed behind the back of the second Lady, between her and the third Lady, goes towards the third Man, passes behind him and places himself at his right side. His Partner follows the same path around the second Man and second[30] Lady, at whose left side she stops.

Fig.3
Tab.IV
The third figure is a Figure of Eight with double passage: the first Man and his Partner cross midway between the two seconds, the Man passes between the two Ladies and the Lady between the Men; she does a full turn round the third Man and her Partner round the third Lady, and the Lady passes behind the second Man and the Man behind the second Lady, and the two firsts stop, having changed places with each other.

Fig.4
Tab.IV
The six persons in the fourth figure all take hands. The first gives his right hand to his Partner's right, who joins her left to the left of the second Lady;[31] he holds right to right with his Partner, who joins her left to the left of the third Man, and he right to right with his Lady. The third Lady begins the walk, passing between the two lines under the arms, her Partner follows her and he is followed by the other Man, then by the second Lady, after her the first Lady and lastly the first Man, and all place themselves in single file, headed by the first to walk; and thus they follow the path and stand one beside the other or place themselves as will be seen in the figurations which will follow.

Fig.5
Tab.IV
The six persons of the fifth figure form a star, being one Man and one Lady on an oblique line, giving right hands.

Fig.6
Tab.IV
The sixth figure refers to the third of the second Table, concerning the three Ladies who are joined by three Men placed at the side, who join their right hands to the Ladies' joined hands, to which figure will be appended the amount of turn.

Fig.7
Tab.IV
The seventh figure was demonstrated in the fifteenth of the preceding Table, with two persons added, and for this no particular explanation is needed; likewise we also omit other figurations of arms, for so many explanations were given in the second and third Tables, all of which can easily be conjectured.

Fig.8
Tab.IV
The Four, standing in a column in the eighth figure, divide to place themselves in two parallel lines. The two Ladies go one behind the other turning round in front of the third Man and, passing by his left side, place themselves in line with him; the second Lady remains at his side and the first is on her right side. Thus the two Men do likewise around the third Lady and similarly stop and each remains opposite his Partner.

Fig.9
Tab.IV
The ninth figure describes a Parallelogram: the three Ladies and the three Men, standing in parallel lines, take hands and walk one following the other and stop on the other two sides of the Parallelogram.

Fig.10
Tab.IV
In the tenth figure the three behind pass in front and vice versa: and as before moving they were face to face, when the walk is ended, as shown by the appended sign, they are back to back.

Fig.11
Tab.IV
In the eleventh figure a walk by all six is shown, linking arms two by two, the second couple following the first, the third following these; and from the two lateral columns, in which they are standing, they form two perpendicular columns, the firsts remaining at the top, the seconds in the middle and the thirds at the bottom.

Fig.12
Tab.IV
A column of six is formed, standing one behind the other, and ordered one Man and one Lady as is shown by those placed in two files in the twelfth figure.

Fig.13
Tab.IV
The thirteenth figure shows another passage stopping on the same line but taking hands, the persons changing places with each other; that is the

first Man in the place of the second Lady and she in that of the first Man; likewise the second Man passes into that of the third Lady and she into his.

Fig.14 From the two lines in which they stand in the fourteenth figure, a
Tab.IV straight line of six is formed but with such order that the Men go one after the other and pass in front of the third Lady, who remains stationary, and place themselves in a file behind her with the second Man next to her; thus the Ladies [place themselves] behind the third Man and all six stay in the line described.

Fig.15 The six positions marked with 15 make one chain of six; as explained for
Tab.IV that of four, so also this is explained and from this is easily recognised the passages that are done and that at one time they give right hands, left hands the next. The only thing remaining to be noted is that half [a chain] of six is marked with three circles, as in the third figuration of the fifteenth figure, and nothing more is done apart from these passages only, three-quarters of a chain as in the fourth figuration of the fifteenth, and a whole chain as in the last.

Fig.16 Another chain is shown in the sixteenth figure, where the Men are all on
Tab.IV one side and the Ladies all on the other. The two firsts begin with the right hand and these are followed by giving the left to the seconds and so on until all are back in their original places.

Fig.17 In the Seventeenth figure the three Ladies take each other by the right
Tab.IV hand and, with the left joined to the left of their own Partners, do their *balletto fermo*, and the Men walk round, letting go of the Ladies' hands. The first Man stops in the place of the second, this one in the place of the third Man who stops in that of the first and when they join they do the *balletto fermo*. The Ladies, having ended the *balletto* referred to, let go of hands and, on the spot, each one turns on her own, and instead of the right, they join left hands between them; and all six remain as seen in the second position of the seventeenth [figure], the third Man beside the first Lady and with his left hand joined to her right, the first Man to the right of the second Lady, the second Man at the side of the third Lady, all taking hands.

Fig.18 In the eighteenth figure the five persons behind pass behind the Lady
Tab.IV who is in front, but simply following one another without taking hands, not as they are seen side by side but one behind the other, then they all form a line beside the Lady who stood still.

§5

Fig.1 In the first figure four Ladies are noted placed in a circle taking hands, and
Tab.V four Men situated laterally join their right to the Ladies' joined hands. The sign of the *balletto* is seen, at the end of which the turn will follow, the amount of which will be indicated by the usual appended sign.

The second figure shows a cross of eight persons. Four Ladies on the

Theoretical and Practical Treatise on Dancing

Fig.2 Tab.V — inside all present right [hands] and the left [hands] are joined to the hands of the Men, who are on the outside.

Fig.3 Tab.V — The third figure is a change of place which, having been done by these four besides whom the sign is appended, will be done by the others.

Fig.4 Tab.V — The chain of eight, which is shown in the fourth figure, has no need of any particular explanation since it is arranged like that of six (Fig. 15 Tab. IV), where the right hand must be given one time and the left the next. The same would be done in a chain which starts from two columns.

Fig.5 Tab.V Contr. XXII fol.11 — In the fifth figure, which is found in figuration 4 of *Contredance* XXII, the four Men move to meet their own partners. The first Man leads, followed by the other three. The first three pass behind the back of the fourth Lady, and the fourth Man, having reached her side without passing behind her, stops in front of her; the others pass in front of the third Lady; on facing her the third Man stops; thus winding their way, the other two follow, each one of whom steps in front of his respective partner, as is seen in the succeeding figuration of the same *Contredance*.

Fig.6 Tab.V — All eight move at the same time in the sixth figure; of those four, who are in a line, the first Man leads, followed by his partner, and she by the second Man and lastly the second Lady; they pass, meeting one another under the arms of the other four, of whom the fourths, taking hands, go in front of them and these are followed by the thirds and so they find themselves as

Fig.7 Tab.V Contr. XXIII fol.17 — In the seventh figure they are seen marked, in which figuration the first Man with the two fourths, after doing the *balletto fermo*, gives hands to form a threesome. The two thirds remain still, and the second and first Lady with the second Man who is between them, taking hands, walk forwards and then return to the same place. The two figurations described will at once be seen in the twenty-third *Contredance*, in the second and third figurations.

Fig.8 Tab.V Contr. XXIV fol.17 — The eighth figure, which is observed in the second figuration of *Contredance* XXIV, is connected up to the fifth figuration, in that the dancers[32] pass one by one, and the person who is passed turns to face the back. The four Ladies always do the *balletto*, but the Men only two at a time, being those whom the Ladies must pass in front of.[33]

Fig.9 Tab.V — The ninth figure is a passage done by the firsts and the seconds and is found at the end of the *Contredances* in which at the beginning not all sixteen persons are marked but only eight, because only eight are always dancing, and the other eight are marked when the passage concerns them alone.

Fig.10 Tab.V — The tenth figure is another passage of firsts to seconds, but as not all sixteen are dancing at the beginning, they are only noted when it is their turn to pass.

Fig.11 Tab.V — In the eleventh figure the two persons who are linking arms pass midway between the two lines and the others follow them; they also link

218

arms when they meet; then they pass outside the lines and, in turning into the place of the firsts, they form one column as is seen

Fig. 12

Tab. V

In the twelfth figure, where the six who are in a column pass under the arms of the other two, who stand taking hands and walk forwards; the column passes under the arms and the couples divide: the Ladies follow the Lady and the Men the Man in the same manner. These are seen in *Contredance* XXXVIII, in figures 22, 23 and 24.

Contr.

XXX-
VIII

fol. 20

So many other signs are left to the discernment of those who have learned these, combining one with another and always having regard to the succeeding figuration as was clearly stated in the general observation made in the first Table.

219

8

Statement on the Starting Positions of the *Contredances*

The *Contredances* of indeterminate number, which may be danced by as many couples as will (Part II, Ch. 4), are not marked by any number other than by those who dance continually, wherefore it must not be thought that only those placed in the figurations are dancing.

In the first Starting Position, only six are marked but an arbitrary number may be placed there. They are situated face to face and, wishing to make them turn towards the starting point, which must be towards the Orchestra (Part II, Ch. 3), the Lady will be to the right of the Man. They begin the figurations that are already marked, which must end with the termination of the Music; the firsts will meet having passed to seconds, and these latter in place of the former. In repeating *da Capo* the *Contredance*, those who at the beginning were seconds and then became firsts, stand still, and the real firsts, although having passed to seconds, continue to dance as firsts, the thirds as seconds, and the fourths, which are not marked here but are inferred, as if supposing the others to be arbitrary, dance as thirds. When the figurations are ended for the second time, the firsts meet, having passed the other dancers, and are in the place of the thirds. And in repeating the beginning of the *Contredance* for the third time, the two couples which passed remain still, the firsts always continuing as firsts; the fourths, who in the second repeat became thirds, here become seconds, and the fifths the thirds. The figuration ended for the third time, the firsts meet having passed three couples; and on beginning for the fourth time, the three couples passed, which are the second, the third and the fourth, also begin to dance, making the second couple the first, the third the second and the fourth the third, and at the same time as the true firsts will dance with the fifths and with the sixths, and thus continuing to pass one couple at a time until they reach the bottom. It remains for me to observe that those couples who pass to the head will remain still as long as they are two couples, but being three they begin to dance with the others, and so on. It is to be noted moreover that, arrived at the penultimate couple, they pass them without dancing, because two couples cannot figure,[34] three being obligatory, and to give way to the last, they are passed without appearing as the second.

In the second Starting Position, eight are to figure, the firsts and the seconds passing to the thirds and to the fourths, as is seen at the end of *Contredances* XI and XII.

The third Starting Position is composed of two Ladies and two Men situated alternately, and eight dance. In passing, all the four firsts pass to the four seconds, and in order to distinguish between firsts and firsts, between seconds and seconds, those in front go to the number distinguished by a dot, and those behind will have no dot on the number.

In the fourth Starting Position, in each row of four persons the Ladies are in the middle and the Men in front and behind; two couples figure between them. In passing, only one of them passes and, arrived at the penultimate, they dance with this couple and do not pass it without figuring, because in the figurations only two couples are necessary, not three.

In the first row, all four are marked by the number 1, and in the second by the number 2, and because you might run into some difficulty distinguishing between one Man and the other, between this Lady and that, both having the same number, I wished to distinguish them with a dot, giving the dotted number to those in front and undotted to all the others behind, as was said in the third Starting Position.

The Fifth does not differ from the one above, except that the Ladies are in the first and third lines, and the Men in the second and fourth. This mode of putting into the *Contredances* four dancers in a row, as also those of three and all the other varieties observed, is one of my inventions for only two rows had been the custom. With this variation of the plans introduced, not only is a more spacious figuration produced and more varied for the multiplicity of Dancers, but it also renders the lines shorter and the ballrooms less crowded, for if twenty-four Gentlemen and as many Ladies, arranged in two lines, might wish to dance, these would be extended to twenty-four people; if however only four occupy half of the said extension, though they are increased in latitude, a great distance exists between the proportion of the diminished length and that of the added width; and apart from this, the dancers who stand at the bottom do not remain long without dancing because, with fewer files passing, the last is quickly reached.

I have done everything to render this divertissement easier and more attractive. Thus succeeding, I might be able to remove the abuse of the extemporaneous *Contredances* and to introduce those prearranged and especially those of determinate number. Then indeed, one could boast of truly good taste in Naples regarding the *Contredances*.

The eminent Signor Lepicq agreed with me in this my desire, since he introduced to this Capital *Contredances* for thirty-two and made to be danced by Gentlemen and Ladies excellent at dancing, that met with universal gratitude, not only for the dancers' fine execution, but also for the famous Inventor's pleasing figurations.

In this Volume I have also annexed some *Contredances* for determinate numbers, one for eight, one for twelve, another for thirty-two, which are the last three; but at the same time, I have recognised that, as something newly introduced and published in printed form, and carried out in performance without the Composer's assistance no matter what the difficulties of putting it into practice, I have abstained therefore from adorning it with vast and intricate figurations which came to my mind, and I have only introduced some easier ones, so that they may be done without confusion and embarrassment.

In the sixth Starting Position the first row is of Ladies, the second of Gentlemen their partners, and so on alternately; in this form of the *Contredances* not only can two files figure between themselves, as in the [aforementioned] *Contredance* and others, but also three and four files, for in the *Contredances* of this kind two files necessarily must pass another two; and those, who will pass into the place of the firsts, must wait for another two to pass before they also begin to dance, not because they cannot already figure, but because there will be no one then with whom to do the passage, for in order to do the said passage four files of dancers are needed. In those where two files figure, if only two of them are placed at the beginning, the other two are added when they must do the passage. In those however where four files figure, all four are placed and although their numbers are the same, those of the firsts are distinguished by the dot and those of the seconds are without a dot. In this kind of *Contredance* two files remain still and two dance, and never do they all dance together.

In the seventh Starting Position three dancers are noted: a Lady in the middle of two Men, and since the three in the first file have the same number as in the second, thus for distinction the number of the latter is without dot, and the number of the former is dotted. Only one file is passed, as was said in the third Starting Position, and two having passed, these also begin to figure.

The eighth Starting Position is done entirely according to the sixth, no difference arising from there being files of four.

These are those Starting Positions that serve for the *Contredances* here noted. I shall publish others when I produce another Treatise with new *Contredances*.

9

Explanation of some *Contredances*

Explanation of *Contredance* XXXVII

*C*ontredance XXXVII of determinate number, in which eight Dancers
dance, without increasing or decreasing the number of dancers or
figures, needs explanation only for the combining of steps which is done in
the third, fourth, fifth and sixth figurations, and the others are easily
understood from the explanations made in the Tables; but in order to make
things clearer, the explanation starts from the beginning and goes through
to the end.

There are eight Ladies and eight Gentlemen,[35] two placed opposite the
others, the Ladies being on the right of the Gentlemen. The *Contredance*
begins with the two firsts and the two thirds taking hands two by two,
walking forwards to meet in the centre and returning to their original
places.

The same is done by the two seconds and the two fourths in the second
figuration.

In the third, the first Gentleman and the third Lady do the sequence of
steps as follows: both do one *chassé* to the right and one *assemblé* with a
ballotté, another *assemblé*, then two *fleurets chassés* circling, giving left hands
with two *demi-coupés forwards* circling, then one *demi-chassé* with the left foot
to the left and one *jeté* with the right foot ending with an *assemblé*, and with
one *contretemps backwards* and another *assemblé* they return to their place, and
the whole path of this sequence will be done as seen marked in the figure.
The whole sequence will occupy twelve bars of Music. When these two
have finished, it will be done immediately by the second Gentleman and
the fourth Lady, as is seen marked in the fourth; in the fifth it is done by the
first Lady and the third Gentleman, and in the sixth by the fourth
Gentleman and the second Lady.

In the seventh the first Gentleman takes his Partner by the hand and they pass between the two fourths; the third Gentleman does the same passing between the two seconds.

And in the eighth, after having done the *balletto fermo* they make two Crosses,[36] the two firsts with the two fourths, the two thirds with the two seconds.

In the ninth the first Gentleman and the third each take their Partners by both hands and return to their original place.

In the tenth the sequence of steps explained in the third begins. It is then repeated four times, as in the above-mentioned 3rd, 4th, 5th and 6th, but for brevity of figures, in all the places where this said figuration enters, only one is shown, although each time it must be repeated in the same way as in those four explained.

What the two firsts and the two thirds did in the seventh figuration, is done in this eleventh by the two seconds.

And in the twelfth the two Crosses after the *balletto.*

In the thirteenth they return to their places.

In the fourteenth, the sequence of steps.

In the fifteenth the four Gentlemen, with left hands, make a Cross and their right hands are joined to the right hands of their Ladies and, without releasing hands, the right hands are passed over the head of the Man, and placed as seen in the

Sixteenth where, having done the *balletto fermo*, they do one full turn.

And in the seventeenth they undo the Cross and each one returns to his place.

The eighteenth shows the sequence of steps.

In the nineteenth they form two columns in front of the thirds as in the

Twentieth where they are seen taking hands, two by two, walking forwards and returning to the same place but facing the opposite direction.

In the twenty-first, the columns break up and they return to their places.

The twenty-second is the usual sequence.

In the twenty-third they form another two columns in front of the seconds.

They walk forwards in the twenty-fourth.

The two columns are broken up and they return to the [square] figure in the twenty-fifth.

The 26th. Sequence of steps.

The 27th. Another two columns behind the firsts.

The 28th. Walk forwards.

The 29th. The columns break up and they return to their places.

The 30th. Sequence of steps.

The 31st. Another two columns behind the fourths.

The 32nd. Walk forwards.

224

The 33rd. Breaking up of the two columns and they return to the [square] figure.

The 34th. Sequence of steps.

The 35th. *Balletto fermo, braccetti*[37] right, and full turn.

The 36th. Another *balletto fermo*, left arms and another full turn.

The 37th. Circle of eight and *balletto fermo*, which ended, the Gentlemen pass their arms over their heads without letting go of hands.

The 38th. The Gentlemen turn to the outside of the circle remaining with crossed arms; they do another *balletto fermo* and the whole circle goes round once.[38]

In the 39th. The circle is broken up and they return to the [square] figure.

In the 40th. The first Gentleman and fourth Lady, the second Lady and third Gentleman, taking hands, meet and do a *balletto fermo*; afterwards

In the 41st. These same make a chain of four and return to their places when it is completed.

The 42nd. The second Gentleman and first Lady, and the fourth Gentleman and third Lady do the same as in the 40th.

The 43rd. Another chain of four is done by these same.

The 44th. The first and fourth Gentlemen go to meet the fourth Lady and do the *balletto fermo* with her; the same is done by the second and third Gentlemen with the second Lady; they form two sets of three and go round once.

The 45th. The first and second Gentlemen go to meet the first Lady and do the *balletto*; the same is done by the fourth and third Gentlemen with the third Lady; they form the two sets of three and make another full circle.

The 46th. Chain of eight.

The 47th. The first Gentleman, first Lady and second Gentleman go one behind the other, the third Lady, third Gentleman and second Lady also one behind the other, passing in two files under the arms of the two fourths and three by three the same named stop in triangles.

The 48th. *Balletto fermo* in two sets of three, then they go round until they reach their own places and the other two make a circle on their own.

The 49th. Another passage under [the arms] of the thirds [as in figure 47].

The 50th. *Balletto* in two sets of three with the circle as above.

The 51st. Another passage under [the arms of] the seconds.

The 52nd. *Balletto* in two sets of three with the circle as at first.

The 53rd. Another passage under [the arms of] the firsts.

The 54th. *Balletto* in two sets of three with the circle as above.

The 55th and 56th. The same as the first and second, with which it ends.

This *Contredance* is a French *Rigaudon* done in a square.[39] In a ballroom, provided that it has the capacity, this same *Contredance* can be done with more squares; that is, with more than one square doing the same Dance, as is customary in the *Minuets*.

Explanation of *Contredance* XXXVIII

This *Contredance* is also for a determinate number, in which twelve always dance, six Gentlemen and six Ladies. All the Partners face each other, and the Gentlemen and Ladies alternate in two lines.

In the first figuration, taking hands six by six they meet in the centre of the dancing space and they all return again to occupy their original places.

In the second, the two Firsts and the two sixths give right hands two by two, and make one full turn.

In the third, the First Gentleman and second Lady, First Lady with the second Gentleman, sixth Gentleman with the fifth Lady, and sixth Lady with the fifth Gentleman give their left hands and make another full turn.

In the fourth, the two Firsts, taking right hands, make a half circle and the same is made by the two sixths.

In the fifth, the first Gentleman with the third Lady, first Lady with the third Gentleman, sixth Gentleman with the fourth Lady, and sixth Lady with the fourth Gentleman, taking left hands two by two, make one full circle.

In the sixth, the first Gentleman and sixth Lady, taking hands, do the *balletto*, the first Lady and sixth Gentleman doing the same; after the *balletto* they do the *Carré* and place themselves in the middle of the two lines.

In the seventh they cross three by three and afterwards they do the *balletto fermo*.

In the eighth they proceed to form a Cross, and at the end of the walk they do their *balletto fermo*.

In the ninth, having formed the Cross, they go round once.

In the tenth, the first Lady, second Gentleman, sixth Lady and third Gentleman, having done the *balletto*, form a circle of four and go round once; meanwhile the sixth Gentleman and the fourth Lady have two arms linked behind their backs and the other two hands are held in front; they do their *balletto* and they turn one full circle, as do the fourth Gentleman and fifth Lady, first Gentleman and third Lady, third Gentleman and second Lady.

In the eleventh, the first Gentleman, third Lady and second Gentleman pass into the place of the third Gentleman, fourth Lady and sixth Gentleman, and these [three] go into the place of the others, having first done the *balletto*; the second Lady, third Gentleman and first Lady, taking hands, walk forwards and return to their original places; the same is done by the fifth Lady, the fourth Gentleman and the sixth Lady.

The twelfth refers to the Tenth; as does
The thirteenth to the Eleventh.

226

In the fourteenth they go three by three into the four corners.[40]

In the fifteenth they proceed two by two in front of the third,[41] who stands still, and they all do the *balletto*.

In the sixteenth, change places.

In the seventeenth two circles go round once in opposite directions.

In the eighteenth the four in the middle break up the circle and go to place themselves in between the others of the outer circle.

In the nineteenth, change so that each finds himself in his own place.

In the twentieth, back to back.

In the twenty-first [with a turn].

These two figurations are repeated another five times each, always changing partners, first going back to back, then the *braccatto*, until they find themselves in their original places.

In the twenty-second, the two firsts with arms behind their backs pass down the middle, the others follow them and turn at the place from where the firsts began, taking their arms similarly; when the firsts arrive at the tail, they divide and pass outside, returning to the head where they begin to place themselves one behind the other, the first Lady leading, until they arrive again at the tail where, meeting, the firsts turn towards the head, taking hands as is seen.

In the twenty-third, the whole column passes underneath the arms [of the firsts], the Gentlemen go behind the first Gentleman, the Ladies behind the first Lady; each two who have passed [underneath] take hands and the others pass underneath, all doing the same. The firsts, arrived at the head, place themselves one behind the other until all form one column, as is seen.

In the twenty-fourth figure, the column divides: the Gentlemen go to the bottom and the Ladies to the top.[42]

In the twenty-fifth the outside four meet in the middle, they do the *balletto*, then the cross making half a turn, and place themselves in the middle of each line.

The 26th and 27th, they do the same.

In the 28th, the *balletto*, then the *mezzo-braccio*[43] to return to their [original] places.[44]

In the last they meet as in the first, and finish.

Explanation of *Contredance* XXXIX

Not only because in *Contredance* XXXIX there are figures which cannot be understood from the information given in the Tables but because not all the movements for every dancer are marked, which would have multiplied the figurations, and all would have been the same as the first; the first movement is shown, by which demonstration the others will be understood with the benefit of the explanation.

This *Contredance* was destined for a masquerade danced by thirty-two

Dancers divided into four Nations, either symbolising four Seasons of the Year or representing the four parts of the World, characters from which to choose as one pleases, four couples by four couples, dressed in distinctive colours, by which distinction a finer order will be observed, a more beautiful symmetry in the figurations, also allowing the liberty of selecting the colour for each character as one pleases, as long as one is totally different from the other in order to give with greatest distinction a more outstandingly beautiful effect. Here I shall give to the four divisions the distinction of Letters. The first four couples will be marked with the Letter A, and with the numbers of 1st, 2nd, 3rd and 4th couple. The second [set of four couples] with the Letter B with the division of the same numbers. The third with C. The fourth with D and the appended numbers.

Not all thirty-two will be placed in the Ballroom at the beginning but all thirty-two will enter from a room off the Ballroom eight by eight. First to enter will be the eight A's: four Men and four Ladies, taking hands two by two, who, turning on entering, divide afterwards and remain in two columns of four Men and four Ladies on the two sides of the door whence they emerged. That done, the eight B's do the same and proceed in file in front[45] of the same two columns, making eight and eight. Then come the eight C's who, after having turned, file in front of the same, making two columns of twelve each. Lastly the eight D's, who similarly turn two by two, and the Ladies in front of the other Ladies and the Men in front of the other Men form the two columns, one of sixteen Men and the other of as many Ladies, as can be seen in the second figuration. These four entrances occupy 40 bars of Music, eight bars for each entrance which, when divided, gives two for each couple. The last [couple] however require sixteen, because in order to join the column they must travel further than the others. Thus by showing only the first and by only describing the other three, drawing all four of them is omitted.

In the second figuration where, as was said, the two columns are placed, Ladies 1A and 2A leave, and their partners follow them as soon as they leave, placed side by side, as also are the Men; all four pass down the centre of the two Columns and go to line up at the head, first the Ladies and next the Men. Thus the next four do likewise and, these having arrived, gradually all follow, forming two new columns, alternately one Man and one Lady as seen in the third figuration; which, to compose this from the second [figuration] would have taken eight figurations, all of which are understood from the one.

In the third, after having done the *balletto fermo*, the Ladies take hands in twos and similarly the Men, these walking obliquely to the right and the Ladies to the left; two Men on the right of the two Ladies form lines of four and the said lines are composed of two Ladies and two Men, as

In the fourth, in which those in the middle make the Figure of Eight round those at the sides, who are doing a *balletto fermo*, and return to the same place.

In the fifth, where the two first A's meet at the head, they part and, passing midway between the two centre files, they form a column of thirty-two, each Partner being behind his Lady and following one after the other as the two first A's did.

In the sixth figure all thirty-two make a serpentine; the Lady 1A begins, she passes midway between her Partner and the Lady 2A, and thus continues to wind her way, her Partner following behind. Having been passed, the Lady 2A follows the other two. All three having passed the Man 2A, he goes behind them, and thus one after the other following until all are moving. Having finished winding their way up and the last Man having passed, who is the 4D, they serpentine their way down once more until they again reach their original places, and thus they are

In the seventh, in which the eight A's form a line to the right of the column. The eight D's in line to the left of the column. And the sixteen in the middle leave in opposite directions, the B's to the left and the C's to the right, and they remain as seen

In the eighth, where all the Men, four by four, take hands, pass behind the Ladies and line up on their left, composing a Parallelogram, squared as in the

Ninth; the eight A's and the eight D's, who are on the opposite sides of the Square, having taken hands eight by eight, meet.

In the tenth the same sixteen, having done their *balletto fermo*, form four Crosses of four by four and, after having gone round once, they divide and return to their original places.

The same is done by the other sixteen, which movement must be supposed; and as they were in the ninth, they are found in the

Eleventh, in which all thirty-two move at once, the Ladies going inside and the Men passing outside, and then they do their *balletto fermo*.

In the twelfth, the *balletto* ended, all partners take left hands and do a half turn, the Men passing inside and the Ladies going outside.

In the thirteenth, after all thirty-two have done the *balletto*, the Men, who are inside, take hands four by four and pass behind the Ladies, paying attention to the numbers and the letters to see which place they have taken in the

Fourteenth, where nothing else is done except that the four Ladies D go to occupy the place of the four A's, meanwhile these change places with them, and in the

Fifteenth the four D's [Ladies] with the four A's [Men] and the four A's [Ladies] with the four D's [Men] take hands turning two by two, and each man is placed at the right side of the Lady; the other Ladies do the same and, turning, take hands and each Lady stops at the right side of the Man, and thus another Parallelogram is formed, the four A's [Men] mixed with the four D's [Ladies], the four D's [Men] with the four A's [Ladies], the four C's [Men] with the four B's [Ladies], and the four B's [Men] with the four C's [Ladies], being one Man and one Lady as is seen

In the sixteenth, from which three circles are formed. That of the inside is composed of the four Ladies at the corners, who are 4A, 1C, 1D, and 4B. The second, that is the middle one, is formed by the four male Partners of the Ladies who formed the small circle from the corners, with another eight Ladies, distributing two for every Man, and these twelve proceed after the four Ladies who formed the inner circle; and the other sixteen compose the outer circle; who these people are, and what their place is, can be observed from the numbers and from the letters; they do their *balletto fermo* and then as

Is observed in the seventeenth, the three [circles] turn in contrary motion, the middle one to the right and the other two to the left,[46] and all three go round once.

In the eighteenth, the three circles are broken up, and each person returns to his place, all thirty-two forming a circle, as is seen

In the nineteenth, where turning just a little until the 1A finds himself in the place where he began, they do their *balletto*, and afterwards four Men, who are 1A, 4C, 4D and 1B, come out of the circle and move backwards and the others move in towards each other, making another circle, as

In the twentieth figure. After having done the *balletto*, four Ladies come out of the circle, moving backwards, and stop in front of the four Men, who were the first to come out. To avoid drawing this figure another six times, I will say that they come out four at a time, and that those remaining always close in to do their *balletto*; and I give as a rule that all those who are to the right of 1A [Man] up to 4C [Man] follow the first [1A], assembling one at a time. Thus do those to the right of 4C up to 4D and [those to the right] of the other two Men to form

The twenty-first [figuration], in which all the Men remain still and only the Ladies move. All the four A's take the place of the four C's. These go into the place of the four D's who take the place of the four B's and these take the place of the four A's.

In the twenty-second all the Men go to meet their own partners.

In the twenty-third, sixteen, four from each side of the Cross, move to form a circle, the other sixteen remaining still in the middle of the said circle in the form of a Cross and, linking hands, they form a circle and a Cross, as

In the twenty-fourth, where they begin to go round and do one full turn.

In the twenty-fifth, the sixteen who formed the circle divide four by four, processing into the middle of the spaces of the Cross, and as

In the twenty-sixth figure they form a six-pointed star[47] which continually goes round, unwinding little by little as two people at a time drop out and, placing themselves one behind the other, they circle around the Cross. To illustrate the whole of this unwinding of the Cross would require sixteen figurations of which I demonstrate only two. The explanation and example of those two helps to understand the unwinding, thus I shall place in order all the persons who come out one after the other; and observe that from where the firsts left, those who are to follow must also leave. First couple 3A leave, and they turn as much as they have to.

In the twenty-seventh, couple 2C separate, having reached the same place where the 3A's separated, then are followed by couple 2D, then couple 3B, then couple 2A, then couple 3C, then couple 3D, then couple 2B, then couple 4A, then couple 1C, then couple 1D, then couple 4B, then couple 1A, then couple 4C, then couple 4D, then couple 1B and they arrive at

The twenty-eighth figure, from which all the eight A's, who found themselves on the four opposite sides of the circle, leave and meet in the centre where they do their *balletto*, and then as

In the twenty-ninth all set out in one direction, the firsts preceding, followed by the seconds, then the thirds and finally the fourths and all leaving the circle dividing, the Ladies on one side and the Men on the other; while these eight are leaving the circle, the eight B's meet and do their *balletto*.

In the thirtieth the first eight are seen to divide, the Men to one side with hat in hand, the Ladies to the other on the outside of the circle, taking leave of one another; the eight B's, who leave the circle and divide up as did the first [eight], follow them, and the eight C's who enter will similarly go out and do the same, thus lastly the eight D's will do this and thus

The thirty-first and last figure; they retire and go through the same door by which they entered, all raising their Hats and saluting the whole Assembly, with which the *Contredance* will close.

LAST CHAPTER

The *Charamente*,[48] the *Amabile*

This Dance, which was so much in use and so prized by the Ancients and was reputed to be one of the most beautiful Ballroom dances, is today seen to have fallen so much into disuse, that there is not one worth talking about; but because I have always held it in the high esteem that such a beautiful Dance merits, I have co-operated in its revival, and because our century is scornful of all that smacks of the Museum, whatever it may be, and has no other love than that of novelty, therefore I have wished to show this ancient and worthy Dance in a new aspect; and thanks to my continual reflection on the subject, I have modified it to a better form, I have filled it with new steps, I have provided it with other Music and have guided it in another direction. In short, it is so new in every way that it is ancient only in name.

For better understanding, I have made a Table in which all the figures of the said *Amabile* are shown and I have transcribed here below which and how many steps comprise each figuration.

I could have noted all the steps in *Chirografia*,[49] but since this would have entailed an endless number of figures, and because I have addressed the Treatise on these Dances to those who know what dancing is, therefore, when speaking of a *pas grave* I presume they know how to do it.

The Beginning of the Table is at the bottom [of the page] because I wanted to draw it just as it is used in a ballroom, so that whoever wishes to study it his own, places the said Table with the beginning towards the chest and traces the path as is noted in this. Before beginning any step, make a brief pause so that, on placing the foot, it falls right on the beat.

§1

In placing themselves, the Man and the Lady must keep a distance of two arms between them and be turned towards each other a little in an oblique line. The position will be the Fourth; the Man will have the right foot in front and the Lady the left. It is to be noted that the Lady does almost all the steps with the opposite foot from that of the Man; therefore it may be supposed that, in the course of the explanation, when speaking about the foot with which the Man does the steps, at the same time I intend that the Lady does them with the opposite foot and therefore I shall not speak of her. I said *almost all* because some steps are done by both with the same foot and in such a case I will give particular notice, saying *both with the foot*, e.g. *the right*. With the *ritornello* of the Music, the two usual *révérences* of the *Minuet* will be done; the second ended, a *coupé forwards* will be done returning to the same place;[50] the *Amabile* begins with a *pas grave forwards*, which is done with the right foot, and with the same foot a *bourrée forwards* is done, and two other *pas grave sur place* immediately follow, the first with the left and the second with the right. These steps will be done in the time of four bars and they compose the whole of the first figuration of the first part. Then with the left foot, which is behind, a *saraband step* is done to the left side; this will occupy only one bar of Music and the Dancers will follow the path marked in the second figuration. An *open pas de bourrée forwards* follows this, with which the third figuration will be taken in the time of another bar. With another two bars a *pas de bourrée under and over* will be done, begun with the right foot, and a *pas grave* with the same right, and with these the fourth figuration will be described and will complete the first part of the Music, which will be repeated once more. The Dancers, on the same Repeat of the first Part of the Music, will follow the fifth figuration which is composed of three *demi-jetés*, the first of which will be done *forwards* with the right, the second *backwards* with the left, and the third like the first; and with the left foot, which is behind, a *saraband step* will be done to the same side and all this will be done within the time of two bars of Music. The sixth figuration is taken with two *demi-pirouettes sur place* which will occupy two bars of Music. Again another three *demi-jetés* are done, but the first and the third with the left foot, and the second with the right, completely opposite to those three aforesaid, and with another *saraband step* to the right side taking another two bars of Music, the seventh figuration will be described; and with the repeat of the two *pirouettes* turned to the right side, another two bars will be filled, and with these is completed the eighth and last figuration of the first part, with which this closes.

§2

The second part begins with both doing two *beaten coupés* with the same foot to the left side and, because they do it facing each other, they will travel in opposite directions; then they will do two *pas de bourrée forwards* travelling in a curved line and, with all of the said four steps, the first figuration of the second part will be taken, occupying four bars of Music. The two dancers will remain side by side and, in order to look at each other, they will turn their heads one to face the other. From here will be done first a *balancé*[51] *forwards* by both with the left, and another *balancé backwards*, both with the other foot; the second figuration will be formed with the *balancé* and will take two bars of Music. The third figuration will be formed by two *coupés*, both doing the first with the left, ending with some beats, the other by both with the right, also ending with some beats, and that will fill two bars, in which the Music of the second part will end and then again be repeated; but the two Dancers continue the fourth figuration with one *chassé sideways* to the left, so that in one bar of Music they come to meet in the centre of the dance floor facing each other. From here one sideways *pas de bourrée under* will be done, turning the body, both to the right, which will make a quarter turn; and with the front foot, which will be the right, another *bourrée forwards* will be done, completing the half circle, and with these steps and two bars of Music, the fifth figuration will be taken. There follows one *saraband step* with another quarter of a turn, and both with the left foot to the left, which will be done in the time of one bar of Music and equals the sixth figuration. After this, one *turning pas de bourrée forwards* is done, both with the left foot to the left with three-quarters of a turn, and with a *coupé disfatto* turning another quarter, still to the left, occupying two bars, the seventh figuration is formed. Then a *fleuret sostenuto*[52] is done by both with the right and a *demi-contretemps* with the left foot, the *fleuret sostenuto* is repeated with the other foot and another *demi-contretemps* with the opposite foot; these steps will fill two bars of Music with which the second part ends.[53]

§3

At the beginning of the third part, the Dancers meet in the centre of the dance floor, staying right side to right, then each does one *pirouette* with the right leg, turning the body three-quarters to the left, in the time of only one bar and that demonstrates the first figuration of the third part. Then in another bar one *coupé forwards* is done, ending with the beats, which equals the second figuration. The third is another *pirouette* done by both with the left foot, turning one full circle to the right in another bar of Music. Doing another *coupé backwards*, at the end of which some beats will be done, another bar of music is filled and the fourth figuration is formed. The fifth is primarily composed of one *demi-coupé sideways* then a *tombé* to the left, to which is joined a *sideways pas de bourrée over* with the right foot and one *pas grave sur place*; all these steps take the time of four bars, where the Music of the third part terminates and returns to the beginning, and the Dancers will continue to form the sixth figuration, which is called the *Chiamata*.[54] Two bars of Music are used for this. The Man in the said figuration does a *demi-chassé beaten on the instep* with the left foot, then a *dégagé* with which the right foot is carried in front, which serves to take another *demi-chassé beaten on the instep* with the same right, after which one beat with the left is done and another with the right. In this sequence of steps I have indicated that the Lady does a *bourrée over and under* first with the right foot and then with the left; but these [steps] for the Lady remain arbitrary whether she does them or does others according to the talent of whoever dances and what will be freer and more brilliant in the said two bars of Music. In the seventh figuration the Lady will do all that has been described for the Man, also in two bars of Music, and the Man will do either what I described for the Lady or other steps to his liking.[55] Then they will do two *pas de bourrée forwards* but travelling in a curved line, almost circular; the first step will be done with the left, the second with the right, and then one *pas grave* with the left, and with these in the time of four bars, the eighth figuration will be done, the last in this third part, with which this ends.

§4

At the beginning of the fourth Part the two Dancers, who are found right side to right, taking right hands, do two *glissades* to the left side of the Lady and the right of the Man, then a *dégagé* carrying the foot to second, from which a *chassé* is taken in two bars of Music and the first figuration of the fourth Part will be formed. One *pas grave forwards* and a *beaten demi-chassé turning* will then be done, the Man to the right, the Lady to the left, after which the left foot is detached in front, thus forming the second figuration in another two bars of Music. The third is done with the same steps as the first, but in the opposite direction taking left hands; the *glissades* will be done to the Man's right side and the Lady's left and, after the *dégagé*, the *chassé* is done to the same sides in the time of two bars. The fourth figuration is formed with another *pas grave forwards* and another *beaten demi-chassé turning* to the same sides as the second in another two bars of Music, which completes the fourth part, the Music of which is repeated. The dancers continue to do the fifth figuration with two *pas de bourrée forwards* travelling in an almost circular line; the first step will be done with the right and the other with the left; these two steps will take two bars of Music and the Dancers will remain in an oblique line; as in the sixth figuration, they will travel along the Diagonal doing one *contretemps forwards*, both with the left, then a *demi-chassé beaten on the instep* done by both with the right foot, and it ends with a *dégagé* done with the left foot, both meeting side by side closer as seen, and these will be done in two bars of Music. The seventh figuration is formed by two *coupés*, both starting with the left foot; each *coupé* will be ended with beats and they will end in second position, which serves to cover ground, and they travel in an oblique line as observed in the said figuration; each *coupé* occupies one bar of Music so that the figuration consists of two bars. Then with the two *pas de bourrée forwards* circling to the right, the Man will be followed by the Lady and they will find themselves in the first situation where they were placed at the beginning.[56] These two steps will take another two bars and with these the tune and the Dance of the *Amabile* will end, to which, without another *révérence*, a *Minuet* is joined, which begins with the *forward step* and will be done at *andante* tempo.

THE END

Warning

I would advise the charitable Reader that for this once he might condone any printing and spelling errors, since lack of time has prevented me from revising the above-mentioned mistakes caused by the Copyist or by the Printer; but I promise that the second Edition will be better corrected, and enlarged, many times more worthy of your kindness than this first one will be.

Notes

Introduction

[1] The term 'Char' applies to a chariot, or car, surrounded by a mobile cloud decoration, also known as the 'Gloire'. This was used for the appearance of the deities from the Heavenly regions.

Part I

[1]   Magri frequently refers to the human body as a machine.

[2]   Those bitten by the tarantula spider.

[3]   Literally, danced pantomime.

[4]   Old-style castanets.

[5]   The Warning to the Courteous Reader seems to have been inserted some time after the original manuscript was sent to the printers, with the result that some page numbers in the 1779 edition overlap.

[6]   Academia della Crusca Firenze was the institution which monitored the purity of the Italian language.

[7]   *Il Galateo* was the title of a manual on politeness published during the first half of the 18th century by Giovanni della Casa, a Florentine by birth.

[8]   Antonio Planelli (1747-1803), author of the treatise *Dell'opera in musica* published in 1772.

9 Magri has slightly misunderstood Noverre here. Noverre wishes the Dancing Master to study Anatomy *not* to be able to depict skeletons but to understand the skeletal structure.

10 By inclining, Magri does not necessarily mean bending the body sideways but moving the body weight onto the supporting foot (the foot which is on the ground).

11 Cadence in dancing refers to fitting the dance phrases to the musical phrases, timing the step according to the music.

12 In the baroque interpretation of Classical Mythology, the furies were the creatures who inhabited the Underworld.

13 A slow *entrée*. The term *entrée* is applied to any dance piece within a ballet.

14 In a sharp, detached manner.

15 *Groteschi* (plural of *grotesco*) who specialised in jumping.

16 A country dance of German origin.

17 Here Magri is stating that the musical metre of the *Chaconne* is constant although the mood is always changing.

18 A *Sospiro* equals a Crotchet rest or the same time value as a Crotchet.

19 In saying that six-eight time is one third slower than Medium time, Magri is making the important point that in the transition typically from duple to triple time, the duration of the beat remains constant, in this case making the bar one third longer. However, his attempt to provide further examples leads to some discrepancy for which it is difficult to account.

20 Two-two time.

21 Magri omits a description of third position here, although he describes it while talking about the false third position.

22 The term used in the text is *andante caminato*, for which 'stepping at a moderate pace' was deemed the most suitable translation.

23 By rising, Magri is referring to the action of straightening the knees. However, rising can also refer to the action of rising onto the balls of the feet (see Ch. 5).

24 Again, the term *Sospiro* is used, equalling a Crotchet rest.

25 *Intercadenza* refers to a syncopated rhythm.

26 Literally, 'low [beat] with a bend'.

27 Literally, 'extended beat', meaning a beat with the working leg straight.

28 Literally, 'high detached'.

29 A corruption of the French *tour de jambe* or *rond de jambe*, meaning 'circling of the leg'.

240

30   *Ballo grave* would be the style performed by the *ballerini seri*. In other words, the serious or noble dance.

31   The word in the Italian text is *su*, which translates as 'on'. This would make the step impossible to perform. Therefore, it is assumed that Magri is using the colloquial meaning of *su*, which is the command 'Lift!'. The command 'turn' in this paragraph refers to the feet which are turned inwards and outwards on the ball of the foot.

32   Facing diagonally to the audience would give a feeling of perspective, hence the art term for this – foreshortened.

33   The noble dance danced by *ballerini seri*.

34   The heroic and *gravi* belong to the *serio* or noble style of dance.

35   Louis XIV.

36   Without moving off the spot.

37   A corruption of *temps d'hanche*, movement of the hips.

38   In Italian, *caduto piegando*, which literally means 'a fall bending'. Therefore, there should be a slight feeling of falling into the *plié* as the feet slide to second position.

39   Literally, 'failed'. In this case, it corresponds to the French *failli*, 'not quite' a step.

40   This explanation seems confused: the second foot will move to its own side, not the opposite as Magri says.

41   A corruption of the French *croisé*, 'crossed'.

42   Demonstration proved that the foot would be carried to third in front, not behind, as described in the next paragraph.

43   The left foot lowers immediately the right is detached.

44   All these steps are explained later in the text.

45   *Groteschi* specialising in jumps.

46   In practice it is highly unlikely that the foot would close behind in fifth. More probably, it is thrown to second as you turn, then the other foot closes behind as you turn another quarter.

47   In practice it seems likely that the first foot is thrown to fourth position on a quarter turn, then the other foot can close in fifth in front or behind, making another quarter turn.

48   A corruption of the French *emboîté*, 'fitted together'.

49   Without the *assemblés*.

50   In Italian, *incerta*, which literally means 'undecided'.

51 Magri has neglected to mention the last movement, the walk.

52 In practice it was found that this step cannot begin with the front foot.

53 The right foot cuts in front of the left, which is simultaneously snatched up to touch the calf of the right.

54 This refers to the *ballonné*.

55 Spring on the right foot, the left foot being raised in the air.

56 The direction 'taken also with the left' refers to the foot in the air, not the foot doing the little spring.

57 The *Chaconne* was popular as an ensemble dance for the finale of an opera or ballet at this time.

58 The North Wind.

59 See page 150 for Magri's explanation.

60 Opening *tableaux* of a dance.

61 A corruption of the French *flic flac*, meaning 'a crack of the whip'.

62 The same as *sbalzato*, meaning 'impetuously', 'with dash'.

63 Here Magri is using the term *in contratempo* to mean 'sudden' or 'unexpected'.

64 People to the north of the Alps.

65 Masked.

66 In Neapolitan Commedia dell'Arte, *Coviello* was the servant and companion of *Pulcinella*.

67 A Neapolitan expression meaning 'fast and detached'.

68 A theatrical expression meaning he does not attempt tragic roles, buskins being the footwear worn by Tragedians.

69 Halfway between low and high, approximately waist level.

70 Each hand faces its own shoulder.

71 Literally, 'vein cutting'.

72 This seems to be a misprint for tragic, although there was a *serio-comic* genre of opera at this time.

73 This refers to the action of the legs, each cut being an opening or closing movement.

74 It should be remembered that this paragraph is an explanation on how to count the cuts only. In the interwoven *caprioles*, both legs move equally during the jump. The Italian term for interwoven is *intrecciato*, which was corrupted by the French into *entrechat*.

75 Meaning 'with the legs drawn up under the body'.

⁷⁶ In practice it will be seen that you do not jump 'on the back foot'. You jump off the front foot while thrusting the back foot forward.

⁷⁷ *le sue passate*, literally meaning 'its passings', the legs passing each other in the air to form the cuts of the *capriole*.

⁷⁸ The supporting leg remains straight under the body, while the working leg opens to second in the air and always closes in the same place, i.e. in front or behind.

⁷⁹ With stretched knees.

⁸⁰ With bent knees. In other words, with both legs in *retiré* position.

⁸¹ The closest proper Italian word to this is *ranocchio*, meaning 'a frog'. Thus it would appear to mean in a frog-like manner, i.e. with the legs drawn up under the body.

⁸² From the Italian *gorgo* meaning 'a whirlpool', as in the French *gargouillade*.

⁸³ Literally, 'an overturned *tordichamp*'.

⁸⁴ In today's dance terminology, *terre à terre*.

⁸⁵ Literally, 'a lock of wool'.

⁸⁶ An overturned jump. In today's dance terminology, a *revoltade*.

⁸⁷ Literally, a 'country sweeper'. The nearest English equivalent would be a plough.

⁸⁸ A jump making a full turn in the air. In today's dance terminology, a *tour en l'air*.

⁸⁹ A 'dry' *salto tondo to the side*. In other words, the jump has little preparation.

⁹⁰ *Salto tondo with a bound.*

⁹¹ Literally, 'a little pistol'.

⁹² Pigeon wings.

⁹³ Young cockerels.

⁹⁴ The 'jump of the hanged'.

⁹⁵ The 'dead jump'.

⁹⁶ Scissors.

⁹⁷ Basque jump.

⁹⁸ Jumping as you raise the foot.

243

Part II

1 In practice it was found that the right foot joins the left in first, with a slight turn happening on the ball of the left foot so that the couple are face to face for the second *révérence*.

2 Magri has neglected to mention that both knees bend during this movement, which is the first movement of the *pas de bourrée*, although he mentions at the end of §6 that the *bourrée* begins from the second *plié*.

3 They look away from each other to acknowledge the spectators.

4 The lady must make three-quarters of a circle.

5 This could mean another repeat of the figure or another arm movement.

6 Anti-clockwise.

7 No *épaulement*, or shading.

8 This appears to be a contradiction of his previous statement to be found in §10 of this chapter, to which the reader is referred.

9 This section lacks a heading at the beginning of Chapter 2.

10 *Piazze*, i.e. dancing spaces. The dance floor was divided into 'areas' in which each couple or set danced.

11 Referring to the number of people attending.

12 This is the first instance where Magri uses the word *figure* to mean a couple. Hereafter they are generally referred to by number, the firsts being the first couple, the seconds being the second couple and so on.

13 All couples face the Orchestra.

14 *Concertino* – the leader or violinist.

15 Magri does not offer a full explanation of the *balletto fermo* but it seems to be a step or a little sequence of steps done on the spot.

16 *Vuoto* – the unaccented part of the bar, or 'off the beat'.

17 'Slave step'.

18 Festival directors from the ranks of the Nobility.

19 An evening party.

20 In this explanatory chapter, the term figure applies to the drawing or plate.

21 On the plate for the third figure of *Contredance* VI, the seconds have been wrongly identified as thirds and vice versa.

22 Here the term figure refers to the individual sign for the dancer.

23 This refers to Figure 6 of Table I in which the dancer is directed to move

244

forwards and not to Figure 8 in which he is directed to move forwards then return to his original place.

24 Magri is here referring to the couple as they appear on the plan. They move from facing north–south to facing east–west.

25 They hold hands behind the Man's back.

26 A turn in the manner of a windmill.

27 The giving of left hands is shown in Figure 20.

28 The plate has been printed sideways.

29 They turn in towards each other.

30 This is a misprint. The first Lady goes round the third Lady, stopping at her left side.

31 This should read second Man.

32 This is the first instance where Magri uses the term figure to refer to individual dancers.

33 The plan shows the Ladies passing *between* the two Men who do the *balletto fermo*.

34 This is the first instance where Magri uses the term figure as a verb, meaning 'to perform the figuration'.

35 According to the plan, there are only four Ladies and four Gentlemen.

36 According to the plan, the Crosses go round once clockwise, i.e. they make a full turn.

37 The term *braccetti* implies that the partners link arms in some way.

38 The term 'goes round once' means that the circle makes a full revolution so that each person ends on the same spot whence he began to move.

39 A set of four couples. In Italian, *a quadriglia*.

40 Magri actually says they go to the sides but the plan shows that they go into the corners.

41 As seen on the plan, the two side dancers move in front of the dancer in the middle; the same happens in each corner.

42 By bottom and top, Magri is referring to the written plan. The Ladies move to their right and the Gentlemen to their left.

43 This could mean taking hands instead of arms as the signs for the arms do not quite contact each other.

44 Some couples will make half a turn, others a whole turn, as shown on the plan.

45 Although from the point of view of the 'presence', or Orchestra, the second set line up one after the other in front of the first set, they are actually behind the first set, all facing away from the Orchestra to the foot of the room.

46   The inner and outer circles turn clockwise and the middle circle anti-clockwise.

47   The plan shows an eight-pointed star.

48   This is probably a mis-spelling of the French *La Charmante*.

49   *Chirografia* – an Italian corruption of the French *Chorégraphie*.

50   Their original places.

51   In the text, this word is given as *balangè* but it seems highly likely that it is a misprint for *balancé*; therefore a *balancé* was performed when reconstructing the dance.

52   There is no description of this type of *fleuret* in Part I but a slow (sustained) *fleuret* does fit the dance at this point.

53   Magri has neglected to mention that these steps form the eighth figuration of the second part.

54   Literally, 'calling'. A more appropriate translation might be 'The Address'.

55   The plates for the sixth and seventh figurations have been printed in reverse.

56   Magri has neglected to mention that these steps form the eighth figuration of the fourth part.

Plates

In the original edition the contredances plates are printed as oversize folding-out pages. For this edition they have each been reduced in size to fit on to a single page.

TAUOLA I.

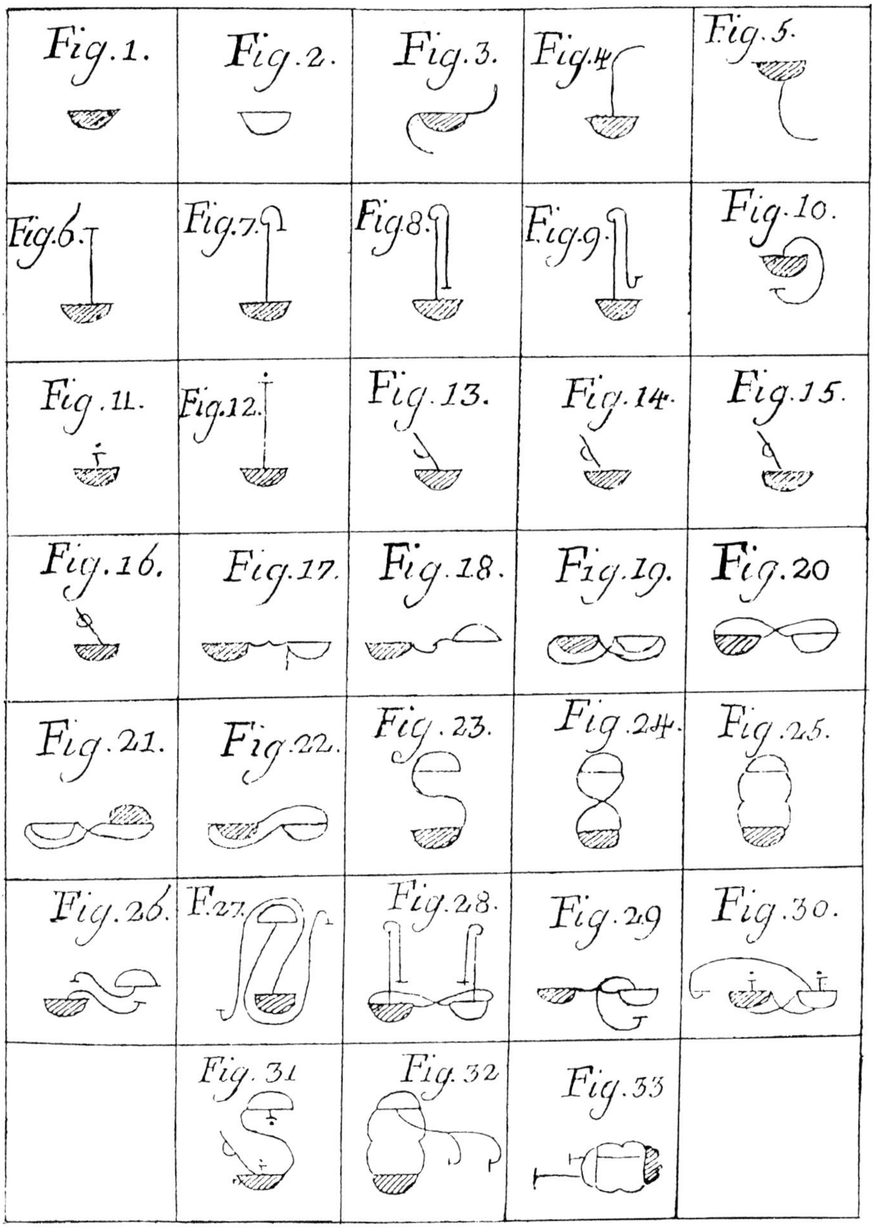

Plate 1

TAUOLA II.

Fig. 1.	*Fig. 2.*	*Fig. 3.*	*Fig. 4.*
Fig. 5.	*Fig. 6.*	*Fig. 7.*	*Fig. 8.*
Fig. 9.	*Fig. 10.*	*Fig. 11.*	*Fig. 12.*
Fig. 13.	*Fig. 14.*	*Fig. 15.*	*Fig. 16.*
Fig. 17.	*Fig. 18.*	*Fig. 19.*	*Fig. 20.*

Plate 2

TAUOLA III.

Fig. 1.   Fig. 2.   Fig. 3.   Fig. 4.   Fig. 5.

Fig. 6.   Fig. 7.   Fig. 8.   Fig. 9.   Fig. 10.

F. 11.   Fig. 12.   Fig. 13.   Fig. 14   F. 15.

F. 16.   Fig. 17.   Fig. 18.   Fig. 19.   F. 20.

Fig. 21.   Fig. 22.   Fig. 13.   Fig. 24.   Fig. 25.

Fig. 26.   26.   26.   26.   26.

Fig. 27.   F. 28.   F. 29.   Fig. 30   Fig. 31.

Plate 3

TAUOLA IV.

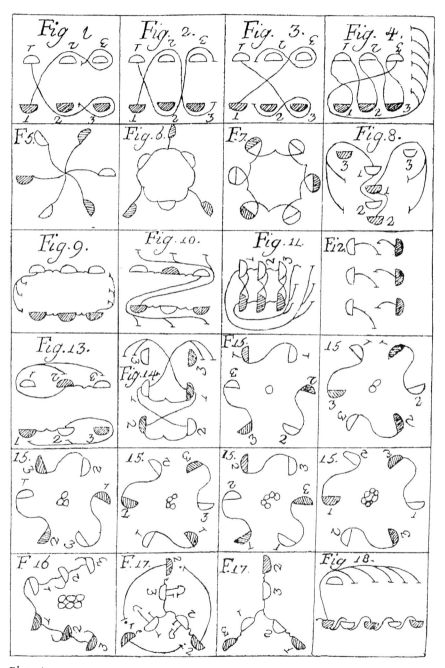

Plate 4

TAUOLA V.

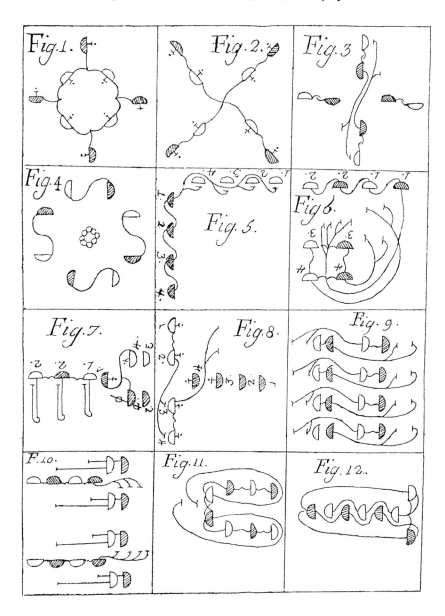

Plate 5

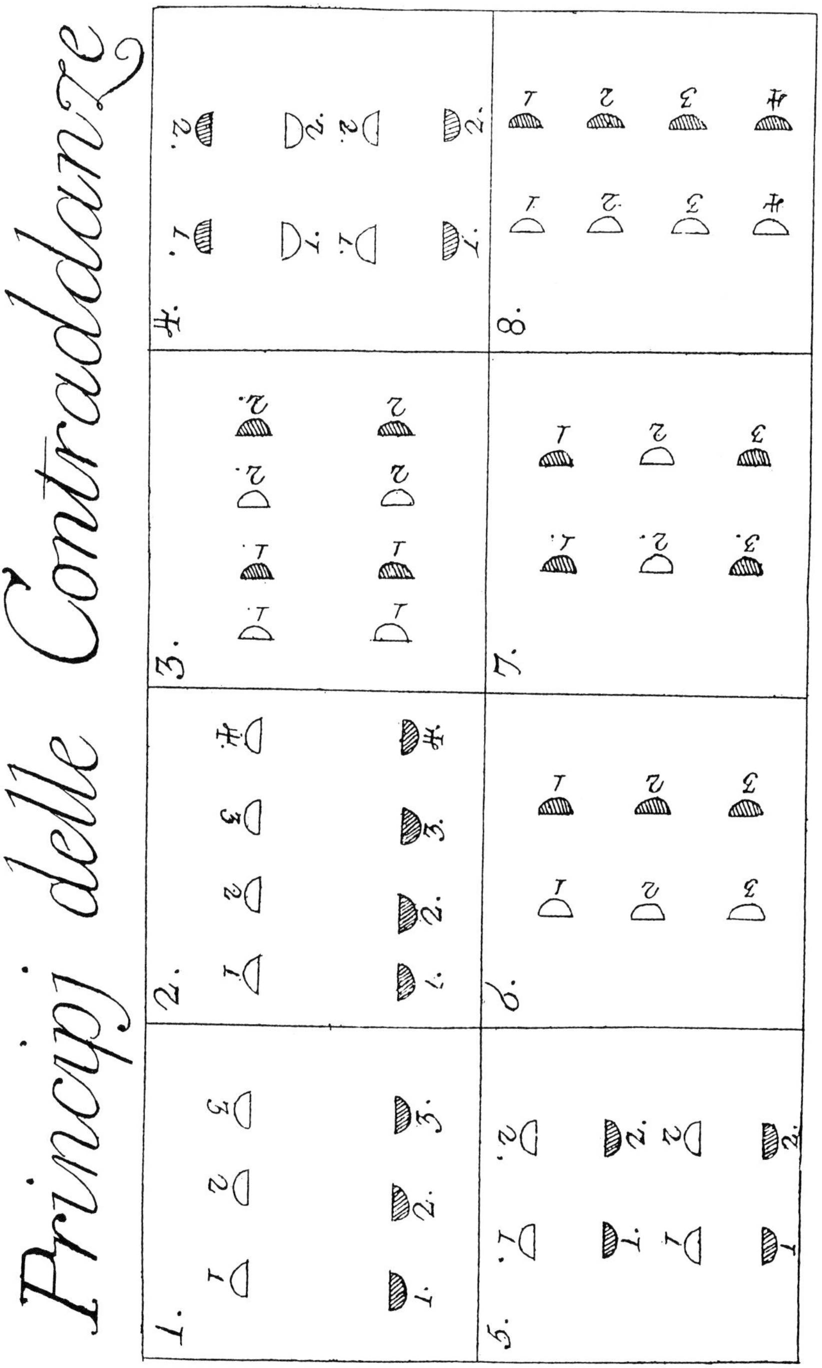
Principj delle Contraddanze
1.
2.
3.
4.
5.
6.
7.
8.

Plate 6

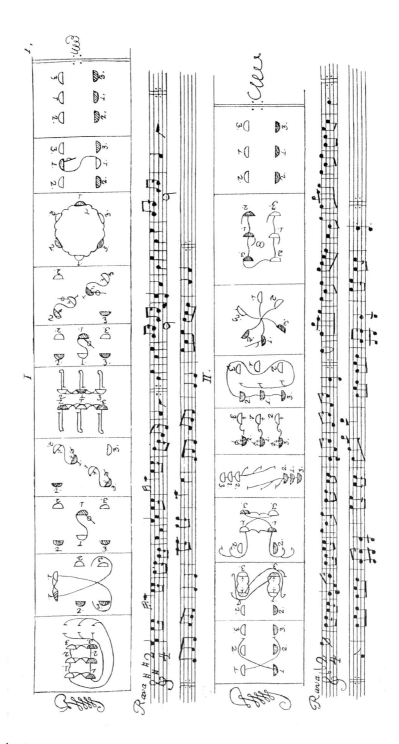

Folio 1

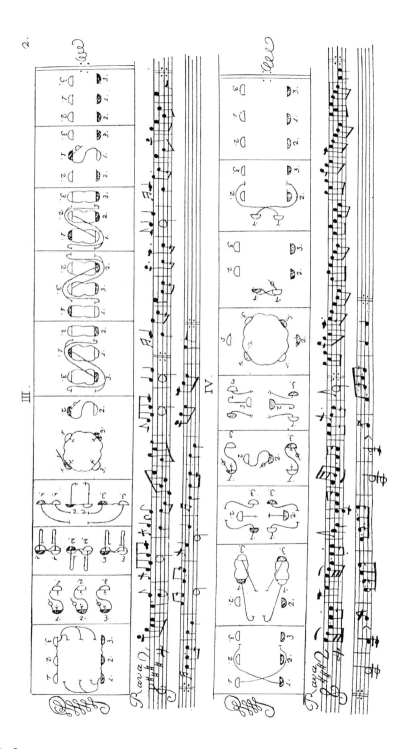

Folio 2

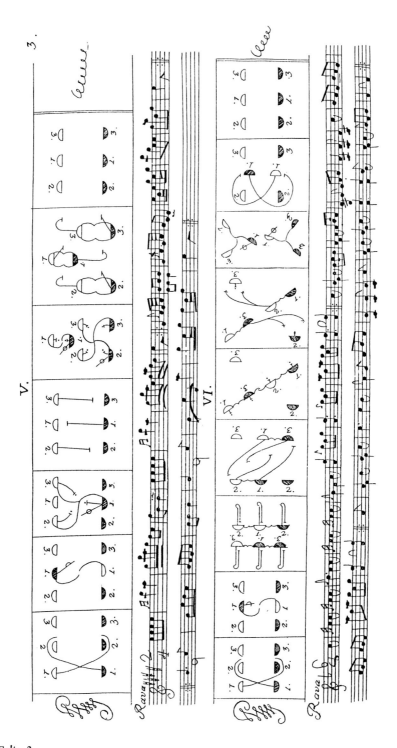

Folio 3

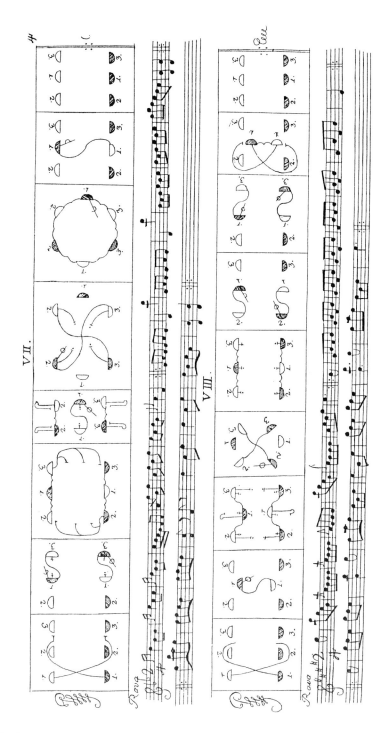

Folio 4

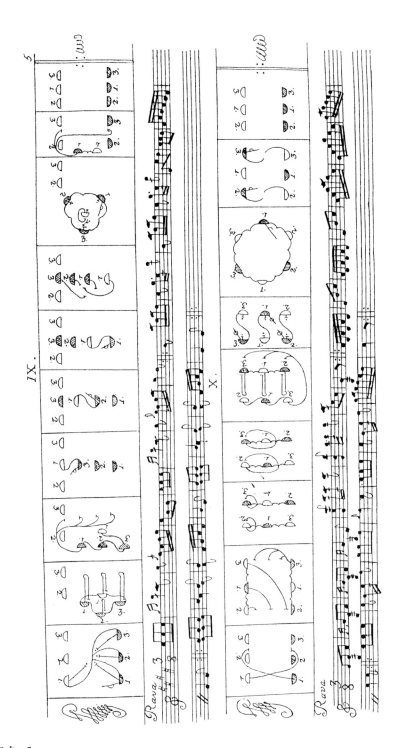

Folio 5

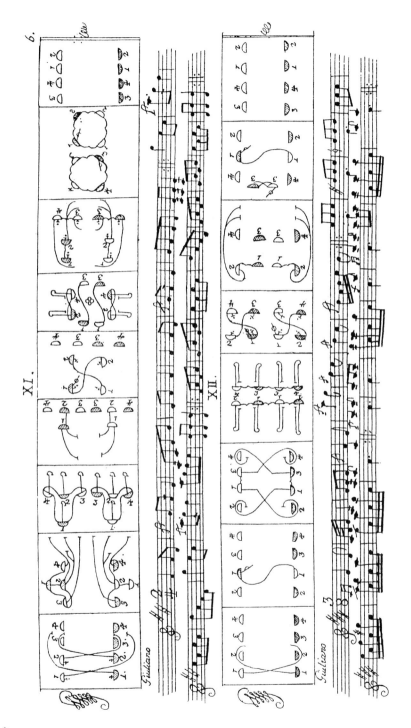

Folio 6

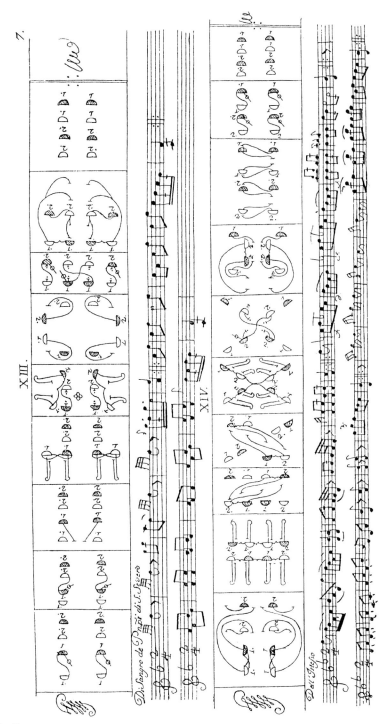

Folio 7

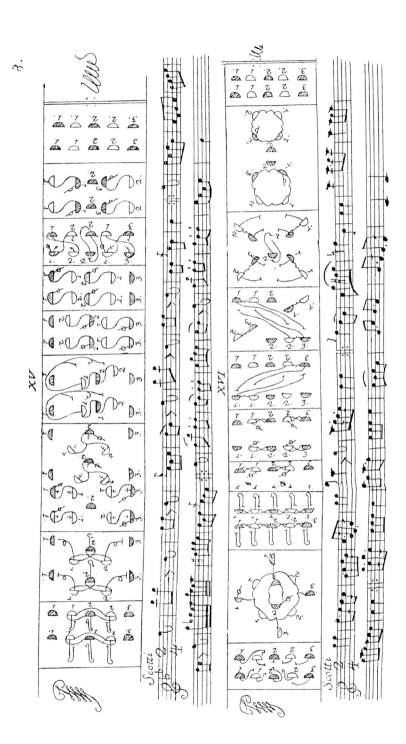

Folio 8

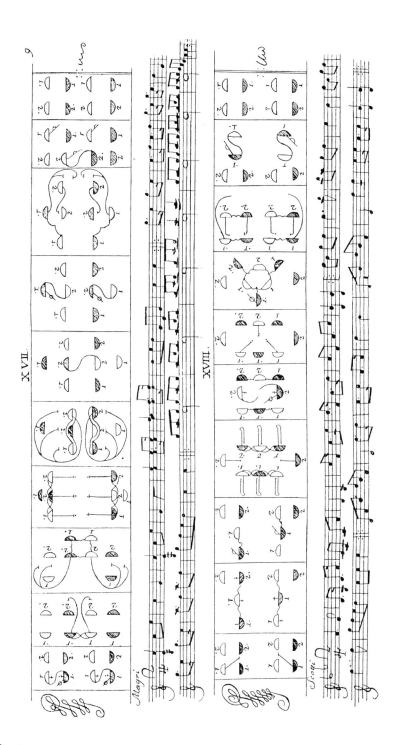

Folio 9

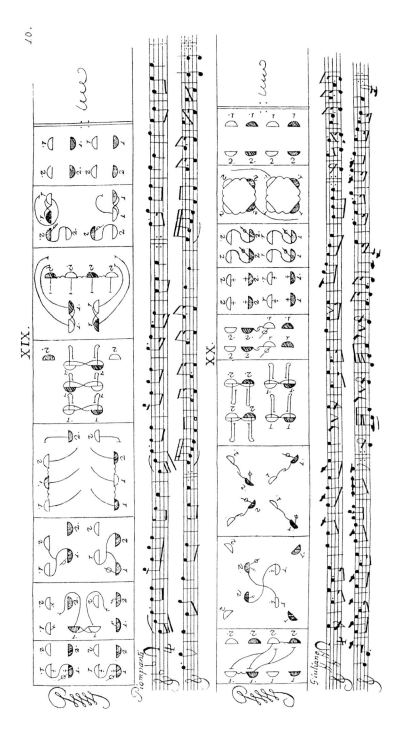

Folio 10

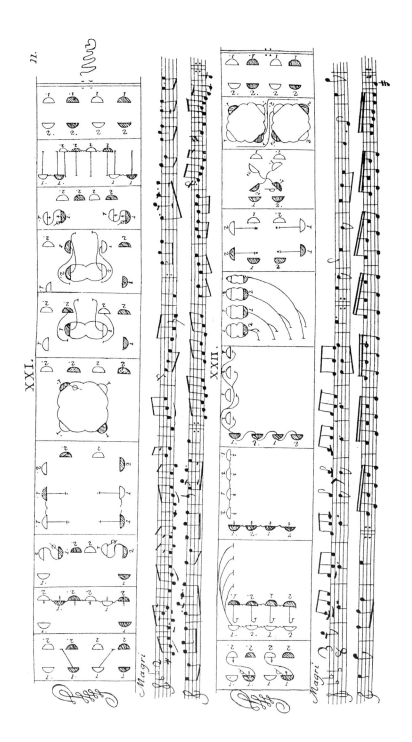

Folio 11

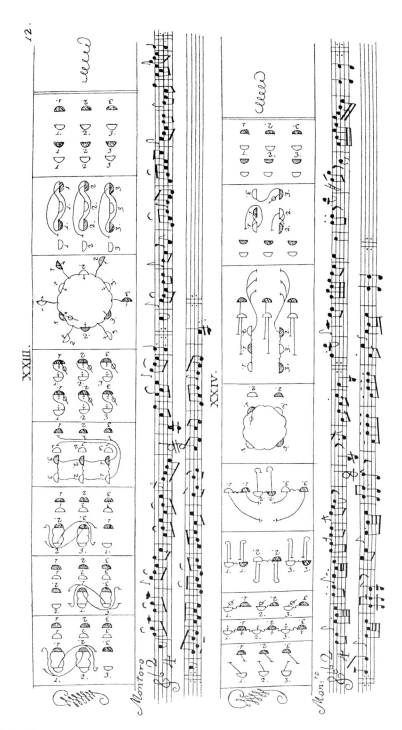

Folio 12

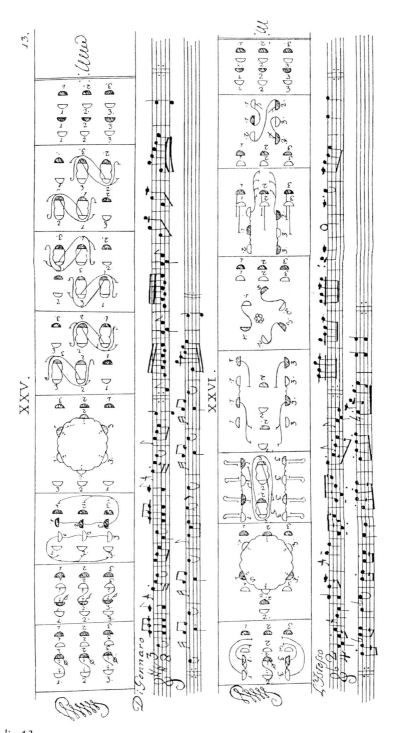

Folio 13

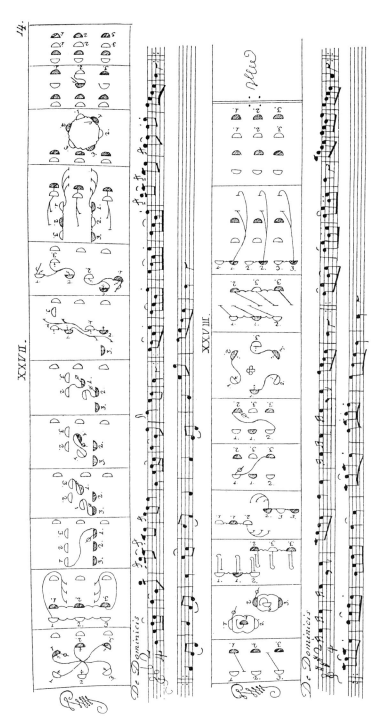

Folio 14

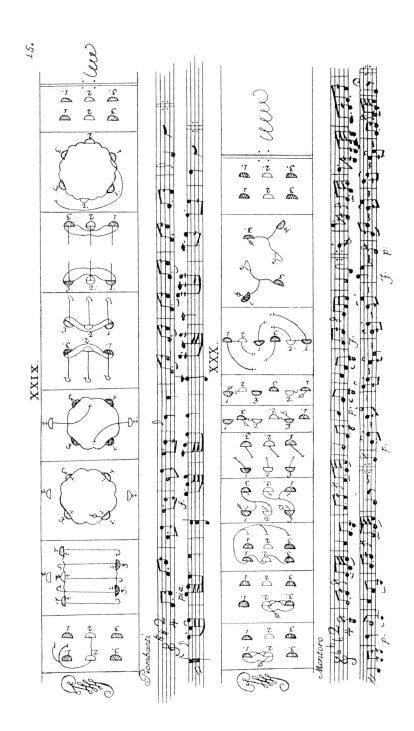

Folio 15

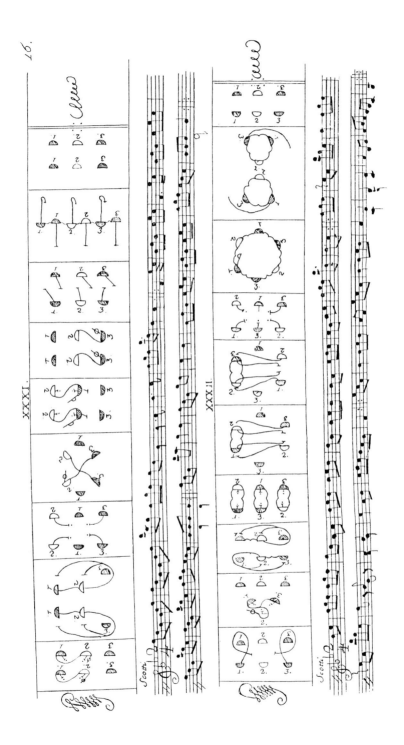

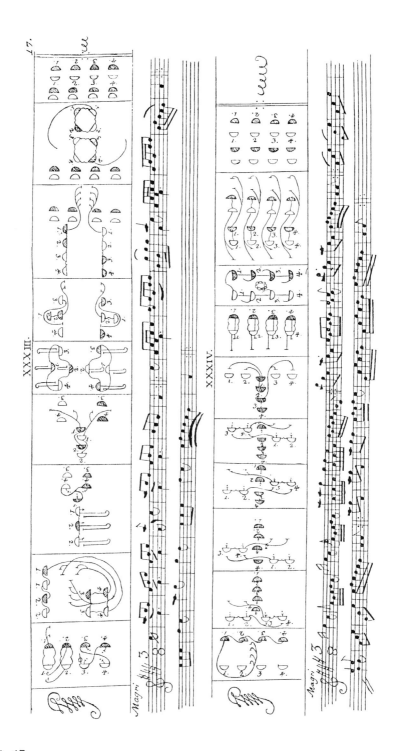

Folio 17

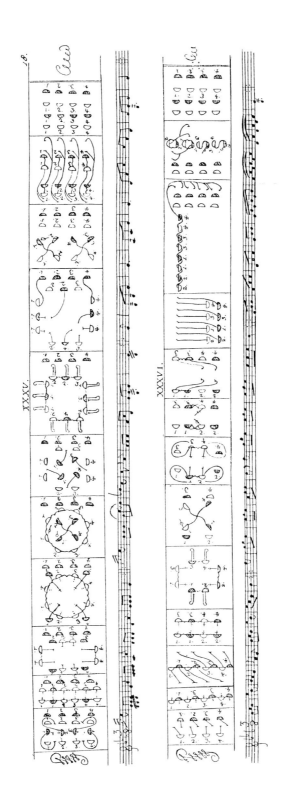

Folio 18

XXXVII

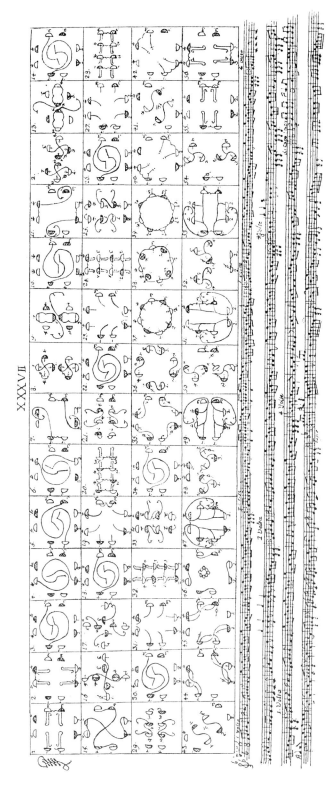

Folio 19

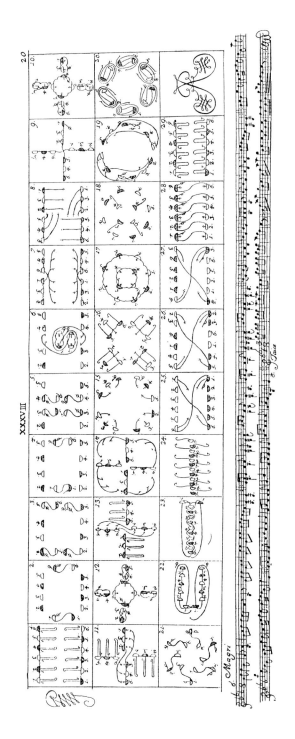

Folio 20

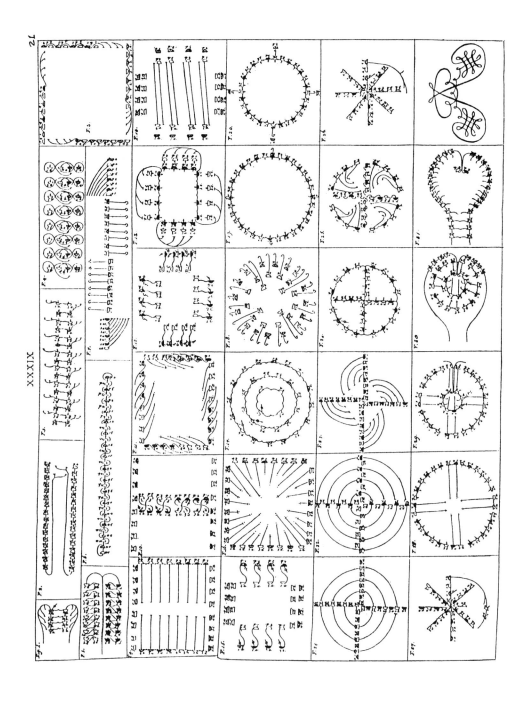

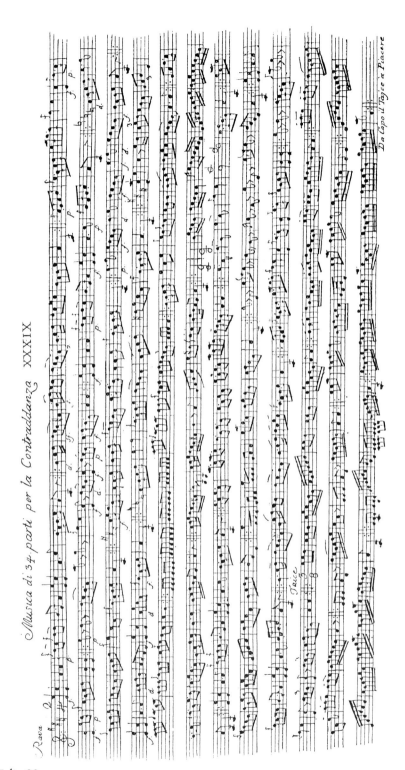

Musica di 34 parti per la Contraddanza XXXIX

Rava

Folio 22

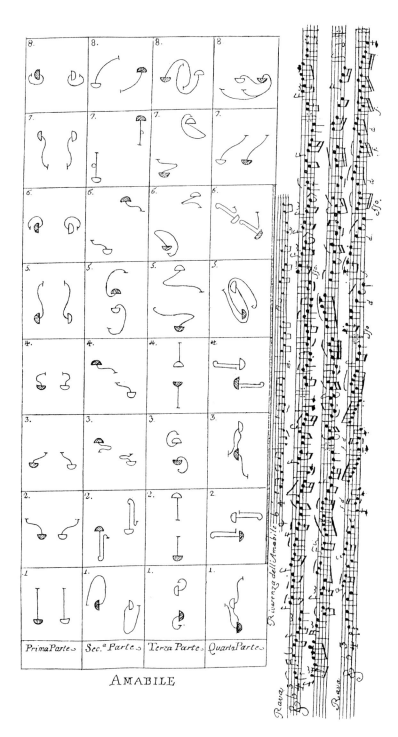

| PrimaParte | Sec.ᵃParte | Terza Parte | QuartaParte |

AMABILE

Folio 23